THE BIBLE BOOK

THE
BIBLE BOOK

RESOURCES FOR READING
THE NEW TESTAMENT

ERASMUS HORT

CROSSROAD · NEW YORK

1983

The Crossroad Publishing Company
575 Lexington Avenue, New York, N.Y. 10022

Printed in the United States of America

Library of Congress Cataloging in Publication Data

Hort, Erasmus
The Bible book.

Includes index.
1. Bible. N.T.—Study—Bibliography. I.Title.
Z7772.L1H64 1983 [BS2330.2] 016.22 83-14446
ISBN 0-8245-0557-3 (pbk.)

65356

CONTENTS

PREFACE

Anyone who contemplates even one year's production of books about the Bible will be impressed not only by the sheer quantity of publications but also by the amazing variety. There are books of every sort, for every level and taste. Those listed here share three characteristics. They are primary resources, basic tools anyone will need for studying the Bible and reading it with greater understanding. Although some are new and some old, they are works of proven usefulness. Finally, they are the best of what is currently available.

Even so, not everything is best for everyone, and the great variety of books reflects the diversity of readers. I have kept foremost in mind the general reader, but the needs of general readers alone range from the most elementary to the most sophisticated. There is no significant difference between what the general reader at the upper end of the range will find useful and what will also meet the needs of teachers, clergy, or even scholars. Therefore, I have tried throughout to indicate instances where I think the level is an important factor by suggesting that a work is elementary or advanced, primarily technical or basically expository.

In general, I think the terms used for such distinctions are obvious enough. For a few, however, a word of explanation might be in order. I have used the term "expository," especially with reference to commentaries, to describe those works that concentrate on unfolding the message of a biblical book and pay less attention to technical details. The term "analytical," in contrast, designates a book that is more technical and likely to be most useful in the critical task of making fine distinctions in literary, historical, and philological matters. The term is appropriate also for works other than commentaries, but in those instances where resources are analytical by their very nature—concordances and lexicons, for example—I have not bothered to state the obvious in each case.

Individual tastes in the study and the reading of the Bible can be quite pronounced, even narrow at times. That is unfortunate if it leads to disregarding valuable resources only because they do not conform to a preconceived point of view. I have deliberately tried to cover a wide range of works suitable for a wide range of tastes and needs, recognizing that there is more than one view about the nature of the Bible, its authority, and the role of the Bible in faith and culture. I have tried to exclude no work that has a contribution to make. From time to time I have used the terms "evangelical" or "conservative" in a description. These words do not lend themselves to simple and rigid definitions, but they are often used by the authors themselves to indicate their theological preferences; when that is the case I have not hesitated to do the same. In contrast, there is no group of authors or readers who call themselves "liberal" or "un-evangelical." Since no such self-designations have been offered, it seemed better not to invent terminology merely for the sake of symmetry. If a particular confessional stance, such as Reformed, or Lutheran, or Roman Catholic, seems to be a salient feature of a work, that is noted. Otherwise, I have made no attempt to call attention to the apparent theological allegiances of authors. Good resources will stand or fall on their own merits. In the case of Roman Catholic scholarship in particular, it is evident that the tools, procedures, and aims are now indistinguishable from those that have long marked work among Protestants. The proof of that is the growing number of primary resources written or edited by Roman Catholic scholars.

In a bibliographical work dates are a constant problem. Librarians and other technical bibliographers distinguish between copyright date and publication date and need to account for every date of every edition. Our needs are simpler. I have tried to provide the original publication date of very old, reprinted works and the most recent date available for everything listed. Even so, there are a few instances where no date can be traced. The few items dated 1983 have been noted in prepublication form and are specifically scheduled to appear in the first four months of that year; but plans sometimes go awry.

Finally, two matters remain: completeness and fairness. It was inevitable that I would overlook some books that should be included. I can only apologize and plead as my excuse the great wealth of material there was to consider. Authors, editors, and publishers who wish to call to my attention what they feel are significant omissions are encouraged to do so. As for fairness, I do not pretend that evaluations did not involve some personal judgments and tastes. I have tried to hold as the norm the entire range of what is available and to ask, in the face of that, whether any single item is as good as the best. Finally, it should be stressed again that everything here does meet a real need and is worth consideration; otherwise it would not be included.

Erasmus Hort

INTRODUCTION
What This Book Is and How to Use It

The Bible Book is a consumer's guide to resources for reading and studying the New Testament. How does one keep track of the hundreds, even thousands, of books that claim to shed light on the Bible and, particularly, on the New Testament? How does one know that a "new" book announced by some publisher is really new and not a reprint of something that appeared a hundred years ago—or, as in one recent case, three hundred years ago? And if a book is an old-timer decked out in new garb, is that necessarily bad? Answering questions like these and many more is what *The Bible Book* is all about.

To speak of a consumer's guide to the New Testament may sound odd, but those who read and study the Bible are certainly consumers. Each year they use and buy thousands of aids and study resources. Some of these are designed for beginners; others are targeted for advanced students, or clergy, or scholars. The range and variety of publications are enormous.

The cost can be enormous too. Many of these resources are expensive and represent a sizable investment—but an investment made only once. They are not going to wear out and cannot be traded in for a newer model. The buyer is going to live with these resources for a long time, and so it makes sense to try to avoid living with mistakes. With that end in view, *The Bible Book* offers a review of what is available, an impartial evaluation of the best materials to have at hand for serious Bible reading and study. *The*

Bible Book does not attempt to list everything, but only works that are distinguished by overall excellence or have special merit. *The Bible Book* includes every major scholarly tool for studying the New Testament, but it is aimed at the general reader whether beginner or advanced.

Why This Book Was Written

Today, more than ever, millions of people enjoy serious and careful study of the Bible. Some do so in church-sponsored groups; others in groups that meet outside any ecclesiastical affiliation. Still others study seriously on their own in the privacy of their own homes. Some have been introduced to biblical studies in schools or colleges. Whatever the motive and the means, taken together these people demonstrate an unprecedented interest in intelligent Bible reading.

Publishers have not been slow to respond. In recent years they have produced an impressive array of helps and resources: dictionaries and encyclopedias; atlases and maps; concordances and commentaries; Greek grammars and Greek interlinear texts—and on and on the list could go. Publication, republication, and reprinting are at an all-time high, and the offerings seem almost endless.

In this sea of possibilities, which are the most reliable prospects? Where does one find the most comprehensive encyclopedia, the most up-to-date atlas? Where, in short, are the very best resources to be found? Titles do not tell us much, nor do the names of authors. Even if one could judge a book by its cover, where could one find all the covers to compare? There are few libraries and probably no bookstores so large that they could, or would, stock more than a fraction of what is available.

The Bible Book is designed to be a balanced and discriminating guide through this material. It will tell what is available and what is the best. If there are several editions of a single work—sometimes from different publishers and in a variety of formats—the differences and similarities are noted. If newer editions have replaced older ones, the differences are explained to determine whether the older edition is truly obsolete—or merely faded.

Finally, there are scores of helps for Bible study that duplicate one another. Yet each has its own virtues and its own drawbacks, which are assessed here.

How to Use This Book

The Bible Book is arranged in chapters that bring together similar resources. It begins with brief descriptions of the standard introductions to the New Testament. Chapter 2 describes the most basic and popular New Testament translations, including some specialized forms of New Testament texts such as synopses of the gospels, and continues with a consideration of books describing the history of the New Testament in English from the first manuscripts to the most recent translations. Each subsequent chapter follows this format and surveys, in turn: concordances; Greek texts of the New Testament (including synopses and interlinear texts); aids to learning or brushing up on Greek; dictionaries and encyclopedias; atlases and maps; commentaries, and more.

Within each chapter the resources are evaluated, usually in four ways. First, an evaluation is already implied by inclusion in *The Bible Book,* since this is a selective consumer's guide and not a mere bulletin board of listings. Every entry in this book has proved its worth. Some entries are certainly more valuable than others, but all those included have survived a process of screening. Second, most chapters and subsections distinguish between "The Best" and "The Rest." In the former category belong a few items that stand out—for different reasons. Some are "the best" because they are the most comprehensive. Others earn that rating because they are the most up-to-date or represent the best value for the money. Individual entries make clear the specific features that make something "the best." If "the rest" are not the very best, they are nonetheless good and worthwhile enough to be listed and described here. These resources have earned their following and claim serious consideration.

Third, the great majority of titles listed here are described and evaluated according to these criteria: (1) Is this book reliable and does it contain what is claimed for it? (2) Does it fill adequately the needs of at least one group of readers—beginners, advanced readers, or professionals? A book may be suitable only for the novice; or it may be a standard in its field without regard to the level of the reader. Some resources are ideal for the specialist but are of limited value to the general reader. Such distinctions are regularly noted. (3) Is this the best edition available? Usually there are no alternatives. Books, after all, are not like household appliances, and one does not expect to find the same book being produced by several different publishers. But that does sometimes happen, especially today with publishers taking such obvious interest in reprinting old classics. As a result it is possible in some instances to get the same book from different publishers in different formats, at various prices.

Finally, at the end of most sections and chapters is a brief summary, which recapitulates the evaluations by spotlighting the very best of the materials surveyed—best buys, most comprehensive, the truly "classical" resource, etc. These brief summaries should not be used in isolation from their context, but they will serve as helpful reminders.

Each entry in *The Bible Book* is furnished with a serial reference number at the left of the entry. These numbers are used throughout for internal reference. They serve as a handy cross-reference system so that any item can be quickly located within the book and easily referred to throughout the book. In addition, at the back of *The Bible Book* is an up-to-date comprehensive listing, the Quick Reference Chart. This chart, ordered according to the numbering system of the book, gives full basic data for each work listed: author or editor, publisher, kind(s) of edition(s) available, International Standard Book Number (ISBN), price, etc.

In the final chapter *The Bible Book* offers a few brief hints on how and where to buy books. Some readers will naturally use this consumer's guide to make library study easier and more efficient. Many others will use it as a guide to purchasing the most appropriate and helpful titles. Since resources for New Testament study are so numerous and varied, no library or bookstore will have them all. With *The Bible Book* the reader need not rely simply on what happens to be available on the shelf at the moment. The concluding chapter, "A Wise Buyer's Guide," offers several suggestions about how to purchase books conveniently and quickly.

1

FOREGROUND AND BACKGROUND
Introducing Yourself to the New Testament and Its Study

This chapter lists and evaluates introductions to the New Testament (part A), books on the historical and religious background of the New Testament (part B), and a few that seek to describe the more difficult aspects of New Testament exegesis (part C).

A. An Introduction to Introductions

Even though in some ways the New Testament is easy to read, it is amazingly complex. It consists of twenty-seven separate documents, through which can be heard a whole chorus of voices and interests. The tradition of generations of serious study and the wide variety of interests among today's readers add to the complexity. Where is one to begin? How does one get a good foundation for reading and understanding the New Testament?

An "introduction" to the New Testament is designed to provide that foundation, but not all introductions are the same. Generally they come in one of three varieties. The first, *analytic introductions* (A-I), are more like reference works and scarcely invite cover-to-cover reading. Like handbooks, they try to sort out all the major interpretive problems, staying abreast of recent developments. The analytic introductions concentrate on who wrote what, when, where, why, and the arguments that back up the various positions. They will also offer a brief synopsis of each New Testament book, and usually there will be an extensive bibliography. Ordinarily, little attention is paid to geography, history, and other matters of background.

A quite different kind of introduction will be found in *textbook introductions,* often written for the college market (A-II). These books may not be elegantly written, but they are written to be read, not just consulted. They combine some of the interests of the handbook with attention to the broader background of the New Testament writings, and they are usually illustrated. Textbooks are less concerned with representing the spectrum of scholarly opinion (though the best are likely to be scrupulously up-to-date) than with helping the general reader get a solid footing in the New Testament and its world. Unfortunately, they are often difficult to purchase, because they are marketed by their publishers in a manner different from that of the more usual trade books customarily found in bookstores.

The third category may be called *introductions for the general reader* (A-III). Usually written by a noted scholar, these are brief, sometimes even breezy journeys through the New Testament with summaries and descriptions of each document and only the highlights of the background information. Some efforts along this line are far better than others; all are designed for the more casual reader.

I. Analytic Introductions

Each of the following meets a slightly different need or has a particular strength. These works are listed in the order of their overall value, but they are not quite interchangeable. They are all advanced and technical, not designed for the casual reader.

1.1   Kümmel, W. G.
       INTRODUCTION TO THE NEW TESTAMENT
       Rev. Eng. ed. trans. by H. C. Kee
       Nashville/New York: Abingdon (1975)

Frequent revisions have kept this book an up-to-date reference for years, first in German, now in English. It is the standard of critical scholarship. Each new edition offers the opportunity to revise the bibliography, which includes a handy list of commentaries on each New Testament book. In addition to covering the technical matters on every New Testament book, Kümmel offers chapters on the synoptic problem, Pauline chronology, apocalypticism, the canon, the manuscript tradition, and the printed texts of the New Testament. This edition brings matters up to 1971 and offers a better translation than any of its predecessors.

1.2	Koester, H.
1.3	INTRODUCTION TO THE NEW TESTAMENT

Vol. 1: *History, Culture and Religion of the Hellenistic Age;*
Vol. 2: *History and Literature of Early Christianity*
Philadelphia: Fortress (1982)

These two large volumes constitute the most recent major introduction to the New Testament. Koester, a scholar of international stature, has followed the classic pattern of the German "handbook" (and has produced an earlier version of this work in German). What is different here is the material to be found in Vol. 1, for such background material is not usually included in this kind of introduction. Vol. 2 also goes beyond the confines of the canon of the New Testament to include some other early Christian writings. By far the most current—and most expensive—option available today, Koester's introduction will probably prove authoritative.

1.4   Marxsen, W.
INTRODUCTION TO THE NEW TESTAMENT
An Approach to Its Problems
Philadelphia: Fortress (1968)

Once more, a German import translated and slightly refitted for the reader of English. Although Marxsen is the very model of conciseness, he covers the same basic material considered mandatory in all such works. Less useful as a reference work, this is the one critical introduction that can actually be read through. Concentrating on the highlights and interested less in bibliographical and scholarly comprehensiveness, Marxsen does try to show what *difference* certain critical choices make, for example, about the purpose of Romans or the authorship of the Pastoral letters. Besides being uniquely concise for an authoritative introduction, Marxsen's book is the least expensive of the classical introductions.

1.5   Moffatt, J.
AN INTRODUCTION TO THE LITERATURE OF THE NEW TESTAMENT
New York: Seabury. 3rd ed. (1918/1961)

Nostalgia alone might prompt mentioning this book, but there are other reasons. Despite its age, "Moffatt" has three virtues. First, it is encyclopedic in its discussion of critical problems up to the time of this edition, 1918. No one has before or since (in English) told so much about the history and range of scholarly debate on technical issues. Second, it pays more attention to Anglo-American scholarship than anything else available (again, up to 1918). Finally, Moffatt's balanced judgments are still worth serious consideration on many points.

1.6   Zahn, T.
        INTRODUCTION TO THE NEW TESTAMENT. 3 vols.
        Minneapolis: Klock & Klock (1909/1977)

Finally, one other venerable introduction bears mentioning, although it is a curiosity. This old work has not been very influential in the past fifty years, but it retains its distinction as probably the most conservative book of its kind ever written by a major scholar. Zahn defends the apostolic origin of every book in the New Testament. Learned and massive, but mostly obsolete.

II. Textbook Introductions

There is considerable variety in the format, level, and general orientation of the standard New Testament introductions published for use in American colleges and universities. Most, however, blend background information with basic attention to literary matters; most use illustrations; and all are written to be read alongside the New Testament as a basic exposition rather than consulted as reference works.

Many of these books never turn up in ordinary bookstores, because they are marketed as "text" books rather than as "trade" books. They can, nevertheless, be ordered. They are listed here under two headings, "readily available" and "others." The distinction does not hold in every case, since it depends solely on a publisher's marketing policies.

Readily Available

1.7   Davies, W. D.
        INVITATION TO THE NEW TESTAMENT
        Garden City: Doubleday (1969)

A Doubleday Anchor book (paperback) by an acknowledged master of New Testament exegesis, this work was written for a general audience and grew out of the author's work on the television series "Sunrise Semester" many years ago.

It is nontechnical, inexpensive, reliable, readable, and written for adults—not many books can make all those claims.

1.8   Grant, R. M.
        A HISTORICAL INTRODUCTION TO THE NEW
        TESTAMENT
        New York: Simon & Schuster (1972)

Another paperback written with attention to style and the needs of the intelligent adult reader, this is surely the most original and sophisticated of all New Testament introductions. Grant attacks the problem and arranges his material in a unique fashion—and with a keen sense of the literary realities. He is independent but moderate in his judgments—and wonderfully concise in his expression.

1.9   Metzger, B. M.
        THE NEW TESTAMENT
        Its Background, Growth and Content
        Nashville/New York: Abingdon (1965)

Cautious and reliable, this work is by a leading American scholar who is respected in virtually all theological camps. Metzger's special expertise is in manuscripts and early versions.

1.10   Guthrie, D.
        NEW TESTAMENT INTRODUCTION
        Downers Grove (IL): InterVarsity. Rev. ed. (1971)

This and the next three entries are somewhat more conservative in judgment than the books above, and they are more noticeably concerned with theological matters. All have proved popular. Guthrie and Martin (1.13, 1.14) are the most comprehensive, but Guthrie is the best at carefully and helpfully tracing the major developments leading to current opinions. The book now needs another revision, but it is still outstanding.

1.11   Gundry, R. H.
        A SURVEY OF THE NEW TESTAMENT
        Grand Rapids: Zondervan. Rev. ed. (1982)

A new edition of a solid survey from a conservative perspective.

1.12   Tenney, M. C.
        NEW TESTAMENT SURVEY
        Grand Rapids: Eerdmans. Rev. ed. (1961)

1.13   Martin, R. P.
1.14   NEW TESTAMENT FOUNDATIONS
        A Guide for Christian Students. 2 vols.
        Grand Rapids: Eerdmans. Vol. 1 (1975); Vol. 2 (1978)

Not quite the standard introduction, but perhaps something better, this useful and thoughtful book surveys the New Testament documents in terms of contemporary issues of debate and interpretation (including method). Martin is never dull and never far away from the arguments and disagreements that make New Testament exegesis lively. He is unusually good at showing the practical consequences of debates that otherwise might seem rather academic.

Others

1.15   Kee, H. C.
        UNDERSTANDING THE NEW TESTAMENT
        Englewood Cliffs (NJ): Prentice-Hall. 4th ed. (1983)

For almost thirty years this has been a standard and widely adopted college and university text. Earlier editions enjoyed the collaboration of F. W. Young and (sometimes) K. Froelich. This entry and the three that follow are all geared to the same market, college and university classes, but each works well without the benefit of supplemental lectures.

1.16   Price, J.
        INTERPRETING THE NEW TESTAMENT
        New York: Holt, Rinehart & Winston. 2nd. ed. (1971)

Noted for its judicious, balanced judgments and its uniformly even coverage. A revised (third) edition is imminent.

1.17   Spivey, R. A., and D. M. Smith, Jr.
        ANATOMY OF THE NEW TESTAMENT
        New York: Macmillan. 3rd ed. (1982)

Spivey and Smith try to break the monotony of bland coverage by focusing on representative small segments within each New Testament document and considering them in detail.

1.18   Perrin, N., and D. Duling
        THE NEW TESTAMENT: AN INTRODUCTION
        Proclamation and Parenesis, Myth and History
        New York: Harcourt Brace Jovanovich. 2nd ed. (1982)

The title sounds pretentious and at times the first edition barely escaped being so. Still, Perrin wrote the most outspoken and challenging college-level text of the previous decade, very much in tune with the critical wing of responsible scholarship. For example, Jesus is treated only in the final chapter and is regarded as the presupposition of or the stimulus to the New Testament rather than as an integral part of it—not everyone's approach, but Perrin was a good spokesman for a certain position. The book is well written but not easy reading and is designed for the more serious nonspecialist. Duling's revision (following Perrin's death) is a genuine improvement and now draws into the discussion the increasing emphasis being paid to the cultural background of the New Testament. Paperback.

1.19   Juel, D., J. S. Ackerman, and T. S. Warshaw
            AN INTRODUCTION TO NEW TESTAMENT LITERATURE
            Nashville/New York: Abingdon (1978)

More compact than most introductions and less detailed technically. Some New Testament books are not covered at all. This volume grew out of experiences in teaching the Bible as literature, and it retains a steady interest in that perspective, making it somewhat different from other introductions.

1.19p   *Same:* paperback

1.20   Perkins, P.
            READING THE NEW TESTAMENT
            An Introduction
            Ramsey (NJ): Paulist (1978)

This small paperback introduction, designed for the novice reader who is also serious, uses a popular and direct style, provides excellent study questions at the end of each chapter, and offers a unique audio-visual bibliography with a listing (including places where individual items may be obtained). Not just another introduction, this is the most simply written of all reliable introductions available. Paperback, and far less expensive than anything else of its quality.

1.21   Connick, M.
            THE NEW TESTAMENT. An Introduction
            to Its History, Literature and Thought
            Encino/Belmont (CA): Dickenson. 2nd ed. (1978)

1.22   Thompson, L. L.
            INTRODUCING BIBLICAL LITERATURE
            A More Fantastic Country
            Englewood Cliffs (NJ): Prentice-Hall (1979)

Covering the entire Bible and not just the New Testament, Thompson concentrates more on the literary features of the material than on historical matters.

III. Introductions for the General Reader

THE BEST

1.23   Beck, B. E.
            READING THE NEW TESTAMENT TODAY
            An Introduction to the Study of the New Testament
            Atlanta: John Knox (1978)

This is a beginner's guide to serious New Testament study. It is lucidly and gracefully written, and its great strength is the way the author takes concrete problems and uses them to introduce the relevance of matters such as manuscripts, the nature of the "meaning" of a text, or the development of the canon. Succinct (154 pages). Highly recommended. Paperback.

1.24   Walton, R. C. (ed.)
            BIBLE STUDY SOURCEBOOK: NEW TESTAMENT
            Atlanta: John Knox (1970/1981)

In this work, originally published (in England) a decade earlier as part of a larger project for church-school teachers, Walton edits notes and essays by outstanding New Testament scholars. Extending beyond the New Testament, the book includes some basic data about the early church and ends with the question of biblical authority. A concluding section offers quick reference for teachers on just about every imaginable topic in the New Testament. It is still better suited to church-school teachers than to anyone else. Eleven simple maps. Paperback.

THE REST

1.25   Briggs, R. C.
            INTERPRETING THE NEW TESTAMENT TODAY
            Nashville/New York: Abingdon (1973)

Standard topics, dealt with in a compact and efficient way. What sets this book apart is its careful attention to some major questions of interpretation and method. Paperback.

1.26   Efird, J. M.
            THE NEW TESTAMENT WRITINGS
            History, Literature, Interpretation
            Atlanta: John Knox (1980)

Simple and brief, this book aims at offering the most elementary introduction in no real depth, but the bibliographies are well constructed to lead to the next step. Paperback.

1.27   Harvey, A. E.
            SOMETHING OVERHEARD
            An Introduction to the New Testament
            Atlanta: John Knox (1979)

1.28   Hendricksen, W.
            A LAYMAN'S GUIDE TO INTERPRETING THE BIBLE
            Grand Rapids: Zondervan (1979)

1.29   Ramsay, W.
            LAYMAN'S GUIDE TO THE NEW TESTAMENT
            Atlanta: John Knox (1980)

SUMMARY

Kümmel (1.1) remains the authority for those who are not daunted by technical discussions. Koester (1.2, 1.3) will prove in time to be of similar stature and looks beyond the confines of the canon in order to understand early Christianity and its literature. The technical introduction most suitable for the nontechnical reader is Marxsen (1.4).

Among the books designed specifically for beginners, here called "textbook introductions," Perkins (1.20) offers the best balance—clear writing, reliable scholarship, and an inexpensive format. Kee (1.15) is a perennial favorite. Spivey and Smith (1.17) provide the clearest and most persistent attention to the theological meaning of the text. Grant (1.8) remains intellectually the most interesting and the most independent in its judgments.

Among introductions for the general reader, the choice is Beck (1.23).

B. New Testament Background

It would be impossible to list here *all* the books that might be useful for illuminating the historical, cultural, and religious background of the New Testament—a background so rich and varied that the range of topics alone can seem intimidating. We have concentrated here on two kinds of resources: books that offer translations of historical and cultural documents of the period and general histories of the era that make New Testament issues their chief concern. The translations include but usually go far beyond "religion" narrowly understood. (Because the Dead Sea Scrolls have generated so much interest—and so much scholarly and popular writing—they are treated separately.)

I. Collections of Texts Illustrating the Background of the New Testament

Three standard collections offer reliable translations from Jewish, Greek, Roman, and later Christian texts. The documents translated, which touch in one way or another on the history and literature of the New Testament and the earliest church, are accompanied by brief introductions and commentaries.

1.30   Barrett, C. K. (ed.)
        NEW TESTAMENT BACKGROUND
        Selected Documents
        New York: Harper & Row (1956)

Barrett offers major sources that shed light on the New Testament world. Some selections are only a few lines long; others run for several pages. The book covers the Roman Empire, papyri and inscriptions, Jewish history, the philosophers, mystery religions, and Rabbinic Judaism and its literature. There are sections on Philo, Josephus, apocalyptic literature, and the Septuagint (the Old Testament in Greek). Much the same material is covered in Kee (1.31). Paperback.

1.31   Kee, H. C. (ed.)
        THE ORIGINS OF CHRISTIANITY
        Sources and Documents
        Englewood Cliffs (NJ): Prentice-Hall (1973)

Kee focuses more on history than Barrett (1.30) does. The selections are somewhat longer and are usually texts that develop central ideas of the New Testament or show parallel literary genres. The collection is very good on issues in Judaism of this period. Paperback.

1.32   Theron, D. J. (ed.)
        EVIDENCE OF TRADITION
        Grand Rapids: Baker (1957/1980)

The subtitle offers a good description: *Selected Source Material for the Study of the History of the Early Church, the New Testament Books, and the New Testament Canon.* The collection includes more than one hundred selections from the first four centuries, with the original Greek or Latin on one page and a good English translation facing it. The second portion of this book, on the history of the New Testament books, goes beyond the scope of Kee (1.31) or Barrett (1.30). There are good tables and lists at the back, and essential notes are provided along the way; but the bibliographies are badly out-of-date in this very recent paperback reprinting.

SUMMARY

If a choice must be made among these three, which do overlap here and there, then the nod goes to Barrett. But all are excellent.

II. The World of the New Testament

THE BEST

1.33   Bruce, F. F.
            NEW TESTAMENT HISTORY
            Garden City: Doubleday (1969/1972)

Bruce brings his early training in classical studies and a lifetime of biblical scholarship to the task of writing a coherent account of the events surrounding the New Testament. The result is a traditional reading of the evidence in a comprehensive but well-written narrative. It is probably the best available, though some would say Bruce ignores problems along the way. Paperback. Easily obtainable.

THE REST

1.34   Ellison, H. L.
            FROM BABYLON TO BETHLEHEM
            The People of God from the Exile to the Messiah
            Atlanta: John Knox (n.d.)

This brief and popular work, while no match for Bruce (1.33), is a clear treatment of intertestamental Judaism that concentrates on what is important in the light of Christianity.

1.35   Filson, F. V.
            A NEW TESTAMENT HISTORY
            The Story of the Emerging Church
            Philadelphia: Westminster (1964)

The major alternative to Bruce (1.33), Filson's book is slightly longer and slightly weaker on the historical setting in the Roman Empire. The famous Westminster maps (see 7.10) are bound with this volume, which also includes a chronological table.

1.36   Lohse, E.
            THE NEW TESTAMENT ENVIRONMENT
            Nashville/New York: Abingdon (1976)

This and the next entry (Reicke, 1.37) are standard introductions to New Testament history by European scholars. Both are solid and reliable; neither has the narrative flow or the appeal of Bruce (1.33).

1.36p   *Same:* paperback

1.37   Reicke, B.
            THE NEW TESTAMENT ERA
            Philadelphia: Fortress (1968)

See the description immediately above.

The remaining entries in this section all have a narrower focus than those above. Some are intended for general readers, and some are scholarly efforts that will appeal only to the avid amateur or to the specialist.

1.38   Freyne, S.
            GALILEE FROM ALEXANDER THE GREAT TO HADRIAN,
            323 B.C.E. TO 135 C.E.
            A Study of Second Temple Judaism
            Notre Dame (IN): University of Notre Dame Press/Wilmington
            (DE): M. Glazier (1980)

A long title for a long book—and a good one—but not for the beginner. Freyne focuses on the geographical territory associated with Jesus' ministry, which is often regarded as culturally and religiously different from the center of Judaism in Jerusalem.

1.39   Goppelt, L.
            APOSTOLIC AND POST-APOSTOLIC TIMES
            Grand Rapids: Baker (1970/1977)

Almost too compressed for the general reader, this is an excellent introduction to the internal development of the early church. The uninitiated will find Goppelt's constant background conversation with the history of scholarship a little perplexing, but he does arrange the New Testament evidence in a clear pattern to illustrate his theory about the line of development.

1.40   Hengel, M.
            JUDAISM AND HELLENISM. 2 vols. in one
            Philadelphia: Fortress (1974/1981)

Intended for the specialist, Hengel's work has already proved quite influential. It is a careful study of the encounter between Greek and Jewish cultures in the intertestamental period. The second volume is all notes. Published in paperback as a single volume.

1.41   Rhoads, D. M.
            ISRAEL IN REVOLUTION, 6–74 C.E.
            Philadelphia: Fortress (1976)

A popular and easy-to-read account of the turbulent times that set the background
for the gospel story and the early church, this is really a modern narrative based
on the evidence in Josephus.

1.41p   *Same:* paperback

1.42   Schürer, E.
1.43   Vermes, G., and F. Millar (eds.)
            THE HISTORY OF THE JEWISH PEOPLE IN THE AGE OF
            JESUS CHRIST (175 B.C.–A.D. 135)
            A New English Version rev. and ed. by G. Vermes, F. Millar,
            and M. Black
            Edinburgh: T. & T. Clark. Vol. 1 (1973); Vol. 2 (1979)

Strictly for the specialist, this excellent book is a complete rewriting of an older
classic that proved influential in its German original and in the English translation.
Vol. 1 deals with the history from 175 B.C. to A.D. 135 and surveys ancient sources
on which it is based. Vol. 2 deals with cultural and religious groups. A third
volume will appear in the near future. This is a scholar's book throughout, and
nowhere more clearly than in the massive bibliographies.

1.44   Simon, M.
            JEWISH SECTS AT THE TIME OF JESUS
            Philadelphia: Fortress (1967/1980)

This brief discussion of the Pharisees, Sadducees, Zealots, and many less well
known groups makes available to the general reader the measured judgments of
an outstanding French Protestant scholar. If the book has a fault it is one shared
with most others that deal with the same topic: it may leave the impression that
we know more about these groups than we do. But it is handy and easy to read,
and its strength lies in the broad coverage it gives to the wide variety of sectarian
phenomena of this period.

1.45   Smallwood, M. E.
            THE JEWS UNDER ROMAN RULE
            Leiden: E. J. Brill (1976/1981)

Now available in both cloth and paper, this extraordinarily expensive book bears
mentioning because it is a careful and scholarly account that is becoming a
standard. Its price is enormous, but so is its value. Obtainable through the Dutch
publisher's New York office.

1.45p   *Same:* paperback

SUMMARY

The best single history is Bruce's (1.33), by any reckoning. Certainly it should be the first choice of the nonexpert. Nothing rivals Schürer (rev. ed., 1.42, 1.43) for depth of coverage of Judaism in this period, and much relevant Roman history is packed into Smallwood's book (1.45). But these are for hearty and seasoned appetites only.

III. The Dead Sea Scrolls: Translations

The chance discovery in 1947 of a "library" of texts has added significantly to our understanding of Judaism in the period just before the New Testament era. Found in caves throughout the craggy heights above the Dead Sea, these texts became known as the Dead Sea Scrolls (or Qumran scrolls after a site in the region of the discovery). Several translations and interpretations are available. Those described here are both the best and, as it happens, the most easily obtainable.

1.46   Vermes, G.
           THE DEAD SEA SCROLLS IN ENGLISH
           Baltimore: Penguin. 2nd ed. (1975)

This is simply the best translation available. It is by an acknowledged expert, and the low cost of this paperback adds to its appeal. The only drawback is Vermes's insistence on using his own (often more accurate) English titles for the documents in place of the more conventional titles usually given to the individual texts.

1.47   Gaster, T. H.
           THE DEAD SEA SCRIPTURES
           Garden City: Doubleday. 3rd ed. (1976)

Every twelve years since he first published his basic book of the scrolls in English translation (1954), Gaster has revised (and expanded) the work. The third edition offers twenty-four texts not found in the second edition. Like Vermes, Gaster uses his own titles for the documents, so that the table of contents may differ from that of other translations, but Gaster offers more notes and more extensive introductions than does Vermes.

IV. The Dead Sea Scrolls: Interpretation

1.48   Vermes, G. (with P. Vermes)
            THE DEAD SEA SCROLLS
            Qumran in Perspective
            Philadelphia: Fortress (1978/1981)

This balanced, up-to-date, and reliable interpretation assesses others' suggestions judiciously and leads the reader to more specialized studies.

1.49   Burrows, M.
            BURROWS ON THE DEAD SEA SCROLLS
            An Omnibus of Two Famous Volumes
            Grand Rapids: Baker (1956–1958)

Burrows was one of the earliest and best interpreters of the scrolls. *The Dead Sea Scrolls* (1956) and *More Light on the Dead Sea Scrolls* (1958) helped correct some exaggerated views and introduced the scrolls both to students and to the larger public. The blend of direct writing and scholarly authority is still evident in this combined reprint. Some of what is said here is now obsolete, but none of it looks foolish even after years of further investigation.

1.50   Cross, F. M., Jr.
            THE ANCIENT LIBRARY OF QUMRAN AND MODERN
            BIBLICAL STUDIES
            Grand Rapids: Baker. 2nd ed. (1958/1980)

Like Burrows (1.49) Cross wrote soon after the discovery. This is surely one of the most influential of all books from a scholar's pen. Designed for the general reader, this revision retains the ability to introduce the novice to a fascinating field.

1.51   Wilson, E.
            ISRAEL AND THE DEAD SEA SCROLLS
            New York: Farrar, Straus & Giroux (1978)

Wilson is almost solely responsible for making the term "Dead Sea Scrolls" a household word. If other discoveries of equal significance are far less well known outside scholarly circles, it is partly because they did not get exposure in *The New Yorker* in essays written by this dean of American letters. Wilson's work shows how a bright amateur confronts the puzzling questions first posed by the scrolls and their early interpreters. His nonspecialist stance is what keeps these essays, now in a revised and expanded edition, appealing. They are readable, and elegantly so.

1.52   LaSor, W. S.
            THE DEAD SEA SCROLLS AND THE NEW TESTAMENT
            Grand Rapids: Eerdmans (1972)

Because Wilson's original articles (see 1.51) raised questions about how the scrolls might alter our interpretation of Christianity and Jesus, there resulted a number of books devoted primarily to that question. It is a narrower interest and usually elicits a confessional response, as here. Although this is not the best of these books, it is as good as any that remain in print today.

1.53   Fitzmyer, J. A.
            THE DEAD SEA SCROLLS
            Major Publications and Tools for Study
            Missoula (MT) [now Chico (CA)]: Scholars Press. 2nd ed.
            (1977)

This is a scholarly resource that guides the reader to all the major research tools. It has no parallel.

SUMMARY

These are but the tip of a publishing iceberg—and the best. The translation by Vermes (1.46) is the most appealing combination of reliability and readability. Vermes's interpretation is the most up-to-date (1.48). Wilson's (1.51) is the best-written book and still will appeal most strongly to the general reader.

C. The Techniques and Methods of New Testament Exegesis

Anyone who begins reading New Testament interpretation soon discovers that it boasts a special vocabulary and a number of distinctive methods—and several arguable issues. These recurring questions hover around topics like the nature of the New Testament text, the origin of the canon, principles of interpretation, the role of historiography in exegesis, and the status of New Testament theology. Weighty issues all, most of these are not addressed directly, or at least not at any length, in the kinds of books described above. The first six volumes listed below are intended to introduce these topics and to explain how New Testament interpretation is—or ought to be—done. The final volume makes a more specialized contribution.

1.54   Harrington, D. J.
INTERPRETING THE NEW TESTAMENT
A Practical Guide
Wilmington (DE): M. Glazier (1979)

This is perhaps the best introduction for the nonspecialist to the methods of modern New Testament study. It is the initial volume in a splendid series of commentaries (see Chap. 9, section B, NTM). Harrington sets forth the basic literary approaches most commonly found in New Testament exegesis today. Each chapter is an exposition of a method with two examples of how that method can be applied to specific texts. The focus is on the traditional methods, not the new experimental approaches. The book is clearly written, very sophisticated, and well done.

1.54p   *Same:* paperback

1.55   Kaiser, G., and W. G. Kümmel
EXEGETICAL METHOD
A Student Handbook
New York: Seabury. Rev. ed. (1981)

Until Harrington (1.54), this was the best book available to illustrate serious exegesis. It is still valuable and appropriately German in its attention to detail and to the nature of the judgments the reader is called on to make. The attitude is "critical" in the technical sense of that term—i.e., analytical, as the term is used here—but the position is quite centrist, not radical. Covers both the Old and the New Testament. Paperback.

1.56   Marshall, I. H. (ed.)
NEW TESTAMENT INTERPRETATION
Essays on Principles and Methods
Grand Rapids: Eerdmans (1978)

These essays, all by evangelical scholars, most of whom are British, deal with central issues and thoughtfully address the purpose and limits of critical biblical study from a conservative theological perspective. A good bibliography makes the essays worthwhile for any reader. This is not a "how to study the New Testament" book but a "how the New Testament is being studied by experts" book that explains the breadth, depth, and limits of various historical and literary approaches.

1.57   Ladd, G. E.
THE NEW TESTAMENT AND CRITICISM
Grand Rapids: Eerdmans (1966)

A general introduction to central methods used in a scholarly reading of the New Testament, this book is designed for nonscholars or for scholars-in-the-making. The position is conservative, and the audience is that wing of conservatism inexperienced in such critical procedures. Ladd explains why and how biblical criticism must be done. The book is easy to read, somewhat older than the Marshall volume (1.56) above.

1.58   Soulen, R. N.
            HANDBOOK OF BIBLICAL CRITICISM
            Atlanta: John Knox. Rev. ed. (1981)

Soulen has compiled a handy dictionary or glossary of the central terms, issues, and problems that figure in biblical scholarship. The compass is wide; the entries are brief and to the point. Though it is well suited to the serious general reader, the scholar will also use it. Helpful tables of abbreviations. An outstanding value in paperback.

1.59   Harrison, R. K., B. Waltke, D. Guthrie, and G. Fee
            BIBLICAL CRITICISM
            Historical, Literary and Textual
            Grand Rapids: Zondervan (1978)

This is a collection of articles gathered from the initial volume of *The Expositor's Bible Commentary* (see Chap. 9, section B, EBC) and here printed in an inexpensive paperback volume. This tells what "criticism" is, why it is necessary, and what its limits are. The orientation is conservative, the scholarship serious and up-to-date, but these authors are slightly less successful than Harrington (1.54) in demonstrating the practical consequences of critical biblical study.

1.60   Henry, P.
            NEW DIRECTIONS IN NEW TESTAMENT STUDY
            Philadelphia: Westminster (1979)

Henry has written a book unlike any other, a stimulating guide through the current fashions and trends in New Testament interpretation that teases out their larger implications. To read this is to hear a gifted teacher at work. He wants to bring New Testament scholarship and theology back together again and has written a fine essay on the intellectual significance of critical New Testament scholarship.

1.60p   *Same:* paperback

1.61   Turner, N.
            HANDBOOK FOR BIBLICAL STUDIES
            Philadelphia: Westminster (1982)

In a brief compass (156 pages), Turner presents information that is often ignored in standard dictionaries and encyclopedias. In addition to basic historical data and maps, he offers examples of ancient scripts, a guide to foreign words used in biblical study, a theological Who's Who, and an excellent glossary of technical terms. Wider in scope than Soulen (1.58) and not quite so easy to use, but filled with valuable ancillary information for those coming to the study of the New Testament on their own.

1.62   Hooker, M. D.
            STUDYING THE NEW TESTAMENT
            Minneapolis: Augsburg (1982)

A brief (224 pages) but complete guide for studying the New Testament comprehensively and systematically, this book was written by a fine New Testament scholar who has taught at London, Oxford, and Cambridge. She includes a plan for working through the New Testament in twelve studies—complete with discussion questions.

1.63   Maas, R.
            CHURCH BIBLE STUDY HANDBOOK
            Nashville/New York: Abingdon (1982)

Maas offers a unique guide for group Bible study, especially designed for use in churches. The arrangement is book-by-book and topical, and it is rich in examples. This is an exegetical handbook for groups rather than for individuals; it focuses on the relationship between the text and the study group. Paperback.

BEST BUYS

The best values in a New Testament introduction are clearly Marxsen (1.4), Perkins (1.20), and Beck (1.23), depending on one's level of interest. Barrett's collection of background documents (1.30) is hard to beat, and nothing rivals Bruce for New Testament history (1.33). The handbooks and guides to New Testament interpretation are not simple equivalents of one another, but for sheer value the choice is Harrington (1.54).

2

THE NEW TESTAMENT
IN ENGLISH

Reading the New Testament in English is sometimes not as simple as it seems, since there are so many versions of the Bible from which to choose. A complete catalogue of these—a comprehensive list of every English translation in all the formats available—would be too overwhelming to be useful, even if it could be produced. But that is not the task at hand; nor is the task to *review* all of the translations that have been influential in the past or are current today. This chapter offers a general overview of the basic and major English versions of the New Testament, followed by a brief listing of *special* types of New Testament texts in English. Some of these comprise portions of the New Testament—for example, a synopsis of the first three gospels; others are multiple translations printed in parallel columns for easy comparison. The third section of the chapter suggests the best books for learning more about the rich history of the English Bible, and the concluding section offers a select group of books that examine more specialized topics, namely, the history of the New Testament textual tradition and the history of the emergence of the canon.

A. Major Versions of the English New Testament (and Bible)

Apart from the most notable achievements of the past, this list, arranged chronologically, focuses on versions currently in use. The abbreviation or popular name of each version is included here and will be used hereafter. The date is that of the publication of the

whole Bible. If the New Testament portion was translated earlier
or later, that date is included in the description.

1382	WYCLIF	The Wyclif Bible was the first complete English Bible. It was based on the Vulgate (Latin) text.
1525	TYNDALE	Tyndale's New Testament was the first *printed* English Bible. Based on the Greek manuscripts available at that time, this version has influenced most modern translations.
1610	DOUAY	The Douay-Rheims Version was the first major Roman Catholic translation (from the Vulgate) into English. The New Testament was translated in Rheims, France, in 1582 and the Old Testament in Douay, (now Douai), France, in 1610.
1611	KJV or AV	The King James Version was for so long *the* Bible in English that it has come to be called simply the Authorized Version (i.e., appointed, or authorized, for public worship). The New Testament text was translated from the third edition of Erasmus's text (3d *Textus Receptus*) of 1551, edited by Stephanus.
1885	RV	The Revised Version (of England) was the first major revision of the KJV. It was motivated by changes in the manuscript tradition behind the translation (which was already some 250 years old) and by the need to update some of the language. This version proved enormously popular in England.
1901	ASV	The American Standard Version was an American Revision of the KJV, an effort to parallel the RV produced a few years earlier in England. This effort to update the KJV was itself revised in 1970 (see NASB below).
1903	WEYMOUTH	*The New Testament in Modern Speech* by Richard Weymouth also appeared forty years later in an American edition.
1926	MOFFATT	*The Holy Bible: A New Translation* by James Moffatt was an effort to translate the entire

Bible as one would any other piece of literature. It offered a new standard in idiomatic biblical translation, despite its very British tone. Moffatt, a Scotsman, was teaching in America, and the influence of his translation in this country was considerable.

1931   GOODSPEED   *The Bible—An American Translation* brought together a New Testament translation (1923) by Edgar J. Goodspeed and an Old Testament translation (1927) by J. M. Powis Smith to form a popular and idiomatic American translation that offered a contemporary alternative to the more British cadences of MOFFATT.

1941   CONFRA-TERNITY   The Confraternity Edition of the New Testament was a Roman Catholic translation based on the Vulgate but influenced as well by Greek critical editions. It reappeared in 1949 as *The New Catholic Edition of the Holy Bible,* which was itself revised in 1967.

1945   BERKELEY   *The Berkeley Version of the New Testament* was translated by G. Verkuyl. Later, a translation of the Old Testament (*The New Berkeley Version,* 1959) was added, and the whole was called *The Modern Language Bible* (1969). This is an updated and annotated KJV.

1949   BASIC ENGLISH   *The Bible in Basic English* is an effort that originated in England (and was subsequently published in the United States in 1950) to translate the whole Bible using a vocabulary of only one thousand words. The New Testament portion appeared in 1941.

1949   NEW CATHOLIC   *The New Catholic Edition of the Holy Bible* is a mixture of the DOUAY version of the Old Testament (except for a few changes in Psalms) and the CONFRATERNITY New Testament translation.

1952   RSV   The Revised Standard Version is the second major revision of the KJV (the first being the RV or ASV). The New Testament appeared in 1946 and the Apocrypha in 1957. Subsequent revisions have provided a common text acceptable to both Roman Catholic and Protestant communities.

1956   KNOX   Ronald Knox's *The Holy Bible,* a fresh translation from the Vulgate, is a heroic undertaking that is famous for its felicitous English.

1958   PHILLIPS   *The New Testament in Modern English* by J. B. Phillips is one of the most successful of the modern translations by a single scholar. The language is contemporary and idiomatic.

1961   NEW   *The New World Translation of the Holy Scrip-*
         WORLD   *tures* is a translation by the Jehovah's Witnesses.

1965   AMPLI-   *The Amplified Bible,* edited by F. E. Siewert and
         FIED   sponsored by the Lockman Foundation, is a synthetic effort to incorporate insights from numerous translations, commentaries, and lexicons. The New Testament portion was completed in 1958.

1966   JB   *The Jerusalem Bible* was originally a French translation produced in Jerusalem by the Dominicans. Based on the Hebrew and the Greek texts rather than on the Vulgate, the JB rapidly became renowned for its combining elegance with contemporary language. The same is true of the English version.

1969   MLB   *The Modern Language Bible* updates the earlier (1945) BERKELEY version (see above).

1970   NAB   *The New American Bible* represents American Roman Catholic biblical scholarship at work in response to modern papal and conciliar pronouncements that have encouraged translations based on Hebrew and Greek manuscripts rather than on the Vulgate.

1971   LIVING   *The Living Bible, Paraphrased* is something of a paradox. It is popular with many whose view of scripture ought to preclude paraphrasing it. The origins of this paraphrase lie in the author's reading the Bible to his children. The simple and

		direct style and the added words that bridge some of the rough spots no doubt explain its great appeal, but no paraphrase is a reliable version for study purposes.
1971	NASB	*The New American Standard Bible* (NT, 1960) comes from the American evangelical Protestant community. It is an attempt to provide a contemporary revision of the ASV of 1901.
1976	TEV (or GNB)	Today's English Version is a simple and contemporary English New Testament translation; it has also been published as *Good News for Modern Man*. It was prepared by R. Bratcher and published by the American Bible Society in 1966. The whole Bible was subsequently published as *The Good News Bible*, although TEV remains the standard tag. This idiomatic translation is designed for all readers of English, including those for whom it is a second language.
1978	NIV	Few recent versions (and there have been many) have appeared with more fanfare and advance sales than *The New International Version* (NT, 1973). Prepared by and for evangelicals, the NIV is the fruit of the labors of more than one hundred scholars from many denominations and countries.
1982	NKJB	*The New King James Bible* is an eclectic arrangement of the old KJV, over which has been laid some new vocabulary. It tries to keep faith with the KJV, which is still the norm for some, while overcoming some obvious disadvantages of a translation almost four hundred years old.

These versions of the Bible—and others less well known—come in an almost endless array of editions. Some boast elegant bindings; other have inexpensive paper covers. Editions can be found with large type or thin paper or with study aids like concordances, notes, etc. Older versions, such as the KJV, are in the public domain, but more recent translations are likely to be copyrighted and licensed to only one or two publishers, which frequently results in higher prices and fewer editions or formats.

B. Comparative Versions

How does an ordinary reader use such a wealth of translations without being overwhelmed by them? The editions of the New Testament (or the Bible) that offer several translations in parallel columns make it possible to compare the translations simultaneously. Such "comparative" versions do not cover all the possibilities by any means, but they do allow for quick reference and easy comparison among the most popular versions.

THE BEST

2.1   THE EIGHT-TRANSLATION NEW TESTAMENT
         Wheaton (IL): Tyndale (1974)

On a double page, the New Testament according to KJV, MLB, PHILLIPS, RSV, TEV, NIV, JB, and NEB. No other volume offers so many of the important contemporary versions.

2.1p   *Same:* paperback

THE REST

2.2   Vaughn, C. (ed.)
         THE NEW TESTAMENT FROM 26 TRANSLATIONS
         Grand Rapids: Zondervan (1967)

This is not a full rendering of the New Testament in twenty-six different versions side by side. Instead, it is a clever, compact index of differences among the translations listed below. Vaughn takes the KJV as the base text and notes every major departure from its wording in ASV, RSV, NASB, NEB, BERKELEY, MOFFATT, PHILLIPS, KNOX, GOODSPEED, LIVING, AMPLIFIED, BASIC ENGLISH, WEYMOUTH, *The Twentieth Century New Testament,* the translations of Lamsa, Conybeare (Paul's epistles), Alford, Broadus, Williams, and several others. Given this format, one cannot here conveniently *read* the New Testament in these versions, but the wording of any passage as it appears in any of the individual translations can be quickly determined.

2.3   THE LAYMAN'S PARALLEL BIBLE
         Grand Rapids: Zondervan (1973)

The entire Bible in four columns to the double page: KJV, MLB, LIVING, RSV.

2.4   THE LAYMAN'S PARALLEL NEW TESTAMENT
                 Grand Rapids: Zondervan (1970)

The New Testament in KVJ, AMPLIFIED, LIVING, and RSV.

2.4p   *Same:* paperback

2.5   Weigle, L. A. (ed.)
                 THE NEW TESTAMENT OCTAPLA. Eight English Versions of
                 the New Testament in the Tyndale–King James Translation
                 New York: Nelson (1962)

On facing pages eight significant translations from 1535 to 1960: Tyndale (1535); Great Bible (1539 and 1540); Geneva Bible (1560 and 1562); Bishop's Bible (1565/1602); Rheims (1582); KJV (1611/1873); ASV (1881/1901); and RSV (1946/1960).

2.6   THE SIX VERSION PARALLEL NEW TESTAMENT
                 Carol Stream (IL): Creation House (1974)

KJV, LIVING, RSV, NEB, PHILLIPS, and JB in six parallel columns.

C. Special Texts:
Portions of the New Testament

The three "synoptic" gospels—Matthew, Mark, and Luke—present special problems because of their unusual literary relationships. For that reason they are often printed in parallel columns for easy comparison. Such a "synopsis" of the gospels may also include all or some of the Gospel of John. Sometimes materials from the apocryphal gospels, especially the *Gospel of Thomas,* are included.

In the same way, it is helpful for studying Paul's letters to have the text of the letters and the relevant material from the Acts of the Apostles printed in parallel columns.

THE BEST

2.7   Aland, K. (ed.)
                 SYNOPSIS OF THE FOUR GOSPELS. English Edition
                 New York: American Bible Society (1982)

There is no better or more up-to-date synopsis of the gospels available in English than this one, and it is also by far the least expensive synopsis on the market. Its "parent" is Aland's bilingual *Synopsis of the Four Gospels* (4.14), but for this English-only edition the Greek text has been omitted. Analytical and now the standard.

2.8   Throckmorton, B. H., Jr. (ed.)
             GOSPEL PARALLELS
             A Synopsis of the First Three Gospels
             Nashville: Nelson. 4th ed. (1979)

An old standard now brought further up to date, this is the second-best synopsis available in English. The page size is ample and the column widths will not frustrate the reader. The text is the RSV. This new edition expands the index of parallel passages not found in canonical New Testament literature (such as the *Gospel of Thomas*). Brief introductory materials increase the usefulness of the book. Analytical and excellent, slightly more expensive and considerably more compact than Aland (2.7), Throckmorton's synopsis offers many fewer parallels from John's gospel and from extracanonical literature.

2.9   Francis, F. O., and J. P. Sampley (eds.)
             PAULINE PARALLELS
             Philadelphia: Fortress (n.d.)

Using the RSV text the editors juxtapose closely related passages from the Pauline epistles and include relevant material from Acts.

THE REST

2.10   Swanson, R. J. (ed.)
             THE HORIZONTAL LINE SYNOPSIS OF THE GOSPELS
             Grand Rapids: Baker (1979)

No other harmony or synopsis of the gospels is arranged this way. The editor has put the synoptic gospels in three parallel lines across the page. For the nonspecialist this makes precise word-for-word comparison far easier than in the conventional format of parallel columns. The RSV text is used.

2.11   Thomas, R. L., and S. N. Gundry (eds.)
             A HARMONY OF THE GOSPELS
             with Explanations and Essays
             Chicago: Moody (1978)

The ostensible reason for publishing this new harmony is its use of the NASB text. In addition to the standard harmony, the editors offer a useful index, which allows the reader to locate any passage quickly. John's gospel is part of the package. There are also tables of cross-references, two maps, some time-lines, and a set of essays at the end. One of these defends the legitimacy of reading the gospel as a harmony, and one attacks the position of modern gospel scholarship. Others deal with special issues such as the birth narrative, chronology, and the accounts of Jesus' death and resurrection. The format is handy for holding but not for reading, because the columns are so narrow. The expressed theological perspective is conservative.

2.12   Robertson, A. T.
            A HARMONY OF THE GOSPELS
            New York: Harper & Row (1932/1974)

D. The New Testament in English

Behind today's rich variety of translations lies a long history of the New Testament in the English language. And behind that is the story of how individual New Testament books were written originally and gathered into a single collection called the canon.

I. How We Got Here: From the Beginnings to the New Testament in English

THE BEST

2.13   Finegan, J.
            ENCOUNTERING NEW TESTAMENT MANUSCRIPTS
            Grand Rapids: Eerdmans (1974)

One of the very best books available for the beginner who wants to know what New Testament manuscripts are like and how scholars go about deciding among variant readings found in them. Part 1 offers a good introduction. Part 2 is unique, providing excellent photographs and detailed analyses of several passages. The reader can learn by doing, so to speak. Strictly speaking, New Testament textual criticism requires knowledge of Greek, but Finegan translates almost everything, making the book accessible to those who do not know Greek and a boon to those who are rusty in that department.

2.14   Metzger, B. M.
            THE TEXT OF THE NEW TESTAMENT
            Its Transmission, Corruption and Restoration
            New York: Oxford. 2nd ed. (1968)

The standard introduction to New Testament textual study and current problems. Metzger is a master of the subject and writes clearly. Although used by scholars, this book is entirely comprehensible to the nonspecialist. It is less exciting for beginners than Finegan (2.13) because it has fewer examples, poses fewer puzzles, and involves the reader less.

2.15   Campenhausen, H. F. von
              THE FORMATION OF THE CHRISTIAN BIBLE
              Philadelphia: Fortress (1977)

This volume offers a reliable and scholarly essay on how the Old and New Testament canons emerged and what influences shaped the Christian Bible. Designed for the advanced reader.

2.16   √   Ackroyd, P. R., et al. (eds.)
              THE CAMBRIDGE HISTORY OF THE BIBLE. 3 vols.
              Cambridge: At the University Press (1963–1970)

2.16p   *Same:* paperback

Also
available
separately:

2.17   Ackroyd, P. R., and C. F. Evans (eds.)
              Vol. 1: FROM THE BEGINNINGS TO JEROME (1970)

2.17p   *Same:* paperback

2.18   Lampe, G. W. H. (ed.)
              Vol. 2: THE WEST FROM THE FATHERS TO THE
              REFORMATION (1969)

/

2.18p   *Same:* paperback

2.19   Greenslade, S. L. (ed.)
              Vol. 3: THE WEST FROM THE REFORMATION TO THE
              PRESENT (1963)

2.19p   *Same:* paperback

Some essays in these three large volumes are quite technical, while others are much less so. Taken together these volumes offer a massive investigation into the origins and the development of the Bible in Western Christianity. Each volume covers one historical period and consists of independent essays written by leading experts in the field. Formidable, but fascinating for the advanced reader.

THE REST

2.20   Bruce, F. F.
              THE BOOKS AND THE PARCHMENTS
              Some Chapters in the Transmission of the Bible
              Old Tappan (NJ): Revell. 3rd ed. (1963)

Covers both the Old and the New Testament in Bruce's clear and authoritative style. Still, there has been much scholarly debate on matters like the canon since the last revision, which leaves this a bit faded.

2.21   Kenyon, F. G.
              OUR BIBLE AND THE ANCIENT MANUSCRIPTS
              New York: Harper & Row. Rev. ed. (1958)

Even older than Bruce's book (2.20), this revision by A. W. Adams kept alive a perennially popular introduction to the history of the biblical text and its transmission. Somewhat more formidable than Price (2.23), this is still an all-time favorite and is reliable up to the time of the last revision. It does not cover translations (i.e., versions).

2.22   Greenlee, J. H.
              AN INTRODUCTION TO NEW TESTAMENT TEXTUAL
              CRITICISM
              Grand Rapids: Eerdmans (1964)

A self-described "primer," this work is not as comprehensive as Metzger (2.14) and is less engaging and less informative than Finegan (2.13). Still, it is a reliable first step.

2.23   Price, I.
              THE ANCESTRY OF OUR ENGLISH BIBLE
              An Account of Manuscripts, Texts and Versions of the Bible
              New York: Harper & Row (1956)

Complete, readable, but not up-to-date. An old standby.

2.24   Metzger, B. M.
              EARLY VERSIONS OF THE NEW TESTAMENT
              New York: Oxford (1977)

A scholar's delight, this book offers a comprehensive survey of every New Testament translation up to A.D. 1000. It features an interesting section discussing the characteristics of eight ancient languages and the problems of translating from the Greek into each.

2.25   Westcott, B. F.
         THE BIBLE IN THE CHURCH
         A Popular Account of the Collection and Reception of the Holy
            Scriptures into the Christian Churches
         Grand Rapids: Baker (1865/1980)

This and the next volume, also by Westcott, offer the views of an influential nineteenth-century scholar. Although this popular treatment is badly out of date in spots, it has been reprinted for good reason: in scope and erudition this is the equal of Campenhausen (2.15) but is considerably more traditional and conservative in many of its judgments.

2.26   Westcott, B. F.
         A GENERAL SURVEY OF THE HISTORY
         OF THE CANON OF THE NEW TESTAMENT
         Grand Rapids: Baker (1855/1980)

Essays on how the New Testament canon emerged are always technical, because the subject is complex. This book, considerably more detailed than Westcott's popular account (2.25), is no exception.

II. Where We Are: The English New Testament in Today's Versions

THE BEST

2.27   Bruce, F. F.
         HISTORY OF THE BIBLE IN ENGLISH
         New York: Oxford. 3rd ed. (1978)

Lively, concise, and authoritative, this is an outstanding book. Bruce starts with the beginning of the English Bible and takes the story up to the present. About a third of the volume deals with translations of the twentieth century. The second edition took account of the NEB, and the third includes the Common Bible, NASB, TEV, and the revised PHILLIPS. Bruce's style gives the reader a feel for the idiom and flavor of each translation. As he says in his preface, those who have tried their hand at translating are likely to come away tolerant of others' efforts. Bruce certainly is. Fair in his judgments and always interesting, Bruce is concerned with uncovering the principles lying behind a particular translation, and he focuses on the truly interesting or exemplary passages.

2.27p   *Same:* paperback

2.28   Lewis, J. P.
              THE ENGLISH BIBLE FROM KJV TO NIV
              A History and Evaluation
              Grand Rapids: Baker (1981)

The heart of this excellent book is a review of *major* English translations of the
Bible, detailing the pedigree and the principles behind each one and giving generous
samples of the various versions. The book needs an index, but the bibliography
is masterful—complete, up-to-date, and organized by specific translations.

2.29   Hills, M. T., and E. J. Eisenhart
              A READY REFERENCE HISTORY OF THE ENGLISH BIBLE
              New York: American Bible Society (1979)

The best brief and inexpensive guide to a perplexing array of Bible translations.
For the money, it has no rivals. The authors offer a survey of the historical
translations, with a listing of versions up to 1978 and brief bibliographies.

THE REST

2.30   Nida, E. A.
              THE BOOK OF A THOUSAND TONGUES
              New York: American Bible Society. Rev. ed. (1972)

First published in 1931, Nida's catalogue in its revised edition lists every language
and major dialect in which at least one Bible book has been translated. It offers
a sample of a few verses of the translation along with complete bibliographic
details. As of 1968 there were 1,399 languages accounted for. Some fascinating
information emerges, such as the fact that Massachuset was the twenty-second
language into which the Bible was translated in a printed version. This was the
first American-language translation—and that in 1663.

2.31   Kubo, S., and W. Specht
              SO MANY VERSIONS?
              Twentieth Century Versions of the Bible
              Grand Rapids: Zondervan (1975)

Concentrates on the proliferation of recent versions.

2.32   Walden, W.
              GUIDE TO BIBLE TRANSLATIONS
              A Handbook of Versions Ancient and Modern
              Duxbury (MA): Livingbooks (1979)

A brief, mimeographed booklet listing English translations by date, giving one or
two characteristics or intentions for each, and naming the translator(s). Nothing

elegant in format or writing style distinguishes this brochure, but it is reasonably complete, very handy, and inexpensive. No judgments are made about the relative merits of the translations. At the time of writing the NKJB and *Reader's Digest* condensation were in progress. Copies can be obtained from the Massachusetts Bible Society.

2.33   Glassman, E.
            THE TRANSLATION DEBATE
            Downers Grove (IL): InterVarsity (1981)

Especially valuable as a nontechnical discussion of the various theories of translation, including the ancient controversy over literal translation versus paraphrase, this book is full of useful background information for the general reader.

2.34   Beekman, J., and J. Callow
            TRANSLATING THE WORD OF GOD
            Grand Rapids: Zondervan (n.d.)

Two missionaries associated with Wycliffe Bible Translators discuss basic principles of Bible translation and illustrate these in several case studies.

2.35   Carson, D. A.
            THE KING JAMES VERSION DEBATE
            A Plea for Realism
            Grand Rapids: Baker (1978)

Carson offers much more than an opinion of the value of the KJV for today's needs. In the process of discussing that translation, he offers a good introduction to textual criticism and translation history. A popular treatment of the tasks and perils of Bible translation and a comparison of the KJV with more modern versions.

BEST BUYS

Anyone interested in comparing modern translations at length will want to consult *The Eight-Translation New Testament* (2.1), while those interested in earlier versions will find Weigle's *New Testament Octapla* (2.5) indispensable.

Synopsis of the Four Gospels, English Edition (2.7) is by far the best synopsis of the gospels available and also the least expensive. *Pauline Parallels* (2.9), while perhaps less crucial, is unique and useful. On the topic of the Greek manuscript tradition lying behind the English New Testament, it is hard to choose between Metzger, *The Text of the New Testament* (2.14), and Finegan, *Encountering New Testament Manuscripts* (2.13). For the beginner, the nod goes to Finegan, but Metzger should be considered the standard.

For one who can read only a single book on the broad subject of the history of the English Bible and contemporary translations, the book should be Bruce's *History of the Bible in English* (2.27). If, however, all one needs is a reference guide to translations, *A Ready Reference History of the English Bible* (2.29) is the best value.

3

CONCORDANCES

A biblical concordance is a wise investment. Most are relatively inexpensive in proportion to their size, and they are filled with useful data. Moreover, a good concordance will not become outdated but will retain its usefulness for generations. There are plenty of concordances in second-hand bookshops, and many are as useful as a new copy. Indeed, some second-hand concordances may actually be better than some new editions, because of type size, for instance, or the durability of the paper. Making a sound choice depends on knowing one's own needs and what is available.

What a Concordance Is and How to Use It

What is a concordance? John Marbeck, who compiled the first concordance of the entire English Bible described his work as ". . . a worke wherein by the ordre of the letters of the A.B.C. ye maie redely finde any worde conteigned in the whole Bible, so often as it is there expressed or mencioned." That was 1540, but the idea is the same today. Concordances really reach back to Hugo de Santo, who in 1230 compiled an index to the Vulgate. To do so he employed the services of five hundred monks. For centuries thereafter making a concordance was painstaking work. Today, the drudgery can be assigned to computers, and new concordances follow new translations in quick succession.

Since a concordance is a list of words in the Bible, it serves several useful purposes. For example, various nuances of one word can be explored by examining all of its biblical contexts. And, of course, the concordance listing will also point to widely separated biblical passages that might be related to one another through the use of common terms.

Word Concordances and Topical Concordances

Strictly speaking, a concordance is an index of *words,* but the term has come to be applied to another kind of Bible index, sometimes known as a "topical concordance" (or "topical Bible," or "index to biblical ideas"). This type of work serves a slightly different purpose. In the case of topical concordances it is not the *word* that counts, but the *thought* or theme. Thus, for example, a survey of biblical texts about "friendship" need not be restricted to the "friend" family of words ("friendly," "friendship," etc.). Topical concordances help solve this problem. Some do it better than others, depending on the range of imagination and the mental discipline exercised by the compiler. When choosing a concordance that lists words—and there are many to choose from—one should consider the text, the range of words, and the edition of the Bible on which the concordance is based.

Which Text?

Since a concordance is a list of words found in the Bible, the actual list depends on the specific version, or translation, being indexed. A concordance to the RSV is of more limited use if you are reading the NAB—and useless if you are reading the Greek New Testament. This inherent limitation can be minimized with cross references, but it cannot be overcome entirely. Thus, the first rule: determine which translation of the Bible (or the New Testament) you want to use, and then look for the proper concordance. (Concordances for currently or perennially popular translations are usually kept in print. For older and more specialized translations—for example, the Moffatt version—you may have to consult a library.)

Which Words?

Which words—and how many—do you need? The answer is not as obvious as it seems. The first concern is the matter of coverage. How complete is a "complete concordance," and how exhaustive is an "exhaustive" one? In titles of concordances, these terms and others such as "unabridged," "full," and "comprehensive," should be taken with a grain of salt. This is because the "little words" are often not included, but a few words of minor significance make up a lot of the Bible—words like *a, an, the, and, he, she, them,* etc. For example, small Greek words—*ho* ("the"), *kai* ("and," "even," etc.), *de* ("but," "and," etc.) and *autos* ("he," "she," "it," "self," etc.) occur thirty-seven thousand times and thus make up one-fourth of the New Testament. Should a "complete" concordance list all such words? Scholars may need them, but others usually do not. Often, therefore, most or all such words are left out, and, if they are included, they are frequently consigned to the briefest possible reference system.

The second concern is the system of citation. The most compact concordances simply list the book, the chapter, and the verse where the particular word appears. With this type of concordance one must look up each reference. A better system is that which cites the word in its context, usually a brief line of the text. Frequently this is enough to jog the memory or indicate whether the citation is worth exploring further. The more context given, the more elaborate the concordance—and, within limits, the better.

Finally, there are concordances that arrange the references for some entries into subgroups. An "analytical" concordance of the English Bible offers a useful breakdown of frequent or especially significant words. For example, the entry for "son" does not simply list every occurrence of the word from Genesis on; references are grouped under headings such as "son of God," "son of Man," "son(s) of Abraham," etc.

Which Edition?

Making a concordance is an enormous task, but if it is well done it needs no revision. For that reason, many of the standard and most famous concordances currently available are actually very old and have been through dozens of editions. If the copyright has expired, they may now be published simultaneously by several publishers in a variety of formats. All these editions, plus older editions that may be found in second-hand bookstores, can make the choice of a concordance a difficult one.

What are the differences and what should one look for? Apart from corrections, the most common change in a "revised" edition of a concordance is the addition of new material to either the front or the back of the book. For example, Young's *Analytical Concordance to the Bible* (3.6) is a perennial favorite. Since 1902 it has concluded with an essay on biblical archaeology, the last version of which was written by W. F. Albright in 1936. This concluding essay will probably be updated again at some point, but this is not the heart of the concordance. The case is similar with two other old standards, Strong and Cruden.

How then should one go about choosing from among competing editions? A concordance is a reference work. It gets hard use and should last a lifetime. For that reason, one should consider the quality of the paper, the binding, and the size of the type. A paperback concordance probably will not wear well, and a second-hand edition in cloth might be a better investment. One way of reprinting books is to reproduce the pages photographically. If at the same time the page size is reduced, there is some loss of clarity, which can result in a page that is difficult to read. Moreover, a generation ago books were printed on paper of better quality than that used in most books today. In a bulky reference work, what is important is the opaqueness of the paper. To keep size down, concordances are usually printed on thin paper. If this paper is not of good quality, print from the other side will show through.

To sum up: Do not buy what you have not seen, and do not buy on the basis of cost alone. If you can find a second-hand concordance of the sort you want, do not hesitate to buy it; it may well turn out to be the best bargain. Otherwise, the few dollars that separate the better new editions from cheaper new editions are probably dollars worth spending. The listings below are rather extensive, but in the case of old standards not all the cheaper alternatives can be recommended.

A. Traditional (Word) Concordances

THE BEST

3.1   Darton, M. (ed.)
       A MODERN CONCORDANCE TO THE NEW TESTAMENT
       Garden City: Doubleday (1977)

This has been referred to as "the first strikingly new concordance of the Bible . . . in many years." Based on the Greek text and originally written in French for use with the Jerusalem Bible (JB), this excellent volume can actually be used with any of six or more major contemporary translations. The arrangement is both by theme (as in a topical concordance) and by word. For each word a subordinate listing of appropriate synonyms, close associates, or derivatives is given. Every Greek word underlying the derivatives is included, together with citations. Thorough, flexible, remarkably helpful—and inexpensive.

3.2   Hartdegen, S. J. (ed.)
       NELSON'S COMPLETE CONCORDANCE OF THE NEW
       AMERICAN BIBLE
       Nashville/New York: Nelson (1977)

This is a well-produced concordance of the New American Bible (NAB), the nationally acclaimed Roman Catholic translation of 1970. The publisher sometimes refers to this volume without reference to the editor's name with the title *Nelson's Complete New American Bible Concordance*.

3.3   Morrison, C. (ed.)
       AN ANALYTICAL CONCORDANCE TO THE REVISED
       STANDARD VERSION OF THE NEW TESTAMENT
       Philadelphia: Westminster (1979)

This new concordance may be, as some claim, "the best English concordance available," but it covers *only* the New Testament. Although it is rather expensive, it must be considered *the new standard* for the most frequently used and cited translation in America today, the RSV New Testament. Morrison's work is designed for readers who do not know Greek, but he does offer the Greek word for every English entry (both in Greek script and in transliteration). The concordance distinguishes different Greek words that are translated by one English word, and a lexicon at the back lists each Greek word in transliteration and in Greek script, followed by a list of every English word used to translate it. The editor has been scrupulous in showing where the RSV omits a Greek word in the text, adds English words that do not reflect the original text, or offers a paraphrase. Although based on the RSV, this volume is arranged so that it has obvious value for readers of *any* contemporary version. Despite its high cost, it is highly recommended for both technical and popular use.

3.4   Strong, J. (ed.)
             THE EXHAUSTIVE CONCORDANCE OF THE BIBLE
             Nashville/New York: Abingdon. Rev. ed. (1980)

Strong's *Exhaustive Concordance* (first published in 1894) is an old favorite based on the KJV (3d AV) and famous for its thoroughness. It actually lists, in one way or another, every word of the Bible, showing where the Revised Version and American Standard Version differ from the Authorized Version (3d KJV). It also offers compact dictionaries of Hebrew and Greek, showing the English translations used in the KJV for each word. All "little words" of the Bible are listed, but forty-seven of the most common are given in a separate, compact list without any citation of context.

     Strong's concordance is famous for its completeness and for having assigned a reference number to each word. Originally designed for internal use within the concordance, this numbering system has been widely adapted to other Bible reference works (see, for example, 4.16, 4.32, 4.40, 4.51, 4.57, 4.59, and 4.60). There is one disadvantage to this concordance, and it causes many users to prefer Young's *Analytical Concordance* (3.6), though both have their fierce defenders. Strong's concordance is not analytical, i.e., it does not gather under subheadings the distinctive uses of a word of repeated occurrence—"son," for example—which can make it harder to use.

     This is standard and applies to *all* editions of Strong's concordance, with the exception of the abridged edition (3.25). This specific Abingdon edition also has an exclusive feature that sets it apart—a tabular listing of the major translation variants among today's most significant versions—called the "Exclusive Key-Word Comparison." "Exhaustive" is indeed the right word for this big book, and Abingdon's new edition stands out.

3.5   *Same:* thumb-indexed

(*For other editions of Strong, see 3.21–3.25.*)

3.6   Young, R. (ed.)
             ANALYTIC CONCORDANCE TO THE BIBLE
             Nashville/New York: Nelson. Rev. ed. (1980)

Young's work goes back to 1873/1881. Current editions are all based on the 1922 revision by W. B. Stevenson. Like Strong's work, then, it is old and has made its reputation. It, too, is based on the KJV. Although less complete than Strong's, Young's work is sometimes preferred because of its more analytical features—common usages of a given word are grouped together. Some users also prefer Young's system of designating the Hebrew or Greek behind each English word. Standard editions offer a supplemental lexicon of Old Testament Hebrew (in both transliteration and Hebrew letters) and a lexicon of New Testament Greek (same format) as well as a list of proper names with suggested pronunciation. Some editions offer a concluding essay on biblical archaeology—those published since 1936 in a (now outdated) version written by W. F. Albright.

A thorough, if not a "complete," concordance, Young's is time-tested, widely available, and adaptable to newer translations. A standard.

Other Editions of Young

In addition to the Nelson edition listed above, there are several others available. These are distinguished mostly by small differences in price.

Young, R. (ed.) ANALYTICAL CONCORDANCE TO THE BIBLE
3.7   Grand Rapids: Eerdmans (1955). Plain
3.8   Grand Rapids: Eerdmans (1955). Thumb-indexed
3.9   Gallatin (TN): Church History Research and Archives (n.d.). Plain
3.10   Gallatin (TN): Church History Research and Archives (n.d.). Thumb-indexed

THE REST

3.11   Cruden, A. (ed.)
            CRUDEN'S UNABRIDGED CONCORDANCE
            Nashville: Broadman (n.d.)

Cruden's was not the first concordance of the English Bible, but after its appearance in 1737 the name Cruden became almost inseparable from the term "concordance." It still is, but the book's age and limitations are evident in the face of newer and more sophisticated works. Nevertheless, by the nineteenth century this concordance was so firmly established that the evangelist Dwight L. Moody regularly recommended it as second only to the Bible itself in importance.

Despite what the title says, Cruden's concordance was never truly complete, and it shows some amazing quirkiness in details. The most valuable feature of many earlier editions—the concordance of the Apocrypha—is not found, alas, in current editions. Broadman's is the best of the current printings. Others, not all of which are particularly worthwhile, are listed below. In general, a "Cruden" of limited size will also prove of limited use.

Other Editions of Cruden

3.12   CRUDEN'S UNABRIDGED CONCORDANCE
            Grand Rapids: Baker (n.d.)

Same as 3.6, but usually priced a few dollars lower.

3.13   CRUDEN'S CONCORDANCE
            New York: Warne (1872)

3.14   CRUDEN'S CONCORDANCE
            Grand Rapids: Zondervan (1949)

3.14p   *Same:* paperback

Short and Incomplete/Abridged Editions of Cruden

3.15   CRUDEN'S COMPACT CONCORDANCE
            Grand Rapids: Zondervan (1968)

3.16   CRUDEN'S HANDY CONCORDANCE
            Grand Rapids: Zondervan (n.d.). Paperback

3.17   CRUDEN'S CONCORDANCE
            New York: Jove Publications (1970). Paperback

3.18   Bullinger, E. W.
            A CRITICAL LEXICON AND CONCORDANCE TO
            THE ENGLISH AND GREEK NEW TESTAMENT
            Grand Rapids: Zondervan (1975)

This concordance indexes the KJV (the text taken from Bagster's *Critical New Testament*) and is based on the old Greek *Textus Receptus,* supplemented with revisions of later editors and manuscript discoveries. Bullinger's concordance is arranged by English words from the KJV. It offers also a Greek index that shows each English word used to translate a Greek word and the frequency of each English word's appearance in the New Testament.

This 1,040-page concordance covers the New Testament only. The old-fashioned format is still handy to use.

3.19   Ellison, J. W.
            NELSON'S COMPLETE CONCORDANCE OF
            THE REVISED STANDARD VERSION BIBLE
            Nashville/New York: Nelson (1957/1978)

The first edition of this concordance, which appeared in 1957, had the distinction of being the first such book produced on a computer. The revised edition keeps pace with revisions in the RSV translation. There are obvious limitations. Hebrew and Greek words lying behind the translation are not listed, nor is the index analytical. Words that occur most frequently in the Bible are omitted—and that encompasses 130 words, almost 60 percent of the biblical text. This is still the best concordance for the entire RSV Bible. For the New Testament, however, Morrison's (3.3) is the better buy.

3.20   [Moody Press Editors]
BIBLE CONCORDANCE
Chicago: Moody (1959)

3.21   Strong, J. (ed.)
STRONG'S EXHAUSTIVE CONCORDANCE OF THE BIBLE
Nashville/New York: Nelson (1977)

This differs from the Abingdon edition (3.4) by omitting the "Key-Word Comparison" system, which monitors variations among modern translations.

3.22   *Same:* thumb-indexed

3.23   STRONG'S EXHAUSTIVE CONCORDANCE
Grand Rapids: Baker (n.d.). Paperback

3.24   STRONG'S EXHAUSTIVE CONCORDANCE
Nashville: Broadman (1978). Paperback

3.25   STRONG'S CONCORDANCE OF THE BIBLE
Nashville/New York: Nelson (1980). Abridgment. (864 pages)

3.26   Goodrick, E. W., and J. R. Kohlenberger III (eds.)
THE NIV COMPLETE CONCORDANCE
Grand Rapids: Zondervan (1981)

One of the most recent concordances to be compiled, this indexes the vocabulary of the New International Version. Evaluated in the light of today's advanced editing techniques and technology, this tool is surprisingly meager in scope—it is far from complete and is not analytical. It is, however, the only concordance to the NIV.

B. Topical Concordances

THE BEST

3.27   Joy, C. R. (ed.)
HARPER'S TOPICAL CONCORDANCE
San Francisco/New York: Harper & Row. Rev. ed. (1976)

Topical concordances and indexes assume that people think in ideas, not words—and that therefore they will find useful a list of biblical references organized by theme. Of those currently available Joy's has stood the test of time. The revised edition is an improvement over the 1961 edition. Quotations are from the KJV; this edition is paperback.

3.28   Viening, E. (ed.)
            THE ZONDERVAN TOPICAL BIBLE
            Grand Rapids: Zondervan (1969)

THE REST

3.29   Griffith, H. K. (ed.)
            THE NEW WORLD INDEX TO THE HOLY BIBLE
            New York: World (1972)

It is unfortunate that this book has been allowed to go out of print so soon after its appearance. It deserves to be republished. In the meantime, it can be found in libraries.

3.30   Nave, O. J. (ed.)
            NAVE'S TOPICAL BIBLE
            Nashville/New York: Nelson (1979)

or

3.31   NAVE'S TOPICAL BIBLE
            Grand Rapids: Baker (n.d.). Paperback

Nave was a chaplain in the United States Army when he compiled this perennial favorite—"in the quiet of army garrisons, apart from the rush and distraction of dense communities"—a century ago. The text used is the KJV. Nave's thematic Bible appeared in 1894 and was revised two years later; by 1904 there were one hundred thousand copies in print. It is still selling, as these and other editions listed below testify. Its popularity results, in part, from the great breadth that Nave offered. In his own words (the subtitle of the book): "Embracing all doctrines of Biblical religion, and all phases of ancient society, history, law, politics, and other secular subjects; archaeology, the arts, sciences, philosophy, ethics and economics; principles of government, equity, and right personal conduct; biography, personal incident, and illustrative facts; geography, the history of nations, states, and cities, and a multitude of common subjects, illustrative of ancient religions, governments, manners, fashions, customs and ideas." That is an honest, if wordy, statement of what *Nave's* offers, even today.

Another reason for its survival is that it was based on sound biblical scholarship of its day. If *Nave's* can no longer be regarded as one of the best, it is because the arrangement now seems outdated. Yet for basic indexing it is still useful. It is available in a paperback edition (3.31), an abridgment (3.32), and an expanded form (3.33).

Other Editions

3.32   Nave, O. J. (ed.)
        NAVE'S TOPICAL BIBLE
        Abridged by Moody Press Staff
        Chicago: Moody (n.d.). Paperback

3.33   Nave, O. J., and S. M. Coder (eds.)
        NAVE'S TOPICAL BIBLE. Enlarged Edition
        Chicago: Moody (1975)

3.34   Monser, H. E. (ed.)
        TOPICAL INDEX AND DIGEST OF THE BIBLE
        Grand Rapids: Baker (1979). Paperback

3.35   Wharton, G. C. (ed.)
        THE NEW COMPACT TOPICAL BIBLE
        Grand Rapids: Zondervan (1972)

It *is* compact—and compatible with *Halley's Bible Handbook* (8.10) and other titles.

3.36   [A. J. Holman Co.]
        HOLMAN TOPICAL BIBLE
        Nashville: Holman (1973)

The range is not wide, and the texts listed are not quoted. It is compact (288 pages) and inexpensive.

3.37   Miller, D. M. (ed.)
        THE TOPICAL BIBLE CONCORDANCE
        Nashville/New York: Abingdon (1977)

Thin in every sense of the word, including cost.

SUMMARY

In the world of topical concordances, less is not more. The best advice: stay with the best concordances; choose a durable binding; watch out for maddeningly tiny print.

C. Greek Concordances

For a complete listing of Greek and Greek/English ("Quick Greek") concordances, see 4.49–4.60.

D. Concordances Arranged by Translation

In addition to the title described above, this list contains a few titles no longer in print. They will often be found in larger libraries. The list is based on the *primary* translation served by each concordance; some concordances can be used with several translations.

THE KING JAMES (or AUTHORIZED) VERSION
Strong: 3.4, 3.5, 3.21–3.25
Young: 3.6–3.10
Cruden: 3.11–3.17
Bullinger: 3.18
[Moody]: 3.20

THE REVISED STANDARD VERSION
Morrison: 3.3
Ellison: 3.19

THE JERUSALEM BIBLE
Darton: 3.1

THE NEW AMERICAN BIBLE
Hartdegen: 3.2

THE AMERICAN STANDARD VERSION
Hazard, M. C. (ed.)
A COMPLETE CONCORDANCE TO THE AMERICAN STANDARD VERSION OF THE BIBLE (1922). *Not in Print*

THE MOFFATT TRANSLATION
Gant, W. J. (ed.)
CONCORDANCE OF THE BIBLE IN THE MOFFATT TRANSLATION (1950). *Not in Print*

THE DOUAY-RHEIMS VERSION
Thompson, N., and R. Stock (eds.)
CONCORDANCE TO THE BIBLE (Douay Version) (1942). *Not in Print*

BEST BUYS

Among concordances covering only the New Testament, Darton (3.1) is, without question, the best buy for its scope, its usefulness with many different translations, and its price. Morrison (3.3), on the other hand, must be acknowledged as the most comprehensive and sophisticated. It is a gold mine, but it is expensive.

Strong (3.4, 3.5, 3.21–3.25) and Young (3.5–3.10) are standards and remain the most complete and sophisticated for the entire Bible. Given their scope, they are wonderful buys. As indicated above, choosing between them requires evaluating certain virtues and faults. Many would prefer Young for ease of use. In both cases, one must choose carefully from among the many available editions.

For a topical concordance, the prize goes to Harper's edited by Joy (3.27). It is solid, tested, easily available, and not too expensive. A cloth edition of the 1976 version is the best buy of all.

4

DO YOU KNOW GREEK?
Essentials for Using
the Greek New Testament

When the apostle Paul was arrested in Jerusalem (Acts 21:27-40), he turned to the centurion in charge and asked for a private word with him. "Do you know Greek?" the surprised soldier asked when he heard Paul's words.

Greek was at that time the closest thing to a common language throughout the civilized world. A single language could be used almost everywhere, not only in Athens or Corinth but also in Jerusalem, Antioch, and Rome. To this day, serious Bible study requires coming to terms with the Greek New Testament and, to a lesser extent, with the Greek version of the Old Testament called the Septuagint. This chapter describes the best resources for using the Greek Bible.

Unfortunately, the days are long past when every educated person studied the classical languages. Even those who once learned some Greek may find it hard to remember the language. This chapter and the one following take these problems into account in two ways.

First, some resources are described that are primarily of technical or advanced interest. These are for serious students and may prove less attractive for more casual use. Second, some items are tagged with the phrase "Quick Greek," which refers to resources that are especially helpful to those who are just beginning Greek or those whose mastery of the language has grown rusty. These tools will help users overcome such deficiencies. "Quick Greek" titles can often make some of the Greek New Testament's riches accessible to those who know nothing more than the Greek alphabet. Such helps include dictionaries, lexicons, concordances, vocabulary lists, and a variety of other books. A summary listing of all of these items will be found at the end of Chapter 5.

A. The New Testament in Greek

I. The Whole New Testament

THE BEST

There are two standard editions of the Greek New Testament currently available.

4.1   Aland, K., with M. Black, C. M. Martini, B. M. Metzger, and A. P. Wikgren (eds.)
             THE GREEK NEW TESTAMENT
             New York: American Bible Society/London: United Bible Societies. Corrected 3rd ed. (1983)99 398

(*In conjunction with this, see also 4.63.*)

and

4.2   Aland, K., with M. Black, C. M. Martini, B. M. Metzger, and A. P. Wikgren (eds.)
             NOVUM TESTAMENTUM GRAECE
             New York: American Bible Society/Stuttgart: German Bible Society. 26th ed. (1979)

These two versions of the Greek New Testament are closely related. The first is referred to as the UBS text, and the second (which bears the name of the original editor, E. Nestle) as Nestle-Aland. They offer exactly the same Greek text (and with the corrected third edition, the same punctuation), but they differ in other ways. One notable difference will be found toward the bottom of the page, beneath the New Testament text. This is called the "critical apparatus" in a Greek Bible, a section that shows how and where different manuscripts offer variant readings. It is also the place where the editors can indicate possible alternatives in punctuation. (Since most manuscripts do not have punctuation, what we find in modern texts has been supplied by those editing the text, and they often must choose from several reasonable alternatives.)

The UBS text provides a select review of a few variant readings. For those it covers, however, it offers very detailed information about dozens of manuscripts. In contrast, the Nestle-Aland text covers many more instances of textual variants but goes into less detail for those it mentions. Scholars will have both texts at hand, but for others the choice may hinge on other concerns. For example, while both are handy volumes to hold, the slightly larger UBS text offers a page that is easier to read, while the Nestle-Aland is easier to tuck into a pocket or purse.

Finally, a word on purchasing these books. Neither is published in this country but both are available from the American Bible Society (ABS) in New York. That organization sells to everyone, dealer or individual customer, at the same price. Therefore, it is best to write directly to the ABS in New York (P.O. Box 5656, Grand Central Station, New York, NY 10163) and place the order with them. All sales are cash in advance, and ABS pays the postage. If a bookstore orders one of these texts, it may save some trouble, but the price will be higher to cover the book dealer's costs and profit.

These two texts also come in other editions with special features:

THE GREEK NEW TESTAMENT (UBS)

4.3	*Same:* (1983)99 398 , but bound with *Greek-English Dictionary* by B. M. Newman, Jr. (4.31).
4.4	*Same:* (1983)99 398 , but in leather binding (the basic edition above is bound in Kivar).
4.5	*Same:* (1975)99 398 , but with a Spanish rather than an English introduction.
4.6	*Same:* (1975)99 398 , but with a Spanish introduction and dictionary.

(*See also* 4.13.)

NOVUM TESTAMENTUM GRAECE (Nestle-Aland)

4.7	*Same:* (1979), but with leather binding (the basic edition above is bound in thin boards).
4.8	*Same:* (1979), but in a study edition featuring large print on large pages, with blank pages interleaved for note taking.

THE REST

Many of the useful older editions are out of print. Among those still available are:

4.9	Kilpatrick, G. D. (ed.) HĒ KAINĒ DIATHĒKĒ New York: American Bible Society/London: British and Foreign Bible Society (1958)

This is the second edition of a standard text that goes back to 1904. It is clear and easy to read.

4.10   HĒ KAINĒ DIATHĒKĒ
New York: American Bible Society/Athens: Bible Society (1967)

This edition features the traditional Greek text of the Greek Orthodox Church, accompanied by a parallel version in modern Greek (Bambas, 1844).

4.11   HĒ KAINĒ DIATHĒKĒ
New York: American Bible Society/Athens: Bible Society (1967/ 1970)

In this edition the traditional Greek text of the Greek Orthodox Church is accompanied by a parallel version in modern Greek (Vellas).

4.12   Friberg, B., and T. Friberg (eds.)
ANALYTICAL GREEK NEW TESTAMENT
Grand Rapids: Baker (1981)

This special (and expensive) new edition of the basic UBS text (4.1) offers a unique feature. Instead of the critical apparatus, there is a "tag" under each Greek word, a symbol indicating the grammatical form and sometimes the function of the word. Nouns, pronouns, verbs, adjectives, and all the rest are readily distinguishable.

This text is no substitute for the UBS or the Nestle-Aland text, and it comes at three times the price. It is useful for "Quick Greek," however, because it allows the novice to sort out grammatical parts and organize words into their proper relationships. Unlike an interlinear text, it does not offer the temptation simply to use the English words and give up on the Greek.

II. Synopses of the Gospels

A *synopsis* of the gospels provides the text of Matthew, Mark, and Luke in parallel columns, so that the reader can quickly notice similarities and differences. In some synopses, relevant material from John's gospel is also included. Synopses in English are listed elsewhere (2.7, 2.8, 2.10–2.12). Those listed here offer the Greek text, though in one case (4.13) an English translation is provided on facing pages.

4.13   Aland, K. (ed.)
SYNOPSIS QUATTUOR EVANGELIORUM
New York: American Bible Society/Stuttgart: German Bible Society. 10th ed. (1978)

65356

There is no question that this is a scholar's synopsis, a technical triumph. It is one of two major Greek synopses (along with 4.15). The Greek text is the Nestle-Aland 26th edition. It also boasts a rich listing of parallels from apocryphal gospels and patristic Christian sources. Nothing comes close to providing so much relevant background material. The introduction appears in both German and English. Technical. A standard.

4.14   Aland, K. (ed.)
SYNOPSIS OF THE FOUR GOSPELS
New York: American Bible Society/Stuttgart: German Bible
Society. 3rd ed. (1979)

This is the "English translation" of the previous entry (4.13). It offers the Greek text of the Nestle-Aland 26th edition and the English of the RSV on facing pages. Something had to be omitted to make room for the English text, and so the rich apocryphal and patristic citations of the original are not found here. There is a valuable apparatus, however, showing variations in the major English translations such as the KJV and the Revised versions, and the rest of the critical apparatus is carried over from the other synopsis. Probably the preferable edition for many without a technical interest. A "Quick Greek" resource.

4.15   Huck, A., and H. Greeven (eds.)
SYNOPSIS OF THE FIRST THREE GOSPELS WITH THE
ADDITION OF THE JOHANNINE PARALLELS
Grand Rapids: Eerdmans. 13th ed. (1981)

"Huck," as it was always called, was *the* Greek synopsis, giving way only recently to the Aland text (4.13). Now a thoroughly revised edition of Huck is available, the first since 1936. Greeven, the modern editor, has provided a newly edited text, making this printed text of the gospels completely independent of the Greek text common to both the UBS text and Nestle-Aland. All descriptive information is provided in both German and English. Technical and, for the scholar, indispensable.

SUMMARY

Each of the three volumes has unique advantages. *Synopsis Quattuor Evangeliorum* (4.13) offers more parallels from the early Christian literature of the period immediately after the New Testament. *Synopsis of the Four Gospels* (4.14) is the best Greek synopsis that also offers a parallel English text. Huck's *Synopsis* revised by Greeven (4.15) makes available an entirely independent Greek text and offers a rich selection of noncanonical "parallel" readings. For a Greek synopsis, the choice is between Huck (4.15) and Aland (4.13). Huck is easier to find or order; it does not offer an English translation as does 4.14.

III. Interlinear Greek New Testaments

An interlinear Greek New Testament presents a running, often literal, English translation immediately below each line of Greek. In addition, many versions offer as a supplement in the margin one or another of the standard English versions such as KJV, RSV, NIV, etc. An interlinear text is a favorite "Quick Greek" resource.

4.16   INTERLINEAR GREEK-ENGLISH NEW TESTAMENT
          Grand Rapids: Baker (n.d.)

This is an older, classic interlinear version of the New Testament; it offers these special features: (1) It is coded to the numbering system used in Strong's *Exhaustive Concordance* (3.4), which means that one can go from the Greek word directly to the pages in Strong's concordance, which show all New Testament usages (and all English words used to translate the Greek, at least in the KJV). (2) This edition includes Berry's *Greek-English Lexicon and New Testament Synonyms* (4.32). (3) It includes also J. Strong's *Greek Dictionary of the New Testament*.

There are some problems with all of this cross-referencing. For example, if you can use the coded numbering system, then presumably you own a copy of Strong's concordance. If so, you do not need the dictionary, since it is already printed in the concordance. On the other hand, if you do not have Strong, then the dictionary may be of some value, but the numbering system is useless. Another drawback is the fact that this edition comes only in paperback binding, which will not stand up to repeated use. Finally, the Greek text is outdated.

4.17   INTERLINEAR GREEK-ENGLISH NEW TESTAMENT
          Grand Rapids: Baker (n.d.)

Essentially another version of the item above (4.16), this edition offers the KJV and, again, Berry's *Greek-English Lexicon and New Testament Synonyms* (4.32). It lacks Strong's *Dictionary* and the numerical coding to Strong's *Exhaustive Concordance* (3.4). A much lower price makes this a better value, but it is still in paper and the text is an antique (see 4.18).

4.18   Berry, G. R. (ed.)
          INTERLINEAR GREEK-ENGLISH NEW TESTAMENT
          Grand Rapids: Zondervan (n.d.)

The text is the old *Textus Receptus,* long since superseded. The interlinear translation runs word for word, and a numbering system is used for tricky sequences. The marginal translation is the KJV. Again, Berry's *Greek-English Lexicon and New Testament Synonyms* (4.32) is included. This cloth edition is a more suitable binding.

4.19   Berry, G. R. (ed.)
     INTERLINEAR GREEK-ENGLISH NEW TESTAMENT
     Nashville: Broadman (1978)

A paperback version of the previous item (4.18).

4.20   Marshall, A. (ed.)
     THE INTERLINEAR GREEK-ENGLISH NEW TESTAMENT
     Grand Rapids: Zondervan (1958)

This version of the interlinear text and the editions of it listed below are preferable to those originally edited by Berry. The Greek text is that of Nestle's 21st edition (1952), old by today's standards but a vast improvement over the old *Textus Receptus*. In addition to a brief introduction by the well-known translator J. B. Phillips, this text features the KJV in the margin. The interlinear translation is well done; and, if the readers heed Marshall's introductory words of caution, they will probably not be tempted to misunderstand what an interlinear text is all about.

4.21   Marshall, A. (ed.)
     THE INTERLINEAR GREEK-ENGLISH NEW TESTAMENT
     Grand Rapids: Zondervan (1958/1976)

Same as the preceding (4.20) but with the RSV in the margin.

4.22   Marshall, A. (ed.)
     THE INTERLINEAR GREEK-ENGLISH NEW TESTAMENT
     Grand Rapids: Zondervan (1958/1968)

Same as the above (4.20) but with the NIV in the margin. For some reason, less expensive.

4.23   Marshall, A. (ed.)
     THE ZONDERVAN PARALLEL NEW TESTAMENT
     IN GREEK AND ENGLISH
     Grand Rapids: Zondervan (1975)

On one page is Marshall's basic Greek text (Nestle) with interlinear translation, and on the opposite page in parallel columns are both the NIV and the KJV.

SUMMARY

Any interlinear New Testament needs to be used with caution. Of those currently available, the Marshall text is definitely to be preferred. While not up-to-date, it does reflect twentieth-century standards. From 4.20, 4.21, 4.22, and 4.23 one can choose the edition that offers the desired English translation.

IV. Greek and English New Testaments

These editions of a Greek text, which offer an English text as well, also deserve the "Quick Greek" tag. Without providing an interlinear translation, they put Greek and English side by side for easy comparison.

4.24   THE NEW TESTAMENT IN GREEK AND ENGLISH
      The Greek Text of the United Bible Societies and Today's
       English Version
      New York: American Bible Society (1966)

A "diglot" (literally, "two-tongued") edition. The Greek text is that of the second edition of UBS. Alongside appears the American Bible Society's own English translation, formerly entitled *Good News for Modern Man* and now called Today's English Version (TEV). This is not always a successful translation, but there can be no doubt that the book is a useful tool. It is available both in hard cover and as a loose-leaf book furnished with its own binder. The wide margins are excellent for note taking. A real value.

4.25   Newberry, T. (ed.)
      THE ENGLISHMAN'S GREEK NEW TESTAMENT
      Grand Rapids: Zondervan (1877/1970)

[4.14]   Aland, K.
      SYNOPSIS OF THE FOUR GOSPELS

(*See 4.14.*)

SUMMARY

Almost all interlinear editions offer a standard translation alongside some version of the Greek text. The truly unique and useful volume is 4.24, the American Bible Society's wide-margin edition. In the loose-leaf version it is a particularly flexible tool for personal research.

B. The Old Testament in Greek

Long before the New Testament came into being, the Hebrew scriptures had been translated into Greek. It was in this version, called the Septuagint (and abbreviated by the Roman numeral LXX), that many New Testament writers knew and quoted the Jewish scriptures.

I. The Septuagint

4.26   Rahlfs, A. (ed.)
                SEPTUAGINTA
                New York: American Bible Society/Stuttgart: German Bible
                Society (1935/1979)

This is the standard reading edition of the Septuagint, the only one readily available in the English-speaking world. The critical text, prepared in 1935, is somewhat dated, but there is no complete edition of better quality available. The introduction is in English (among other languages).

II. The Old Testament in Greek and English Versions

There are also available two editions of an earlier work.

4.27   Brenton, C. (also catalogued as
                Lee-Brenton, Sir Lancelot Charles)
                THE SEPTUAGINT VERSION: GREEK AND ENGLISH
                Grand Rapids: Zondervan (1844/1970)

This was first published in 1844, and the Apocrypha was added in 1851 (see 4.28). This offers the Greek text of the Old Testament as found in one important manuscript, Codex Vaticanus, along with the editor's translation into English.

4.28   Brenton, C. (also catalogued as
                Lee-Brenton, Sir Lancelot Charles)
                THE SEPTUAGINT WITH APOCRYPHA: GREEK AND
                ENGLISH
                Grand Rapids: Zondervan (1844–1851/1972)

The only difference between this edition and the preceding one is the inclusion of the Old Testament Apocrypha in Greek. Since one definition of the term "Old

Testament Apocrypha" is the books of the Greek Old Testament not found in the Hebrew Old Testament, it is odd that a publication called "Septuagint" would omit them.

SUMMARY

There is no complete text to rival Rahlfs (4.26). It is also the best buy and the technical standard. If you want an English translation of the Septuagint text close at hand (which can be useful, since the Septuagint text does not always correspond to the text of the English Bible), then Brenton's larger edition with Apocrypha (4.28) is the best choice.

C. Lexicons and Dictionaries of New Testament Greek

THE BEST

4.29   Abbott-Smith, G. (ed.)
        A MANUAL GREEK LEXICON OF THE NEW TESTAMENT
        Greenwood (SC): Attic Press. 3rd ed. (1937/1977)

The term "manual" indicates that this is not a huge reference work but one you can hold in your hand. Being "handy" is Abbott-Smith's main attraction. It also offers some other good features: etymologies (which make building vocabulary easier), citations of Hebrew words underlying the Septuagint and New Testament Greek usage, and synonyms. For completeness Abbott-Smith is no match for Bauer-Arndt-Gingrich-Danker (4.30), and it is less complete than old Thayer (4.38). But there is nothing like it for quick, easy reference, and no other lexicon crams so much information into such a small package.

4.30   Bauer, W., W. F. Arndt, F. W. Gingrich
        A GREEK-ENGLISH LEXICON OF THE NEW TESTAMENT
        AND OTHER EARLY CHRISTIAN LITERATURE
        Revised and augmented by F. W. Gingrich and F. W. Danker
        Chicago: University of Chicago Press/Grand Rapids: Zondervan.
        2nd ed. (1979)

Without question, this is *the* lexicon of New Testament Greek. It is also rich in coverage of early Christian literature from the period just after the New Testament.

The first edition (1957) was based on a well-known German lexicon by W. Bauer. That dictionary was soon revised, and this second edition of the English translation reflects these and many other more recent changes. It expands the survey of Greek papyri, taking account of recent secondary literature. New words have been added and the range of textual variants is extended. This is by far the most complete and up-to-date lexicon of New Testament Greek available. No scholar would be without it, and no one who reads the New Testament in Greek should miss its wealth of information. Casual users and those who want some help with Greek will find a derivative item (5.60) of interest.

4.31   Newman, B. M.
        A CONCISE GREEK-ENGLISH DICTIONARY OF THE NEW
        TESTAMENT
        New York: American Bible Society/London: United Bible
        Societies (1971)

This brief lexicon was specifically designed for use with the UBS *Greek New Testament* (4.1). It is available separately or bound with that New Testament text. Place names are located on endpaper maps; irregular verbs are cited both alphabetically and according to their proper primary forms. This is not the last word in dictionaries, but it is hard to beat for the money.

THE REST

4.32   Berry, G. R. (ed.)
        BERRY'S GREEK-ENGLISH NEW TESTAMENT LEXICON
        WITH SYNONYMS
        Grand Rapids: Baker (1980)

This original paperback is actually a separate reprinting of material found in Berry's interlinear New Testament (4.18). The lexicon is coded to the numbering system of Strong's *Exhaustive Concordance* (3.4). The chief virtues of this lexicon are its portability and its usefulness for "Quick Greek."

4.33   Gingrich, F. W.
        A SHORTER LEXICON OF THE GREEK NEW TESTAMENT
        Chicago: University of Chicago/Grand Rapids: Zondervan
        (1957/1965)

An abridgment of the *first* edition of Bauer-Arndt-Gingrich, *A Greek-English Lexicon* (for the *second* edition, see 4.30). It confines its listings to the basic meanings of words and to citations from the New Testament. Textual variants are noted. It is reasonably up-to-date and handy, fuller than Newman (4.31) but less useful all around than (the older) Abbott-Smith (4.29).

4.34   Moulton, J. H., and G. Milligan
        THE VOCABULARY OF THE GREEK TESTAMENT
        Illustrated from the Papyri and Other Non-Literary Sources
        Grand Rapids: Eerdmans (1949)

This is a technical and specialized tool, not a general New Testament Greek lexicon. At the turn of this century it became clear that the language of the New Testament had much in common with nonliterary papyri such as those turning up in profusion in Egypt. "Moulton and Milligan," as it is called, is a scholarly lexicon of Greek words that appear also in the papyri and similar sources. It supplements other major lexicons and is of greatest interest to technical users.

4.35   Sophocles, E. A.
        GREEK LEXICON OF THE ROMAN AND BYZANTINE
        PERIODS
        New York: Scribner (1887/1957)

This, too, is a specialized volume appealing primarily to the technical and scholarly user. This is *the* standard lexicon for Greek of the period 146 B.C. to A.D. 1100.

4.36   Hickie, W. J.
        GREEK ENGLISH LEXICON TO THE NEW TESTAMENT
        Grand Rapids: Baker (1977)

Paperback. Very brief and very inexpensive.

4.37   Souter, A. (ed.)
        POCKET LEXICON TO THE GREEK NEW TESTAMENT
        New York: Oxford University Press (1916)

This old favorite has the virtue of being handy and compact. It is vastly preferable to Hickie (4.36). Souter remains in demand because so much reliable information is compressed into fewer than three hundred pages. Although not as up-to-date, this is a clear alternative to the abridged version of Bauer-Arndt-Gingrich (4.33). Relatively expensive.

4.38   Thayer, J. H.
        GREEK-ENGLISH LEXICON OF THE NEW TESTAMENT
        Grand Rapids: Zondervan (1889/1956)

Thayer's classic lexicon appeared in 1885–1886 as a translation of a German effort, the Grimm-Wilde *Clavis*. It was revised a few years later and became the standard New Testament lexicon until the appearance of the first edition of Bauer-Arndt-Gingrich (4.30). Thayer remains popular and can be found in a variety of inexpensive (but not very durable) new editions. Most have been reproduced by reducing the page size, which makes the book harder to read. This edition is available in cloth binding. For the others, see the next two entries—better yet, find an older second-hand copy.

4.39   Thayer, J. H.
THAYER'S GREEK-ENGLISH LEXICON OF THE NEW
TESTAMENT
Nashville: Broadman (1889/1978). Paperback

4.40   Thayer, J. H.
THAYER'S GREEK-ENGLISH LEXICON OF THE NEW
TESTAMENT
Grand Rapids: Baker (1889/n.d.). Paperback

This edition, in paperback, is keyed to the numerical code of Strong's *Exhaustive Concordance* (3.4). Good for "Quick Greek."

4.41   Kubo, S.
A READER'S GREEK-ENGLISH LEXICON OF THE NEW
TESTAMENT AND BEGINNER'S GUIDE
Grand Rapids: Zondervan (1975)

"Quick Greek."

4.42   Moulton, H. K.
THE ANALYTICAL GREEK-ENGLISH LEXICON REVISED
Grand Rapids: Zondervan (1978)

This is an updated version of a very much older lexicon; it lists alphabetically not only every New Testament word but also every *form* of every word. The emphasis in such "analytical lexicons" is not just on the meaning of the Greek words but also on recognizing the specific form of each. "Quick Greek," this book is designed for the beginner.

SUMMARY

For a full-scale lexicon, Bauer-Arndt-Gingrich-Danker (4.30) in the second edition is the best choice; for a handy-sized but reasonably full lexicon, Abbott-Smith (4.29); and for quick reference and conciseness, Newman (4.31).

D. Major Greek Reference Works

There are a few reference works that are so important they belong in a class by themselves. Those described here fall into two categories: standard lexicons of Greek literature and standard reference works covering Greek Christian literature.

4.43   Liddell, H. G. and R. Scott (eds.)
              A GREEK-ENGLISH LEXICON
              New edition, rev. by H. A. Jones, with a supplement by E. A.
              Barber
              New York: Oxford. 9th ed. (1968)

The standard in Greek dictionaries. Nothing rivals it for covering the whole range
of Greek literature. Because early Christian Greek is so well served by other
resources, however, Liddell-Scott pays less attention to it than to other areas. Still,
this is *the* dictionary that settles arguments about the meaning of Greek words.
It has been around so long that many second-hand copies are available. Those
published before 1968 do not contain Barber's supplement; otherwise there have
been no changes since 1940.

4.44   Liddell, H. G. and R. Scott (eds.)
              INTERMEDIATE GREEK-ENGLISH LEXICON
              New York: Oxford (1889/1957)

A considerable abridgment of the above. Easy to use for quick reference, but not
definitive.

4.45   Liddell, H. G. and R. Scott
              ABRIDGED GREEK-ENGLISH LEXICON
              New York: Oxford (1953)

Still briefer. Designed for classroom use.

4.46   Lampe, G. W. (ed.)
              A PATRISTIC GREEK LEXICON
              New York: Oxford (1961/1968)

This is a huge volume, almost as large as the unabridged Liddell-Scott (4.43),
which it is actually designed to supplement. Lampe catalogues the Greek vocabulary
of the early church. Like every other book in this section, it is highly technical,
definitive, and expensive.

4.47   Kittel, G., and G. Friedrich (gen. eds.)
              THEOLOGICAL DICTIONARY OF THE NEW TESTAMENT
              An Unabridged English Translation by Geoffrey W. Bromiley. 10
              vols.
              Grand Rapids: Eerdmans (1963–1976)

Unlike the other books listed above, "Kittel' is marketed for both the scholar and
the general reader and is often featured at discount prices. Nevertheless, it should
be remembered that this is still a technical and formidable work. Encyclopedia-
like entries cover every major *Greek* word in the New Testament. These may run
from one or two paragraphs to more than one hundred pages. The entries are
given in (Greek) alphabetical order, and later words get much fuller treatment
than many of those coming earlier in the alphabet. The standard approach for

each entry is to show the word's range of meanings in earlier Greek, to canvass the Greek Old Testament and the meanings of Hebrew equivalents, and then to trace the uses of the word throughout the New Testament. An extensive scholarly bibliography is provided at the bottom of every page.

Kittel is really a scholarly and technical tool that *can* be used by others who have a serious interest in word study, provided they can recognize the Greek alphabet. Vol. 10 has an excellent index (by Greek words, by Hebrew words, and by New Testament passages), which enormously expands the usefulness of the other nine volumes.

4.48   Cremer, H.
            BIBLIO-THEOLOGICAL LEXICON OF NEW TESTAMENT
            GREEK
            Edinburgh: T. & T. Clark. 4th ed. (1895)

Although frequently reprinted after the appearance of the fourth edition in 1895, Cremer is now badly out-of-date. Readers with technical interests will prefer Kittel (4.47), while more general readers will find Brown (6.42) more suited to their needs. Still, Cremer was for a long time the only such work available, and it still offers some interesting essays, arranged alphabetically by Greek words.

SUMMARY

Except for Cremer (4.48), these are standard technical tools, although Kittel (4.47) is also very theologically oriented and of somewhat greater appeal. Among lexicons, if one has Bauer-Arndt-Gingrich (4.30), then the abridged editions of Liddel-Scott (4.44, 4.45) hold little appeal.

E. Greek Concordances of the New Testament

On concordances in general and the meaning of terms such as "complete" in their titles, see the introductory note in Chapter 3. Several of the concordances listed below combine the use of Greek words with English translations, making them useful for "Quick Greek."

THE BEST

4.49   [Institut für neutestamentliche Textforschung und
            Rechenzentrum der Universität Münster-Westphalia]

COMPUTER KONKORDANZ ZUM NOVUM
TESTAMENTUM GRAECE VON NESTLE ALAND 26.
AUFLAGE, UND ZUM GREEK NEW TESTAMENT
New York: Walter de Gruyter. 3rd ed. (1980)

The German title (not to mention the name of the institutional "editor") may sound intimidating, but in English this is usually referred to simply as the "Computer Concordance." This is the most complete and useful concordance to the Greek New Testament available today. While not exactly inexpensive, it is, at least for the moment, the standard by which all others are measured.

The "Computer Concordance" is based on the Greek text common to both UBS (4.1) and Nestle-Aland (4.2). Behind this effort lies an even larger project, a genuinely "complete concordance to the Greek New Testament," which is appearing a few pages at a time. That edition will be monumental and truly definitive, showing practically every variant reading in every significant Greek text edition since Tischendorf. It will also be monumentally expensive. In the meantime, and presumably for a long time, this is the best. Standard. Technical.

4.50   Smith, J. B. (ed.)
GREEK-ENGLISH CONCORDANCE TO THE NEW
TESTAMENT
Scottdale (PA): Herald Press (1955)

It is unfortunate that very few people know about this fine work, but the publisher has kept it in print nevertheless. For the general reader of the Greek New Testament this is the most helpful tool available in opening up the Greek text. Scholars will find it less useful, perhaps.

Smith's tabular and statistical Greek-English concordance is based on the KJV and includes an English to Greek index. The tabular arrangement conveys an enormous amount of information quickly. It enables the reader to see at a glance the whole range of translations of any particular Greek word and to determine the number of occurrences, book by book, in the New Testament. With the English-Greek index it is possible to start with an English word and turn to the proper Greek word for all the information. Best of all, the price is surprisingly modest. Highly recommended.

4.51   Moulton, W. F., and A. S. Geden
A CONCORDANCE TO THE GREEK TESTAMENT
According to the Texts of Westcott and Hort, Tischendorf, and
the English revisers
Greenwood (SC): Attic Press. 5th ed. (1978)

For generations "Moulton and Geden" has been the standard Greek New Testament concordance in English. It was based on Westcott and Hort's version of the Greek New Testament with other Greek versions accounted for. The third edition of 1926 was widely reprinted; and in the last revision of 1978, a number of "small" words, previously only listed, were fully included. The whole is now keyed to the numbering system of Strong's *Exhaustive Concordance* (3.4). Until the new

"Computer Concordance" (4.49), this was the standard Greek New Testament concordance; it remains a basic, reliable technical resource, even it it has been eclipsed.

4.52   *Same*

4.53   Schmoller, A. (ed.)
            HANDKONKORDANZ ZUM NEUEN TESTAMENT
            New York: American Bible Society/Stuttgart: German Bible
            Society. 15th ed. (1973)

Schmoller does not rival the previous entries for completeness, but it is the best *compact* concordance of the Greek text available—one every scholar will have close at hand. It is less useful for more general readers. The definitions of Greek words are given in Latin. Although of limited range, this is a fine technical tool. Standard.

THE REST

4.54   Gall, J.
            LAYMAN'S ENGLISH-GREEK CONCORDANCE
            Grand Rapids: Baker (1974)

This concordance is brief and less than adequate for serious work. As the title suggests, the listing is by English words. Very inexpensive.

4.55   Stagenga, J.
            THE GREEK-ENGLISH ANALYTICAL CONCORDANCE
            OF THE GREEK-ENGLISH NEW TESTAMENT
            Jackson (MS): Hellenes-English Biblical Foundations (1963)

Based on the *Textus Receptus* (of 1550), this concordance offers Greek words with English translations. Good for "Quick Greek."

4.56   Wilgram, G. V. (ed.)
            THE ENGLISHMAN'S GREEK CONCORDANCE OF THE
            NEW TESTAMENT
            Grand Rapids: Zondervan (1883–1889)

An old classic admired by those who want to look up words in Greek and find the citations translated into English. Based on older Greek New Testament editions, it is not up-to-date. But it is still popular, as the next two entries suggest.

4.57   Wigram, G. V. (eds.)
            THE ENGLISHMAN'S GREEK CONCORDANCE OF THE
            NEW TESTAMENT
            Numerically Coded to "Strong's Exhaustive Concordance."
            Grand Rapids: Baker (1883/1980)

Same as preceding work (4.56) but in paperback.

4.58   Wigram, G. V. (ed.)
            THE ENGLISHMAN'S GREEK CONCORDANCE OF THE
            NEW TESTAMENT
            Nashville: Broadman. Rev. ed. (1883/1980)

Same as 4.56 but in paperback.

4.59   Winter, R. D. 9ed.)
            THE WORD-STUDY CONCORDANCE
            Wheaton (IL): Tyndale (1978)

4.60   *Same*

This is basically the same concordance as that described in the three entries
immediately above. Winter, however, has added extra features here and there,
whether or not they improve the work may be debated. The basic information
from Wigram is preserved: Greek concordance in alphabetical order with citations
following in the English of the KJV. Added to this is a series of codes at the top
of the entry; for example, the number assigned by Strong's *Exhaustive Concordance*
(3.4) along with the number of times the word appears in the New Testament.
Winter also located the page in Bauer-Arndt-Gingrich where the word appears
(but these references are to the first edition, not the revised edition, 4.30) and the
page number in Moulton and Geden's Greek concordance (4.51). Finally, this
scheme of numbers and symbols gives the volume and page in Kittel's Theological
Dictionary (4.47) where the word is discussed. Since all of these books are
arranged alphabetically anyway and since Kittel has a superb index volume of its
own, there is some question about the usefulness of all this numbering. On the
other hand, for "Quick Greek" this book works like a central switchboard
connecting the reader with other major reference works.

Unfortunately, Winter's concordance is available from Tyndale only as part of
a set, the other volume being *The Word-Study New Testament,* which is actually
the American Bible Society's large type KJV of the New Testament accompanied
by Strong's (ubiquitous) numbering system. All of this adds up to much ado about
little.

F. Greek Concordances to the Septuagint

In this area there are not many alternatives.

4.61   Hatch, E., and H. A. Redpath (eds.)
            A CONCORDANCE TO THE SEPTUAGINT AND THE
            OTHER GREEK VERSIONS OF THE OLD TESTAMENT
            (INCLUDING THE APOCRYPHAL BOOKS). 2 vols. and
            supplement
            New York: International Publications Service (1892–1906/1975)

This is a 1975 reprint of the standard Greek Old Testament concordance first published between 1892 and 1906. A scholarly and technical tool of long-standing significance, Hatch-Redpath is specialized, technical, expensive, and authoritative.

4.62   Morrish, G. (ed.)
        A CONCORDANCE OF THE SEPTUAGINT
        Grand Rapids: Zondervan (1900/1976)

In contrast to Hatch-Redpath (4.61), this is an older and less complete concordance—but one that is available at one-tenth of the price. It is probably adequate for all but the most technical users.

G. Greek Manuscript Commentary

4.63   Metzger, B. M. (ed.)
        A TEXTUAL COMMENTARY ON THE GREEK NEW
        TESTAMENT
        A Companion Volume to the United Bible Societies' Greek New
        Testament (Third Edition)
        New York: American Bible Society/London: United Bible
        Societies (1971)

This volume is literally in a class by itself. In format it is identical to the UBS Greek New Testament (4.1). It offers descriptive summaries of the major variant readings chosen in that Greek text, explaining how and why the editorial committee made its decisions and what the most salient issues are in each case. Serious students of the Greek New Testament will not be without it. Others, if they can read even a bit of Greek,, will find that this volume offers a world of insight into reading New Testament manuscripts and into the process of making a single Greek New Testament from five thousand of these. There is nothing like it, and it is very inexpensive.

BEST BUYS

The "Computer Concordance" (4.49) is the top of the line and will remain so until its even more complete parent publication is finished. Scholars will gravitate toward these and away from the older Moulton-Geden (4.51). Those who need some help in moving from Greek to English will particularly value Smith (4.50), even though it uses the KJV for its English text. The best overall value in an all-Greek concordance remains Schmoller (4.52).

Among interlinear texts Marshall's various editions (4.20–4.23) have the edge because one can choose KJV, RSV, or NIV English text.

5

DO YOU KNOW GREEK?
How to Learn—
and Learn More—
New Testament Greek

Reading the New Testament in Greek brings unique satisfaction. Nothing—and no one—stands between you and the text; you are not reliant on the opinions of others. In addition, a whole array of helpful resources, closed to those who do not know Greek, suddenly becomes available—commentaries, dictionaries, concordances, encyclopedias, and more.

It is regrettable that learning Greek takes special effort, but there are many helpful resources. A number of theological seminaries offer intensive summer courses in simple New Testament Greek, and often classics departments of colleges and universities teach courses that concentrate on New Testament Greek. There is an alternative that requires some patience and discipline, to be sure, but very little money: teach yourself.

Listed below are the best Greek grammars available today. Some are specifically designed for self-instruction. Others are more conventional and can be divided into three categories: elementary grammars, those designed for intermediate level use, and advanced reference grammars. In addition, standard reference works for classical Greek have been included here, along with a variety of special study aids designed to consolidate one's command of Greek grammar and to build vocabulary quickly. Finally, at the conclusion is a list of all of those books designed for "Quick Greek" that have been described in this and the previous chapter. These are especially useful for those who are just beginning Greek or those whose knowledge has grown rusty.

A. Teaching Yourself New Testament Greek

While a reasonably diligent reader can probably learn New Testament Greek from any of the many basic grammars reviewed below, some books have been especially designed for self-instruction. Others, although not really designed for this purpose, work well because they offer a key to the exercises in the grammar book, which enables readers to check their own work. The items described in C-II below will also prove particularly helpful to those who are studying on their own.

THE BEST

5.1   Hudson, D. F.
       TEACH YOURSELF NEW TESTAMENT GREEK
       New York: David McKay (1979)

The best of the self-teaching books, this is part of a magnificent series from which thousands, over the years, have learned any one of a score of languages. In this case the focus is specifically on New Testament Greek. The writing is clear, the exercises (with a key at the back of the book) are pertinent. The book provides everything except paper, pencil, and will power. Accents, a bothersome but standard part of Greek, are not used in this book.

5.2   Wenham, J. W.
       THE ELEMENTS OF NEW TESTAMENT GREEK
       New York: Cambridge University Press (1965)
and

5.3   Wenham, J. W.
       KEY TO ELEMENTS OF NEW TESTAMENT GREEK
       New York: Cambridge University Press (1965)

Wenham set out to revise a classic older grammar (written by H. P. V. Nunn) and wound up writing a new book instead. Its most obvious feature, apart from a very pleasing typography, is the absence of accents (as in Hudson, 5.1). But, as Wenham reminds us, they were also missing for the first seven hundred years of the New Testament; and he makes clear those rare instances where only the accent distinguishes between words.

The book begins with the basic features of grammar in general, using English to refresh a lagging memory. With the accompanying key, every exercise can be converted into a self-instruction unit. Wenham uses every word occurring more than thirty times in the New Testament, a help in building a working vocabulary. The presentation of material is a model of clarity.

5.4   Nunn, H. P. V.
         A SHORT SYNTAX OF NEW TESTAMENT GREEK
         New York: Cambridge University Press. 5th ed. (1938)

Strictly speaking, this book does not belong here, since it is not really a full-fledged grammar and it is not designed to be read lesson by lesson. Instead, it takes up major points of Greek syntax in systematic fashion. Nevertheless, Nunn's work is particularly valuable for those using some other text, such as the two above, for self-instruction. Nunn begins with a refresher course in basic parts of speech, sentence structure, etc. Starting with English, he gradually introduces the reader to the Greek equivalents. It takes much of the mystery out of syntax, and that is why the book has lasted for more than seventy years. It is an excellent supplement to Hudson (5.1) and Wenham (5.2).

THE REST

5.5   Powers, W.
         LEARN TO READ THE GREEK NEW TESTAMENT
         Grand Rapids: Eerdmans (1982)

This is a versatile book, suitable for self-instruction as well as for use in classrooms or in study groups. Powers puts the emphasis on early translation and uses linguistic principles to achieve his goal. The focus is on mastery of basic Greek structure and elementary proficiency. Large and rather expensive.

5.6   Goodrick, E. W.
         DO IT YOURSELF HEBREW AND GREEK
         Everybody's Guide to the Language Tools
         Grand Rapids: Zondervan (1976/1980)

This is a very general introduction to the significance of Greek and Hebrew for Bible reading and study. It lists major tools that presuppose these languages, and the large format includes lessons and worksheets as well as answer keys. The level is introductory. By itself Goodrick's book will not teach you Greek, but it is a place to begin for those who want to start slowly. It is of some use also for those who want to use Greek-language reference tools but do not want to study the language.

5.7   Werner, J. R.
         GREEK: A PROGRAMMED PRIMER. 3 vols.
         Philadelphia: Presbyterian and Reformed (n.d.)

The scope is somewhat broader than New Testament Greek alone. This three-volume set is designed specifically for self-instruction.

5.8   Jay, E. G.
           NEW TESTAMENT GREEK
           An Introductory Grammar
           New York: Seabury (for SPCK, London) (1961)

and

5.9   Jay, E. G.
           A KEY TO THE REV'D DR. E. G. JAY'S
           NEW TESTAMENT GREEK GRAMMAR
           New York: Seabury (for SPCK, London) (1961)

If this book were readily available in the United States it would be listed with the best, for it is excellent. Jay tries to erase some of the distinction between beginning and intermediate levels of instruction and bridges the gap between New Testament and classical Greek. It is excellent for self-instruction because of the accompanying key. One particularly helpful feature is that, wherever possible, Jay illustrates grammatical points from the Gospel of Mark. After finishing this book, one is ready to read that gospel in Greek with understanding.

B. Standard New Testament Grammars

So many grammars are available that we list here only the best and the most widely used (see also C. Special Study Aids). Distinguishing "the best" from "the rest" is rather a subjective matter, since different styles and approaches appeal to different individuals. There is, however, another important distinction. Some grammars are designed for beginners; these are listed here under the heading "Learning New Testament Greek." Others are written to help intermediate students: "Improving Your New Testament Greek." Still others are for advanced readers and serve primarily as "Reference Grammars."

I. Learning New Testament Greek

THE BEST

5.10   Machen J. G.
           NEW TESTAMENT GREEK FOR BEGINNERS
           New York: Macmillan (1923)

This may be the all-time favorite introductory grammar for New Testament Greek. It was so well done sixty years ago that it is still in print in its original edition. Among the secrets to its success are logical organization, clear presentation, and a good index. It is not the best for self-instruction, and those wishing a more inductive approach—learning by doing—may prefer something like LaSor (5.18). But "Machen" is almost in a class by itself.

5.11   Colwell, E. C., and E. W. Tune
          A BEGINNER'S READER-GRAMMAR FOR
          NEW TESTAMENT GREEK
          New York: Harper & Row (1965)

Features good reading exercises.

5.12   Davis, W. H.
          BEGINNER'S GRAMMAR OF THE GREEK NEW
          TESTAMENT
          New York: Harper & Row (1923)

One of the great names in New Testament philology was A. T. Robertson (see 5.28, 5.39). This book was written by one of Robertson's pupils and was designed to bring those with no knowledge of Greek up to a level where they could use Robertson's more sophisticated grammars. Such a pedigree would be unimportant but for the fact that Robertson and his students insisted on distinguishing eight cases for the Greek noun, while everyone else uses five. This grammar, which is an excellent introduction, does the same. The reader, however, should also know that the eight-case distinction is now something of a relic.

5.13   Goetchius, E. van N.
          THE LANGUAGE OF THE NEW TESTAMENT
          New York: Scribner (1966)

and

5.14   Goetchius, E. van N.
          THE LANGUAGE OF THE NEW TESTAMENT:
          WORKBOOK
          New York: Scribner (1966)

A reputable introduction featuring a separate workbook. Handy format. High price.

5.15   Moulton, J. H. (edited by H. G. Meecham)
          AN INTRODUCTION TO THE STUDY OF
          NEW TESTAMENT GREEK
          New York: Macmillan. 5th ed. (1955)

Although small, this is a formidable—and informative—introduction. One of its finest features is a "first reader" at the end, a synthetic set of texts of increasing difficulty. Not the simplest book for self-instruction.

THE REST

5.16   Drumwright, H. L.
            INTRODUCTION TO THE GREEK NEW TESTAMENT
            Nashville: Broadman (1980)

Designed primarily for seminary students.

5.17   Greenlee, J. H.
            A CONCISE EXEGETICAL GRAMMAR
            OF NEW TESTAMENT GREEK
            Grand Rapids: Eerdmans (1963)

A slender introduction to the principles of New Testament grammar.

5.18   LaSor, W. S.
            HANDBOOK OF NEW TESTAMENT GREEK
            An Inductive Approach Based on the Greek Text of Acts. 2 vols.
            Grand Rapids: Eerdmans (1973)

As the subtitle indicates, the approach is inductive. The student starts out with the briefest introduction and begins quickly to read Acts under LaSor's guidance, building a knowledge of grammar as the reading progresses.

5.19   Mare, W. H.
            MASTERING NEW TESTAMENT GREEK
            A Beginner's Grammar, Including Lesson Plans for Intermediate
                and Advanced Greek Students
            Grand Rapids: Baker (1979)

Uses both inductive and deductive methods.

5.20   Marshall, A.
            A NEW TESTAMENT GREEK PRIMER
            Grand Rapids: Zondervan (1981)

5.21   Story, C. I. K., and J. L. Story
            GREEK TO ME. Learning New Testament Greek
            Through Memory Visualization
            San Francisco: Harper & Row (1979)

Thin.

5.22   Summers, R.
              ESSENTIALS OF NEW TESTAMENT GREEK
              Nashville: Broadman (1950)

Better as a beginner's "reference" tool than as an actual introduction.

5.23   Argyle, A. W.
              AN INTRODUCTORY GRAMMAR OF NEW TESTAMENT
              GREEK
              Ithaca: Cornell University Press (1966)

Compact.

5.24   Gignac, F. T.
              AN INTRODUCTORY NEW TESTAMENT GREEK COURSE
              Chicago: Loyola University Press (1973)

II. Improving Your New Testament Greek

THE BEST

5.25   Dana, H. E., and J. R. Mantey
              A MANUAL GRAMMAR OF THE GREEK NEW
              TESTAMENT
              New York: Macmillan (1927/1957)

This is the best handy ("manual") one-volume intermediate grammar available. The arrangement is sensible and the examples numerous. Greek texts cited to illustrate a point are translated on the spot, something an intermediate student welcomes. Those who understand what is in Dana and Mantey are well on their way to understanding all the Greek of the New Testament. Outstanding.

5.26   Moule, C. F. D.
              AN IDIOM BOOK OF NEW TESTAMENT GREEK
              New York: Cambridge University Press. 2nd ed. (1959)

Exasperated students like to call it "an idiot's book," but they would not be without it. This is a difficult volume to classify, but it is indispensable. Not a reference grammar of the usual sort, Moule's compact survey concentrates on the major characteristics of New Testament Greek; it highlights most of the difficult phrases and ambiguous passages. Worth its weight in gold, it can be purchased for about that amount in cloth, and considerably less in paper.

5.26p   *Same:* paperback

THE REST

5.27   Chamberlain, W. D.
                AN EXEGETICAL GRAMMAR OF THE GREEK NEW
                TESTAMENT
                Grand Rapids: Baker (1941/1975)

This paperback reprint of a classic title represents the intermediate step between
Davis (5.12) and Robertson's large reference grammar (5.39). Chamberlain, who
was Robertson's pupil, also uses the eight-case division for nouns (see the
description of 5.12). Solid.

5.28   Robertson, A. T., and W. H. Davis
                A NEW SHORT GRAMMAR OF THE GREEK NEW
                TESTAMENT
                For Students Familiar with the Elements of Greek
                Grand Rapids: Baker. 10th ed. (1933)

Robertson wrote this specifically as an intermediate grammar. As a philologist
and a historian of the Greek language, he included in this intermediate-level book
much that is not ordinarily found in such efforts. Particularly noteworthy are the
grammatical examples from papyri and inscriptions, which make the book meatier
than most intermediate grammars and somewhat more sophisticated. But for the
same reason, this grammar is more difficult to use. It is the richest, if not the most
efficient, intermediate grammar.

5.29   Zerwick, M.
                BIBLICAL GREEK
                English Edition Adapted from the 4th Latin Edition by J. Smith
                Chicago: Loyola University Press (1963)

Zerwick was for many years at the Pontifical Biblical Institute in Rome, where
this book was written—in Latin—for seminarians beginning their study of the
Greek New Testament. The English translation is welcome, for this slender volume
covers much ground. The translation takes on added significance, however, because
Zerwick later wrote a grammatical analysis of the entire New Testament (see 5.52
and 5.53) that is keyed to paragraph numbers in this grammar. Thus, when a
puzzling turn of grammar comes up in the New Testament and Zerwick solves
the puzzle, he also refers the reader to a larger discussion in this book. A superb
tool.

5.30   Vaughn, C., and V. E. Gideon
                A GREEK GRAMMAR OF THE NEW TESTAMENT
                Nashville: Broadman (1975/1979)

III. Reference Grammars

A few giants dominate this field. Each has its distinctive characteristics and virtues, and it is difficult to say that one is "better" than another.

5.31   Funk, R. W. (ed.)
        [F. Blass, A. Debrunner]
        A GREEK GRAMMAR OF THE NEW TESTAMENT AND
        OTHER EARLY CHRISTIAN LITERATURE
        A Translation and Revision of the ninth-tenth German edition
            incorporating supplementary notes of A. Debrunner
        Chicago: University of Chicago Press (1961)

5.32   *Same:* Grand Rapids: Zondervan (1961)

"Blass-Debrunner" has long been *the* standard Greek reference grammar for studying the New Testament. This translation and revision, by R. W. Funk, established the same reputation in the English-speaking world. But it is an unusually awkward book to use. Revised editions of the German original appeared over the years with appendixes tacked on to the main entries. When the English translation was made, this format was followed. As a result, the user must usually check two or three places in any paragraph entry to find all the relevant material. In addition, the writing is very concise—almost cryptic at times.

The newest German edition has streamlined all this and offers a completely rewritten, integrated, and coherent grammar. This new book is simplicity itself to use and still upholds the great reputation of the authors. But that does not help those who want the book in English. Whatever the problems of format, Blass-Debrunner-Funk is a recognized authority.

5.33   Burton, E. DeW.
        SYNTAX OF THE MOODS AND TENSES OF NEW
        TESTAMENT GREEK
        New York: Seabury. 3rd ed. (1898/1976)

Burton's book is not a full-fledged reference grammar, but it is the last word in comprehending and classifying New Testament verbs. In almost a century there has been nothing to match it.

5.34   Moulton, J. H.
        A GRAMMAR OF NEW TESTAMENT GREEK
        Vol. I: PROLEGOMENA
        New York: Seabury (for T. & T. Clark, Edinburgh). 3rd ed.
        (1908/1978)

5.35	Vol. II: ACCIDENCE AND WORD FORMATION Ed. by W. F. Howard New York: Seabury (for T. & T. Clark, Edinburgh) (1922/1979)
5.36	Vol. III: SYNTAX Ed. by N. Turner New York: Seabury (for T. & T. Clark, Edinburgh) (1963/1978)
5.37	Vol. IV: STYLE Ed. by N. Turner New York: Seabury (for T. & T. Clark, Edinburgh)/Greenwood (SC): Attic Press (1976)
5.38	*Same:* four-volume set

Taken together, these four volumes cover all of New Testament Greek. For most users the third volume, Turner's on syntax, is the most important one for everyday use. It is a full-fledged reference grammar. Concise and well indexed.

5.39	Robertson, A. T. A GRAMMAR OF THE GREEK NEW TESTAMENT IN THE LIGHT OF HISTORICAL RESEARCH Nashville: Broadman. 4th ed. (1923/1934)

This bulky book is nothing short of monumental. Robertson stood alone in his generation of American New Testament scholars when it came to Greek grammar, and this is his great work. It is the only advanced grammar that can be read like a book, for it was written like an extended essay. That also makes it harder to use for quick reference purposes. Robertson had a few quirky views, but this grammar is the doorway to the history of the Greek language and to viewing the New Testament from that vantage point.

5.40	Owings, T. A CUMULATIVE INDEX TO NEW TESTAMENT GREEK GRAMMARS Grand Rapids: Baker (1983)

Owings has taken major New Testament Greek grammars of the intermediate or advanced level and indexed their coverage of specific New Testament passages to save the reader the time required for consulting each index individually. This 160-page index of indexes covers:

> Dana and Mantey (5.25)
> Moule (5.26)
> Robertson and Davis (5.28)
> Zerwick (5.29)
> Blass-Debrunner-Funk (5.31)
> Moulton-Howard-Turner (5.34–5.38)
> Robertson (5.39)

C. Special Study Aids

Dozens of books and pamphlets appear every year offering supplementary help for learning or remembering Greek. Those of value fall into three categories: summaries of grammar and syntax; vocabulary lists, either based on New Testament frequency or arranged according to the Greek roots from which the words are derived; and detailed, verse-by-verse grammatical analyses of part or all of the New Testament.

I. Quick Review of Grammar and Syntax

5.41   Chapman, B.
NEW TESTAMENT-GREEK NOTEBOOK
Grand Rapids: Baker. 2nd ed. (1978)

In a loose-leaf format identical in size and style with the UBS *Greek New Testament* (4.1), Chapman has assembled a small handbook of New Testament Greek. Chapter 1 deals with vocabulary, arranged by parts of speech (prepositions, conjunctions, etc.). Other lists are arranged by common roots and by frequency. There is a basic grammar review with patterns of inflection, an inconsequential essay on translation theory, another on exegesis, a fine section on syntax, and two or three other helps. A good refresher course. Elementary.

5.42   Chapman, B.
GREEK NEW TESTAMENT INSERT
Grand Rapids: Baker (1978)

A sixty-page condensation of 5.41 in a format that allows it to be pasted in the back of the UBS *Greek New Testament* (4.1). Thin, but good on syntax.

5.43   Chapman, B.
A CARD-GUIDE TO NEW TESTAMENT EXEGESIS
(I AND II)
Grand Rapids: Baker (1977)

Laminated plastic cards to fit a three-ring binder showing basic elements of syntax and grammar. Concise, well organized, elementary.

5.44   Chapman, B.
A CARD-GUIDE TO NEW TESTAMENT GREEK
Grand Rapids: Baker (1976)

The abc's of Greek forms, on laminated plastic cards to fit in a three-ring binder. Handy, but nothing not found in any simple grammar.

5.45   Mueller, W.
            GRAMMATICAL AIDS FOR STUDENTS OF NEW
            TESTAMENT GREEK
            Grand Rapids: Eerdmans (1972)

Text and charts to supplement a standard grammar.

5.46   Peterson, D.
            THE GREEK NEW TESTAMENT SLIDAVERB
            CONJUGATION CHART
            Grand Rapids: Zondervan (n.d.)

This updating of the old "verb wheel" is a compact way to list verb paradigms.

5.47   Boyer, J.
            A MANUAL OF GREEK FORMS
            Winona Lake (IN): BMH Books (n.d.)

II. Vocabulary Building

5.48   Metzger, B. M.
            LEXICAL AIDS FOR STUDENTS OF NEW TESTAMENT
            GREEK
            Geneva (AL): Allenson. 3rd ed. (1969)

Metzger's little book long ago won its laurels. It offers lists of New Testament vocabulary arranged by frequency, a guide through the maze of prepositions, and solid grounding in Greek roots for rapid vocabulary building. Next to a grammar, it is the best thing a beginner can have.

5.49   Morrison, C. D., and D. H. Barnes
            NEW TESTAMENT WORD LISTS
            Grand Rapids: Eerdmans (1964)

Designed for the beginning student, these lists include words (apart from proper nouns) occurring fewer than ten times in the Greek New Testament. Lists are arranged alphabetically according to the chapter (or synoptic section) in which they appear. It complements Metzger (5.48).

5.50   Rogers, T.
            GREEK WORD ROOTS
            Grand Rapids: Baker (1968)

On the theory that mastering Greek roots is the quickest way to build vocabulary, Rogers offers a large but well-chosen selection of such roots and the words derived from them, based on frequency in the New Testament. Excellent and inexpensive.

5.51   Berry, G. R.
              A DICTIONARY OF NEW TESTAMENT GREEK
              SYNONYMS
              Grand Rapids: Zondervan (1897/1979)

The material in this older work is also found in 4.16, 4.17, and 4.18.

III. Exegetical Aids

These resources are designed to help in the actual word-by-word reading of the New Testament. Some parse words, others offer more complex analyses of grammar. All belong to the category of "Quick Greek."

5.52   Zerwick, M., and M. Grosvenor
5.53   A GRAMMATICAL ANALYSIS OF THE GREEK NEW
              TESTAMENT
              Vol. 1: GOSPELS–ACTS (1974)
              Vol. 2: EPISTLES–APOCALYPSE (1979)
              Chicago: Loyola University Press (1974–1979)

This compact philological analysis of the New Testament went through three editions in Latin before it ever found its way into English. The two volumes offer a concise analysis of every significant form and grammatical construction in the Greek New Testament. The grammatical points are illustrated by referring to specific sections of Zerwick's *Biblical Greek* (5.29), although having that book at hand is not essential for using these. Each volume is introduced by a glossary of technical terms and a list of New Testament words occurring more than sixty times. While scholars usually regard books of this sort as beneath contempt, Zerwick's work is so good he makes the genre respectable. It is preferable to the next entry.

5.54   Rienecker, F.
5.55   A LINGUISTIC KEY TO THE GREEK NEW TESTAMENT
              Trans. and rev. by C. L. Rogers
              Vol. 1: MATTHEW–ACTS (1976)
              Vol. 2: ROMANS–REVELATION (1980)
              Grand Rapids: Zondervan (1976–1980)

This is a thorough revision and translation of a long-standing favorite among

German theological students. It does essentially what Zerwick does, but less concisely and more expensively. The heart of the book consists of linguistic helps, but theological notes appear here and there.

5.56   *Same:* one-volume edition

5.57   *Same:* two-volume set

5.58   Holly, D.
            A COMPLETE CATEGORIZED GREEK-ENGLISH
            NEW TESTAMENT VOCABULARY
            Greenwood (SC): Attic Press (1978)

Holly has divided his vocabulary list into four sections: (1) all New Testament words appearing ten times or more, classified by "types" of conjugations, declensions, etc. (following the patterns of E. G. Jay's *New Testament Greek* [5.8]); (2) all words occurring fewer than ten times, by decreasing frequency, in alphabetical order, showing proper declension, conjugation, etc.; (3) all proper nouns, with declension pattern; (4) a master summary list, which serves as an index. Further notes account for discrepancies between these lists and those found in other publications, including the Nestle-Aland New Testament (4.2) and Moulton-Geden's *Concordance* (4.51). Topping off this amazing book are a grammatical index, a list of differences in spelling and accent between Bauer-Arndt-Gingrich-Danker (4.30) and Moulton-Geden (4.51), and a list of words found only in single New Testament books. Technical, brilliant, useful to the beginner and seasoned veteran alike. There is nothing quite like it.

5.59   Holly, D.
            A COMPLETE CATEGORIZED GREEK-ENGLISH
            NEW TESTAMENT VOCABULARY
            Grand Rapids: Baker (1980)

The same as 5.28 but less elegantly prepared, this volume is bound in paper at a much reduced price.

5.60   Alsop, J. R.
            AN INDEX TO THE REVISED BAUER-ARNDT-GINGRICH
            GREEK LEXICON, SECOND EDITION, BY F. W. GINGRICH
            AND F. W. DANKER
            Grand Rapids: Zondervan. Rev. ed. (1981)

In its preface this book claims to be a time-saver for novice and veteran Greek reader alike. Alsop takes in order every word of the New Testament beginning with Matthew 1:1 and gives a reference to the subsection of the main entry in Bauer-Arndt-Gingrich-Danker (4.30), along with the page and the quadrant on the page where this use is listed and discussed. Beginners will perhaps find it helpful, and it has utility for "Quick Greek"; otherwise it represents a needless step. Paperback.

5.61   Han, N. E.
          PARSING GUIDE TO THE GREEK NEW TESTAMENT
          Scottdale (PA): Herald Press (1971)

This guide to every verb of the New Testament begins with Matthew 1:1 and follows the Greek text of Nestle-Aland's 25th edition of 1963. Those using the 26th edition (4.2) will notice a few differences here and there, but not enough to detract from this book's overall usefulness for the novice.

D. Classical Greek Grammars

5.62   Crosby, H. and J. Schaeffer
          AN INTRODUCTION TO GREEK
          Boston: Allyn & Bacon (1928)

This time-tested introduction to classical Greek is still used in many schools. It is preferred by some because of its extensive use of English derivatives of Greek words as an aid in memorizing vocabulary.

5.63   Goodwin, W. W.
          GREEK GRAMMAR
          New York: St. Martin. 2nd ed. (1879)

Venerable and still valuable, but see the next item.

5.64   Goodwin, W. W. and C. B. Gulick
          GREEK GRAMMAR
          New Rochelle (NY): Caratzas Bros. (1958)

A classic revision of a classic text, this work is available in both cloth and paper. Preferable to 5.63.

5.64p   *Same:* paperback

5.65   Smyth, H. W.
          GREEK GRAMMAR
          Rev. ed. by G. M. Messing
          Cambridge: Harvard University Press (1920/1956)

In 1956 Messing revised Smyth's famous grammar, which was once described as "the very epitome of an English school grammar." It remains the standard one-volume reference grammar for Greek available in the English language—the equivalent for all of Greek of Blass-Debrunner-Funk (5.30) or Moulton-Howard-Turner (5.34–5.38).

E. The Greek of the Old Testament

5.66   Conybeare, F. C., and St. G. Stock
            A GRAMMAR OF SEPTUAGINT GREEK
            Grand Rapids: Zondervan (1909/1980)

This is a recent reprinting, taken from an older and larger work published in 1905. This grammatical description of the grammar of Septuagint Greek has not lost its relevance, and nothing like it is available.

F. "Quick Greek" in Review

In this and the preceding chapter we have noted books that are especially useful for "Quick Greek." These are designed to help the novice read better or to help the person with little or no Greek use some of the reference resources involving Greek words. The amount of knowledge and background they require varies; in each case knowledge of the Greek alphabet is essential, and for some that is all the Greek that is needed. "Quick Greek" resources are also useful for polishing up rusty language skills.

Here is a list of the works from Chapters 4 and 5 that belong in the category of "Quick Greek":

The New Testament in Greek: 4.12, 4.14, 4.16, 4.17, 4.18, 4.19, 4.20, 4.21, 4.22, 4.23.

Greek and English New Testaments: 4.24, 4.25.

The Old Testament in Greek and English versions: 4.27, 4.28.

Lexicons and dictionaries of New Testament Greek: 4.32, 4.40, 4.41, 4.42.

Greek concordances of the New Testament: 4.50, 4.51, 4.54, 4.55, 4.56, 4.57, 4.58, 4.59, 4.60.

Standard New Testament grammars: 5.40.

Special study aids: 5.41, 5.42, 5.43, 5.44, 5.46, 5.47, 5.48, 5.49, 5.50, 5.51, 5.52, 5.53, 5.54, 5.55, 5.56, 5.57, 5.58, 5.59, 5.60, 5.61.

BEST BUYS

Some books stand out from the selections in this chapter because they are the very best. For teaching yourself New Testament Greek the choice is Hudson (5.1), and for a more conventional grammar covering the same material, Machen (5.10). If you are on your way but need help in consolidating your gains, Dana and Mantey is the best buy (5.25). Despite all its limitations, Blass-Debrunner-Funk (5.31) is probably the best reference grammar in the area of early Christian Greek literature. If you want a more comprehensive Greek reference grammar, choose Smyth (5.65), but it is not so useful for the early Christian texts.

Finally, there are all the gadgets designed to help you review grammar and syntax quickly. Few offer anything that is not found in a standard introductory grammar book. Two aids do stand out, however. One is an excellent investment for vocabulary building: Metzger (5.48). The other should be used with caution, since it can become a crutch; but for beginners who want to read the New Testament without having to look up every word, there is Zerwick (5.52, 5.53) or, failing that, Rienecker (5.54, 5.55), which is almost as good.

6

DICTIONARIES
AND ENCYCLOPEDIAS

Dictionaries and encyclopedias are common enough, but those designed for use with the Bible need a word of introduction. The two terms are not always clearly distinguished in the titles of biblical reference works. Ordinarily one expects a *dictionary* to have brief definitions and an *encyclopedia* to have longer essays; but there are dictionaries of the Bible that run to five volumes and there are one-volume encyclopedias.

In general, it helps to keep these criteria in mind when trying to choose a reference work:

Coverage. How detailed and far-ranging is the scope of the work? Multi-volume sets are usually more detailed, but sometimes they offer only more illustrations, not better or longer articles. Some reference works are all but exhaustive on subjects within the Bible but pay insufficient attention to historical, geographic, or religious contexts, and thus lack depth. Others may emphasize these very topics.

Level. Dictionaries and encyclopedias appeal to different audiences. Some are written for children, others for the advanced reader. Some are very general, while others serve the needs of specialists and scholars. Those listed here are all suited to the general reader, but many will also serve a more specialized or advanced audience; if so, that is noted.

Perspectives. Reference works of this sort often assume one of two basic orientations. The *traditional* perspective emphasizes the theological significance of biblical materials above all other concerns (but not necessarily to the exclusion of all other interests). If this includes an emphasis on the agreement between biblical "doctrines" and classic statements of Christian orthodoxy, then the perspective can also be called a conservative one. The *analytical* orientation, in contrast, puts the primary emphasis on historical or literary matters (though again, not necessarily exclusively so).

One last word—about becoming obsolete. Producing these reference works requires an enormous investment of time and money, which often is recovered only slowly over many years. Keeping reference volumes of this sort really up-to-date—especially in the case of the largest sets—is difficult. Revisions may be made only every forty or fifty years, if at all. Therefore, much of what is to be found both in libraries and in bookstores is old. For some topics this is a less critical concern than it is for others. Archaeological and historical information is the likeliest to be obsolete after a few years. Theological interests and tastes change too, but more slowly and usually with less drastic consequences.

A. Standard Bible Dictionaries and Encyclopedias

I. One-Volume Dictionaries

THE BEST

6.1   Douglas, J. D. (ed.)
        THE NEW BIBLE DICTIONARY
        Wheaton (IL): Tyndale. 2nd ed. (1982)

Douglas's work is a major one-volume reference work, enlarged in its second edition and shaped by a predominantly British and evangelical group of subeditors and contributors. W. F. Albright once (overenthusiastically) called the first edition "the best one-volume dictionary in the English language." He was wrong, but the work did prove popular with evangelicals and conservative readers.

Perhaps Albright was only premature, for this second edition more nearly deserves such superlatives. The theological commitment is still that of the Tyndale Fellowship for Biblical Research, which accepts the accuracy of the Bible in all matters. That will please some readers and leave others looking for more refinement and discrimination on specific historical and geographic topics. It must be said, however, that there is diversity in the viewpoints reflected within the pages of this very large dictionary; and no apparent effort has been made to herd the more than 150 contributors into narrow confines.

More than that, no recent work of this sort for the general reader comes even close in terms of clear entries that also contain excellent references to other places where the issues, including scholarly debates, can be pursued further. In bringing the nonspecialist into the ongoing discussion of biblical topics, the NBD sets a new standard in *this* edition. If differences of opinion on theological matters are left aside, this is the best and most up-to-date dictionary available in one volume. The editors include F. F. Bruce, J. I. Packer, R. V. G. Tasker, D. J. Wiseman, D. Guthrie, and A. R. Millard.

6.2   McKenzie, J. L.
            DICTIONARY OF THE BIBLE
            New York: Macmillan (1965)

Douglas's dictionary (6.1) gets a lot of advertising and attention. In contrast, McKenzie's work is far less well known than it deserves to be. One has to admire it simply because it was *written*—not merely edited—by *one* person, and in only six years. The coverage is thorough and the writing is clear. Throughout, it serves the interests of the general reader. Here and there one notices a Roman Catholic position, but on the whole this is solid scholarship packaged appropriately for the nonspecialist. It is not as up-to-date as Douglas (6.1), of course. With black-and-white photographs and adequate maps.

6.2p   *Same:* paperback

6.3   Miller, M. S., and J. L. Miller (eds.)
            HARPER'S DICTIONARY OF THE BIBLE
            Rev. by B. M. Bennett and D. H. Scott
            San Francisco: Harper & Row (1978)

6.4   *Same:* thumb-indexed

The Millers first produced this dictionary in 1952 after their *Encyclopedia of Bible Life* (6.50). Since then the publisher has updated it with frequent revisions. Its strengths include a reasonably nontechnical style well suited to the general reader who wants a quick-and-ready reference source. It concentrates on historical matters and leaves alone traditional theological concerns. It offers plentiful illustrations and maps and is comparatively reasonable in cost. Somehow, however, this volume is less exciting than either Douglas (6.1) or McKenzie (6.2).

6.5   Gehman, H. S. (ed.)
            THE NEW WESTMINSTER DICTIONARY OF THE BIBLE
            Philadelphia: Westminster (1970)

6.6   *Same:* thumb-indexed

A revision of a classic (see 6.9), this standard dictionary has long appealed to a wide range of general readers and to those with more specialized interests as well. The new edition, reasonably up-to-date, retains the handy format of its predecessors. Standard equipment includes the useful Westminster Bible maps.

6.7   Alexander, P. (orig. ed.)
           EERDMAN'S FAMILY ENCYCLOPEDIA OF THE BIBLE
           Grand Rapids: Eerdmans (1978)

The best of the dictionaries specifically designed for readers of all ages. The coverage is broad rather than deep, and the format is unusually attractive, with ample illustrations. Somewhat lightweight in terms of content.

THE REST

6.8   Alexander, P. (ed.)
           EERDMAN'S CONCISE BIBLE ENCYCLOPEDIA
           Grand Rapids: Eerdmans (1981)

This is a paperback version of the previous item (6.7) without the color and most of the pictures. Much less appealing.

6.9   Davis, J. D. (ed.)
           DICTIONARY OF THE BIBLE
           Grand Rapids: Baker. 4th ed. (1954)

"Davis" is an old favorite and a trusted name in Bible dictionaries, as the next few entries will show. Originally published in 1898, it is badly outdated even in this fourth edition. The original was replaced by the *Westminster Dictionary of the Bible* (1944), which itself has been thoroughly revised (see now 6.5, 6.6). Because of its very traditional stance on many issues and the fact that it is in the public domain, "Davis" is widely reprinted in various editions and marketed, despite the fact that it shows its age on every page.

6.10   Davis, J. D. (ed.)
           DAVIS' DICTIONARY OF THE BIBLE
           Old Tappan (NJ): Revell. 5th ed. (1972)

Modest revisions do not overcome the problem of age.

6.11   Davis, J. D. (ed.)
           DAVIS' DICTIONARY OF THE BIBLE
           Nashville: Broadman (1973)

6.12   Davis, J. D. (ed.)
           DAVIS' DICTIONARY OF THE BIBLE
           Gallatin (TN): Church History Research and Archives (n.d.)

6.13   Smith, W. (orig. ed.)
           Lemmons, R. G., et al. (eds.)
           NEW SMITH'S BIBLE DICTIONARY
           Garden City: Doubleday (1966)

Smith is almost a brand name, like Cruden in concordances. In fact, however, most dictionaries using his name have only the slightest connection with the original William Smith and his four-volume work, which was first published in America in 1870. An exception is the reprint of the original work (6.38). Smith was determined to be comprehensive and noncontroversial at the same time. His dictionary often offers more than one entry on a topic—to account for differing views in matters of both history and theology. Without doubt the work is now a museum piece, but it does retain its interest because of unparalleled comprehensiveness and balance. None of the one-volume editions bearing his name retains the flavor of the original. Of those listed here, this and the next four entries are the best; but none is up to contemporary standards.

6.13p   *Same:* rev. ed., 1979; paperback

Inconsequential revisions do not offset the higher price and the poorer binding.

6.14   *Same:* thumb-indexed

6.15   Peloubet, F. N., and M. A. Peloubet (eds.)
SMITH'S BIBLE DICTIONARY
Nashville: Nelson (1979)

6.15p   *Same:* paperback

6.16   SMITH'S BIBLE DICTIONARY
Nashville: Holman. Rev. ed. (n.d.)

6.17   *Same:* thumb-indexed

6.18   SMITH'S BIBLE DICTIONARY
New York: Jove Publications (1967)

Designed for children. Paperback.

6.19   SMITH'S BIBLE DICTIONARY
Old Tappan (NJ): Revell (n.d.). Paperback

6.20   SMITH'S BIBLE DICTIONARY
Grand Rapids: Zondervan (1955). Illustrated

(*See also 6.38 for the original "Smith's."*)

6.21   Unger, M. F. (ed.)
UNGER'S BIBLE DICTIONARY
Chicago: Moody. 3rd ed. (1961)

Noted for its conservative stance. Not up-to-date.

6.22   *Same:* thumb-indexed

6.23   Smith, B. (ed.)
            THE WESTMINSTER CONCISE BIBLE DICTIONARY
            Philadelphia: Westminster (1981)

An up-to-date, reliable, but *very* compressed dictionary in paperback format, this
work comes from a publisher long known for a more solid Bible dictionary (see
6.5).

6.24   Hastings, J. (ed.)
            DICTIONARY OF THE BIBLE
            Rev. ed. by F. C. Grant and H. H. Rowley (eds.)
            New York: Scribner (1963)

First published in 1909 as a shorter version of the five-volume Hasting's dictionary,
this has long been a classic work. It was thoroughly revised in a new edition of
1963. Strong on historical interests, Hastings covers the apocryphal materials
better than most one-volume dictionaries, and this is its strength. It is reliable but
rather dull, perhaps because of a bland style, or a rather old-fashioned format.
Weak on bibliography and *very* expensive.

6.25   Tenney, M. C. (ed.)
            THE ZONDERVAN PICTORIAL BIBLE DICTIONARY
            Grand Rapids: Zondervan. Rev. ed. (1963/1967)

Lively entries get to the point in this dictionary, which was designed for pastors
and church-school teachers. Its most obvious feature is hundreds of photographs;
but the format is crowded and not very pleasing to the eye, and the entries are
rather thin. The text of the Bible is the KJV (with spellings from ASV and RSV
in parentheses). Ten printings in six years attest the popularity of this dictionary.

6.26   *Same:* thumb-indexed

6.27   Bryant, A. (ed.)
            THE NEW COMPACT BIBLE DICTIONARY
            Grand Rapids: Zondervan (1967)

6.27p   *Same:* paperback

6.28   Boyd, J. P. (ed.)
            BOYD'S BIBLE DICTIONARY
            Nashville: Holman (n.d.)

The original title, *Vest Pocket Bible Dictionary,* suggests the scope of this
paperback.

II. Multi-Volume Dictionaries and Encyclopedias

THE BEST

6.29 √ Buttrick, G., and K. Crim (eds.)
THE INTERPRETER'S DICTIONARY OF THE BIBLE. 5 vols.
Nashville/New York: Abingdon (1976)

The original four volumes of this standard Bible encyclopedia were published in 1962; consequently, the work as a whole is not as recent as the date above indicates. Fourteen years later a supplementary volume added new articles and brought previous entries up to date. To use the dictionary, therefore, one must watch for cross-references in the first four volumes to the supplement, and vice-versa.

The focus is moderately technical, the slant analytical. "Biblical theology" is more evident in the original volumes than in the supplement. The writing is good, as encyclopedia writing goes, and the material is reliable. Lists of contributors read like a scholarly Who's Who in America. The bibliographies are outstanding; the maps and illustrations adequate.

6.30 Hillyer, N. (ed.)
THE ILLUSTRATED BIBLE ENCYCLOPEDIA. 3 vols.
Downers Grove (IL): InterVarsity (1980)

The text is that of the revised *New Bible Dictionary* (6.1) with hundreds of illustrations in a pleasing and useful format: three columns to a page with a marginal column for the legends that identify the accompanying illustrations. This is a rare instance where adding illustrations, because it was done imaginatively, has improved the dictionary. For example, a color wheel is used to distinguish among the various colors described in the Bible, and the Greek and Hebrew terms used in each passage cited are given in transliteration. Although this is hardly a necessary piece of information, it is graphic and certainly engaging.

The photographs are of stunning quality but not always relevant to the text under discussion. The line drawings are of medium detail, and these *are* relevant and appropriate. The bibliographies are quite selective, but they usually do cite the basic literature. On the text itself, see the comments above (6.1).

6.31 Bromiley, G. W. (ed.)
6.32 INTERNATIONAL STANDARD BIBLE ENCYCLOPEDIA
4 vols. (in process)
Grand Rapids: Eerdmans. Vol. 1 (1979); Vol. 2 (1982)

6.33 *Same:* two-volume set

What began as a revision of an old favorite has emerged as a "completely reconstructed encyclopedia" now being published in four volumes. The old favorite was *The International Standard Bible Encyclopedia* (see 6.36). Like the earlier volumes, these are comprehensive and conservative; in their use of authors they are international and interdenominational. This current edition is somewhat less idiosyncratic than its predecessor, reflecting a certain shift away from confrontation between "criticism" and "faith"—an issue more characteristic of the era of the previous edition. Here, in contrast, the emphasis falls on the "critically aware" positions of many contemporary scholars, who predominate among contributors.

ISBE seeks to be comprehensive, and broad coverage is one of its strengths. Historical minutiae and theological conundrums are all here in impartial alphabetical order. The bibliographies are selective but of course very current. The maps (Hammond's) are outfitted with a good index.

One oddity of this edition is the retention of old entries from the previous edition in the same or only slightly altered form: 38 percent of the text is held over from more than fifty years ago. The unfortunate result is that some of the material sounds very old-fashioned, and the theological topics are more likely to have an antique ring than are the historical entries.

In sum, this set is Protestant and conservative in its tone (and English, too, in its accent) and carries on the tradition of a classic. It will no doubt itself become one. Since the quality of the new contributors and their articles is high, it is disappointing that so much that is so old was retained.

THE REST

6.34   Tenney, M. C. (ed.)
        THE ZONDERVAN PICTORIAL ENCYCLOPEDIA
        OF THE BIBLE. 5 vols.
        Grand Rapids: Zondervan (1975)

The same basic editorial team that produced the *Zondervan Pictorial Bible Dictionary* (6.25) produced this more comprehensive work a decade later. It is a far more detailed guide, still lively in tone and much more pleasing visually. Illustrations continue to be a conspicuous feature. Five volumes do not make the handiest format, but the work does have superior breadth and depth. KJV, RSV, and ASV are all used. Excellent, but expensive.

6.35   Pfeiffer, C. F., H. F. Vos, and J. Rea (eds.)
        WYCLIFFE BIBLE ENCYCLOPEDIA. 2 vols.
        Chicago: Moody (1975)

A Companion to the *Wycliffe Bible Commentary* (9.8) and the *Wycliffe Historical Geography of Bible Lands* (7.23), this two-volume set strives for a balance between comprehensiveness and conciseness. Four printings in five years attest to its success. The format is crowded, and illustrations are less effective than in the new

International Standard Bible Encyclopedia (6.31–33). This book is for nonspecialists and offers good basic coverage of standard areas by more than two hundred contributors, mostly American and largely evangelical.

6.36   Orr, J. (gen. ed.), and J. L. Nielsen, E. Y. Mulling, M. O. Evans, and M. G. Kyle (eds.)
THE INTERNATIONAL STANDARD BIBLE
ENCYCLOPEDIA. 4 vols.
Grand Rapids: Eerdmans (1939/1957)

This is a 1957 reprint of a 1939 revision of a 1929 text. The 1939 revision concentrated on updating information about a few archaeological sites; consequently most of the text is now quite old. Furthermore, it has recently been replaced by the new edition of the same title (6.31–6.33), of which two volumes have now appeared. Presumably, when that new version is complete, this one will be allowed to fade. In the meantime, it is an old standard showing its age. The accent is on theological interests, but historical coverage is broad, if badly out-of-date. Some two hundred contributors, about half of whom were American, reflect an attitude described in the preface as "reasonable conservatism."

6.37   Cheyne, T. K., and J. S. Black (eds.)
ENCYCLOPEDIA BIBLICA. A Critical Dictionary
of the Literary, Political and Religious History, the Archaeology,
Geography and Natural History of the Bible. 4 vols.
New York: Gordon Press (1899–1903/1977)

Now something of an antiquity itself, EB, as it has long been known, was a monumental work. Its emphasis falls on historical and technical matters, and it is more appropriate for advanced readers than for beginners. Where its judgments once seemed (to some, at least) hypercritical, they often look less so today because of changing perspectives. But the heavy use of scholarly conjecture to fill in the gaps in our historical understanding seems more dubious than ever. Still, some of the essays are masterful in their coverage and rigorous in their argument. The reprint is *very* expensive.

6.38   Smith, W. (ed.)
SMITH'S BIBLE DICTIONARY. 4 vols.
Grand Rapids: Baker (1870/1981)

Several "Smith's" dictionaries were described above (6.13–6.20). This is the original. It is very old, and it never did have the incisive individuality of EB (6.37); but it, too, is a classic. This multi-volume set is famous for sometimes offering more than one entry on a given topic, allowing competing points of view to be expressed. The retrospective glimpse afforded into earlier academic and scholarly debates is fascinating. Dated, but still useful.

B. Dictionaries and Encyclopedias of Biblical Theology

Among general dictionaries and encyclopedias such as those described above, some may stress theological interests while others stress historical matters. Reference volumes of "biblical theology" are a distinctive group. They make no claim to comprehensiveness in matters of geography, archaeology, history, and the like. Instead, they offer articles describing and defining biblical ideas, themes, concepts, and doctrines. They vary greatly in size and scope (see also Kittel, 4.47).

THE BEST

6.39	Brown, C. (ed.)
6.40	THE NEW INTERNATIONAL DICTIONARY OF
6.41	NEW TESTAMENT THEOLOGY. 3 vols.
6.42 (set)	Grand Rapids: Zondervan (1975–1978)
	Vol. 1 (1975); Vol. 2 (1976); Vol. 3 (1978)

This ambitious reference work is arranged alphabetically by English words. Each word-entry also shows all the Greek words it translates throughout the New Testament. The strength of the dictionary is its range of compact articles on every major term and topic. In addition, there are several essays on general topics—for example, the resurrection in contemporary theological thought. All of these features distinguish this from Kittel's *Theological Dictionary of the New Testament* (4.47) and make it more attuned to the needs of the general reader, more up-to-date, and more concerned with contemporary theological thought. These volumes are useful to the nonspecialist but will not be overlooked by more advanced readers. The bibliographies are somewhat selective and even quirky here and there, perhaps because this is a translation of a German reference work.

6.43	Bauer, J. B. (ed.)
	THE ENCYCLOPEDIA OF BIBLICAL THEOLOGY
	The Complete *Sacramentum Verbi*
	New York: Crossroad (1970/1981)

A recent one-volume unabridged reprint (1,180 pages) of an original three-volume work (*Sacramentum Verbi*) of international scope and reputation. Written largely by European scholars, this work has a Roman Catholic perspective, but not narrowly so. Major ideas and terms are discussed in fifty-three articles, which are masterful and, more important, clear. The emphasis within articles falls on the development of terms and ideas and on distinguishing between biblical ideas or expressions and later developments in dogmatic and ecclesiastical thought.

6.44   Rahner, K. (ed.)
          ENCYCLOPEDIA OF THEOLOGY
          The Concise *Sacramentum Mundi*
          New York: Crossroad (1975)

Based originally on the work of six hundred experts and displaying Rahner's strong influence, this encyclopedia goes far beyond biblical theology. Many of the articles were written especially for this revision and abridgment of an earlier, larger work. The perspective is postconciliar Roman Catholic, and the book abbreviates major Catholic reference encyclopedias by leaving out many scholarly specialities. Thus, while it is a serious and challenging volume, it is suitable for the nonspecialist (1,856 pages).

6.45   Leon-Dufour, X. (ed.)
          DICTIONARY OF BIBLICAL THEOLOGY
          New York: Seabury. Rev. ed. (1973)

This dictionary first appeared in 1967. It is based on theological themes and ideas rather than on actual biblical words. Imaginative and broad in scope, it is a reference work specifically designed for the general reader and for parish clergy. There is a noticeable Roman Catholic flavor here and there. Its most welcome feature, however, is its comprehensiveness. With superb organization and clever use of tables and cross-references, this does the work of multi-volume tools twice its size, which is 752 pages.

6.46   Leon-Dufour, X. (ed.)
          DICTIONARY OF THE NEW TESTAMENT
          San Francisco: Harper & Row (1980)

Independent of the earlier dictionary described immediately above, this focuses on the New Testament only and again shows a flair for organization and an interest in meeting the needs of the general reader. Illustrated; 448 pages.

6.47   Vine, W. E.
          AN EXPOSITORY DICTIONARY OF NEW TESTAMENT
          WORDS
          Nashville: Nelson (1978)

First published in 1940, this reference volume is arranged alphabetically by English words. It is not a standard dictionary but a series of essays on specific words from the New Testament vocabulary. Some knowledge of the Greek papyri has influenced Vine, but the interest is more theological than historical. Both the KJV and the RV are used, and the differences between the two are often noted.

6.48   Vine, W. E.
        AN EXPOSITORY DICTIONARY OF OLD AND
        NEW TESTAMENT WORDS
        Old Tappan (NJ): Revell (1981)

This includes the material from the book above, plus Vine's treatment of several Old Testament words.

6.49   Cruden, A. (ed.)
        CRUDEN'S POCKET DICTIONARY OF BIBLE TERMS
        Grand Rapids: Baker (1976)

Included in Alexander Cruden's famed concordance (see 3.11) were brief essays describing the significance of key words. These were given at the head of the entry of the word discussed, before the actual concordance listings. This is a compilation of these brief essays. Old and thin. A reprint.

C. Supporting Encyclopedias and Dictionaries

I. Biblical Times and Manners

6.50   Miller, M. S., and J. L. Miller (eds.)
        Rev. by B. M. Bennett and D. H. Scott
        HARPER'S ENCYCLOPEDIA OF BIBLE LIFE
        San Francisco: Harper & Row (1978)

Compact and nontechnical, this book concentrates on biblical names, customs, and conditions of daily life. It includes ample illustrations (primarily photographs) and good indexes (including an index of biblical passages). This edition revises the first, published in 1944. Bennett, one of the revisers, has also written *Bennett's Guide to the Bible* (8.9).

II. History of Christianity

6.51   √ Cross, F. L., and E. A. Livingstone (eds.)
        THE OXFORD DICTIONARY OF THE CHRISTIAN
        CHURCH
        New York: Oxford University Press. 2nd ed. (1974)

This premier one-volume dictionary of the Christian church offers a great amount of information on the early church and the period immediately after the New Testament. There are no illustrations and only basic bibliographies, but the material is solid scholarship, slanted toward the needs of the advanced reader and the specialist (1,550 pages). Those with more general interests should see 6.53.

6.52   Douglas, J. D., and E. E. Cairns (eds.)
THE NEW INTERNATIONAL DICTIONARY
OF THE CHRISTIAN CHURCH
Grand Rapids: Zondervan. Rev. ed. (1974/1978)

A handy and reliable encyclopedia of church history, this work is the conservative-evangelical counterpart of *The Oxford Dictionary* (6.51). An ecumenical project but basically Protestant in orientation. Strong on biographical essays.

6.53   Livingstone, E. A. (ed.)
THE CONCISE OXFORD DICTIONARY
OF THE CHRISTIAN CHURCH
New York: Oxford University Press (1978)

An abridgment of the second edition (1974) of *The Oxford Dictionary of the Christian Church* (6.51), which "provides as Gregory the Great said of Scripture, water in which lambs may walk and elephants may swim. The aim of the present work is to offer basic information for the lambs who do not need, and perhaps cannot afford, the elephants' swimming pools" (from the Preface).

6.53p   *Same:* paperback

6.54   Brauer, J. C. (ed.)
THE WESTMINSTER DICTIONARY OF CHURCH HISTORY
Philadelphia: Westminster (1971)

This work shows a more noticeable interest in American matters than the three preceding titles. The treatment is middle-of-the-road, but on biblical topics it is weaker than others (904 pages).

6.55   Dowley, T. (ed.)
EERDMAN'S HANDBOOK TO THE HISTORY OF
CHRISTIANITY
Grand Rapids: Eerdmans (1977)

Designed as a companion to *Eerdman's Handbook to the Bible* (8.2), this volume is richly illustrated and basically sound, but a bit breezy. It is designed for the general reader, unlike more standard dictionaries of church history.

III. Comparative Religions

6.56   ✓   Roth, C. (ed.)
ENCYCLOPEDIA JUDAICA. 16 vols.
New York: Macmillan (1971–1972)

Most topics of interest to the reader of the New Testament are also important in the study of early Judaism. A reputable Jewish encyclopedia can shed considerable light on the background of the New Testament. This is the standard in English, an up-to-date reference work of great range and scholarship. It is a worthy successor to the *Jewish Encyclopedia* (6.57). Vol. 1 contains introductory information and a general index.

6.57   ✓   Singer, I. (ed.)
             THE JEWISH ENCYCLOPEDIA
             New York: Ktav (1901–1906/1964)

Now eclipsed and replaced by *Encyclopedia Judaica* (6.56), this still is a valuable library reference resource despite its age. (It was first published from 1901 to 1906.) Of the two encyclopedias only this older one is currently available.

6.58   *Same:* New York: Gordon Press (1901–1906/1976)

6.59   ✓   Hastings, J. (ed.)
             ENCYCLOPEDIA OF RELIGION AND ETHICS. 13 vols.
             New York: Scribner (1908–1927)

This was originally published from 1908 (Vol. I) to 1922 (Vol. XII), and an index appeared in 1927. As the title indicates, the scope is broader than the New Testament, and even broader than the Bible as a whole. Even though the work is old, its essays are still referred to regularly, if only because they were so valuable in comparing historical and religious matters. The collection has not been rivaled or replaced and is unaltered in the current reprint.

BEST BUYS

There are many reference works from which to choose, something for almost every taste. Nevertheless, theological fashions and taste seem to be less important in such reference works than they were a few decades ago. There is nothing parochial about these resources, although they come from Roman Catholic, conservative Protestant, or other Protestant sources.

For a one-volume dictionary nothing rivals the new edition of Douglas's *New Bible Dictionary* (6.1). *The Interpreter's Dictionary of the Bible* (6.29) is the best of more extensive sets published in several volumes, but *The Illustrated Bible Encyclopedia* (6.30) is far more pleasing visually and better suited to the general reader. It does not, however, offer more information or a broader scope than Douglas; in fact, the text is the same. The most recent edition of the *International Standard Bible Encyclopedia* (6.31–6.33), now being edited by Bromiley, will prove influential when it is completed. For biblical theology, Brown's *New International Dictionary of New Testament Theology* (6.39–6.42) is truly impressive; nothing like it has ever before been available that did not require a knowledge of Greek. The *Encyclopedia of Biblical Theology* (6.43), however, is handier and better written.

For a dictionary of the church, the nod still goes to *The Oxford Dictionary of the Christian Church* (6.51) for the specialist, and to the smaller edition (6.53, 6.53p) for other readers.

All of these resources are expensive, but it is possible to buy such large reference works at discounted prices (see Chapter 10). If there is a true *value* among these books, it is Douglas (6.1).

7

THE LAY OF THE LAND
Atlases, Archaeology, and New Testament Geography

The archaeology of the biblical lands fascinates experts and general readers alike. Part of its attraction grows out of a desire to corroborate the historical data in the Bible. But even where that is not the case, the archaeologist's patient sifting and uncovering produces tangible artifacts for all to admire. One can see and touch an object and somehow suddenly bridge the centuries.

The results of archaeological excavations at New Testament sites eventually make their way into commentaries and encyclopedias; but there are other facets of the physical world of the Bible that also command our attention. The territory of New Testament history is the ancient Mediterranean rim, vast and varied, occupied by Roman legions. It ranges from high mountains to water basins below sea level, from fertile plains to arid wastes. It is the purpose of geographical descriptions of the New Testament and the biblical world to explain the significance of these features.

Finally, there is the atlas, the all-purpose tool that helps readers get their bearings in the real world. An atlas is not just a map or a series of maps; most Bible atlases also provide a text that blends the geographical detail with historical narrative. It may be the maps that sell an atlas, but it is the text that makes it better or worse. Because a good atlas can be quite expensive, most readers will probably have to depend on a library for this tool. We have listed here two or three that are either out of print or available only from foreign publishers, but they are outstandingly good and worth consulting even if you cannot own them.

In general, an atlas will begin to show its age—but not necessarily in the maps—twenty years or so after publication, unless it is revised. The text is more likely to need revision, along with the information about archaeological sites.

A. Atlases of the Bible

THE BEST

7.1   ✓   May, H. G. (ed.)
          OXFORD BIBLE ATLAS
          New York: Oxford University Press. 2nd ed. (1974)

This is perhaps now the most popular Bible atlas. It abounds in excellent and easy-to-read maps (twenty-six in full color), which have become widely used since their introduction (they are found in Oxford Bibles, for example). It is handy in size and available in an inexpensive but sturdy paper binding as well as in cloth. The text is a model of brevity but still quite extensive in coverage. Finally, the publisher is willing to keep it updated. This is a revision of the first edition (1962). In either binding, a best buy.

7.1p   *Same:* paperback edition

7.2   Wright, G. E., and F. V. Filson
          THE WESTMINSTER HISTORICAL ATLAS TO THE BIBLE
          Philadelphia: Westminster. Rev. ed. (1956)

Although widely regarded as *the* standard atlas, this has not been quite so successful in its revision. The large format and excellent maps (now found in dozens of other publications) established this volume when it first appeared. That format is still important today, for—while it makes the book oversized—it lends unusual clarity to the maps. Smaller versions of these maps are also available separately (see 7.10).

7.3   Grollenberg, L. H.
          THE PENGUIN SHORTER ATLAS OF THE BIBLE
          Baltimore: Penguin (1978)

The least expensive alternative of this trio, this atlas reprints the 1959 version of Grollenberg's atlas (7.9), an atlas that was classic but is no longer in print. "Shorter" means shorter than the original Grollenberg.

7.4   Monson, J. (general consultant)
                        STUDENT MAP MANUAL
                        Historical Geography of the Bible Lands
                        Grand Rapids: Zondervan (1979)

In appearance this is very different from any other atlas. The maps are arranged on an east-west orientation. When the book is held with the binding at the top, the east-west axis runs the length of the page; south is at the bottom of the page. No gimmick, this is the most logical way to display a map of biblical Palestine: with the Dead Sea on the right, the Sea of Galilee on the left, and the Mediterranean coast at the bottom. This is the most innovative atlas yet published for biblical studies. It is part of a larger project originating in Israel, and references to other materials and resources (such as slides) not contained here are frequent throughout the atlas.

Sixteen large-scale regional maps concentrate on topography, ten more show archaeological sites, and seventy-eight maps cover the historical period between Canaanite and Byzantine times. Four additional archaeological maps are devoted to Jerusalem. The New Testament world outside Palestine is *not* covered. There is a sequence of indexes for place names. Strictly a reference volume, this offers no text covering historical events, but the high quality of the maps, the amount of information contained in them, and the accompanying tables are truly impressive. Very expensive.

THE REST

7.5   Aharoni, Y., and M. Avi-Yonah
                        THE MACMILLAN BIBLE ATLAS
                        New York: Macmillan. Rev. ed. (1977)

Instead of featuring a few large maps and arranging a text around them, this atlas traces a historical path through the Bible using a running text and 262 small two-color maps illustrating specific events and conditions from Canaanite to early Christian times. It is unusual in other ways as well. Originally an Israeli production, this atlas offers more insight into Jewish life in the intertestamental and Second Temple periods than do most Bible atlases. But the New Testament material is sketchy. This tool is excellent for those interested primarily in history, but less useful to those primarily interested in geography.

7.6   Bruce, F. F.
                        BIBLE HISTORY ATLAS
                        Popular Study Edition
                        New York: Crossroad (1982)

This ninety-six-page volume is packed with lavish maps and completed with a succinct text covering the highlights of biblical history. Bruce writes well for the general reader, and the result is a compact, uncluttered, and elementary volume of particular value to beginners.

7.7   Blaiklock, E. M. (ed.)
             THE ZONDERVAN PICTORIAL BIBLE ATLAS
             Grand Rapids: Zondervan (1969)

Sixteen chapters of text and nine full-color maps (by Rand McNally and taken from their earlier Bible atlas) make up this standard volume. There are sixty-eight one-color maps throughout, ranging from a third of a page to a full page in size. The text is clear and easy to read. Four appendixes cover the cities of the Bible, archaeology and the Bible, the languages of Bible lands, and the geology of these areas. Even the most technical portions are well written.

7.8   Pfeiffer, C. F.
             BAKER'S BIBLE ATLAS
             Grand Rapids: Baker. Rev. ed. (1961)

A geography of the Bible containing nineteen colored maps, dozens of black-and-white photographs, and several black-and-white maps. Organized according to the biblical text, beginning with Genesis, this atlas offers also a brief review of biblical archaeology.

7.9   Grollenberg, L. H.
             ATLAS OF THE BIBLE
             New York: Nelson (1956)

Although it is not currently in print, this volume deserves mention for those who might come across it in a second-hand bookshop or who wish to use it in a library. It is one of the finest biblical atlases of this century; some would say it has never been equalled.

B. Bible Maps

These are not full-fledged atlases but convenient and inexpensive editions of Bible maps. Often the maps in this format are reduced in size from the atlas in which they originally appeared.

7.10   Wright, G. E., and F. V. Filson
             WESTMINSTER HISTORICAL MAPS OF BIBLE LANDS
             Philadelphia: Westminster (n.d.)

No better buy can be found than the sixteen now-famous Westminster maps (see 7.2) in a paper booklet along with the map index.

7.11   Frank, H. T. (ed.)
ATLAS OF BIBLE LANDS
Maplewood (NJ): Hammond. Rev. ed. (1977)

The Hammond maps (here and in the next entry) are noted for clearness and simplicity and are fairly recent. The format is larger than in the equivalent set of Westminster maps (7.10).

7.12   THE COMPACT BIBLE ATLAS WITH GAZETTEER
Grand Rapids: Baker (1979)

This uses nineteen of the Hammond Bible maps and offers a gazetteer listing 1,300 entries.

C. Other Useful Atlases

Biblical history is part of world history. In the case of the New Testament this means it is part of the history and geography of classical antiquity. Readers of the New Testament can learn much from reference works dealing primarily with the classical world, as do the following.

THE BEST

7.13   Hammond, H. G. L. (editor-in-chief)
ATLAS OF THE GREEK AND ROMAN WORLD IN
ANTIQUITY
Park Ridge (NJ): Noyes Press (1981)

This superb volume realizes an unfulfilled goal of Oxford University Press—to produce an atlas of the world of antiquity. The editor's name adds luster, but it is the cartographer's pen (he is David Cox) that puts this new volume in a class by itself. Forty-eight maps (plus insets) cover the Western world from Neolithic times to the sixth century of this era. No special emphasis is given to the New Testament or to early Christianity. The index of 12,500 place names is itself worth the price of the book. The maps are only two colors but use skillful shadings; the format is oversized. The British editor is a noted classical scholar. These maps are not to be confused with those produced by an American publisher of the same name (7.11).

7.14   Scullard, H. H., and A. A. M. van der Heyden
SHORTER ATLAS OF THE CLASSICAL WORLD
New York: E. P. Dutton (1962/1967)

This paperback is not an abridged version of the classic, which is now out of print (7.18), but a largely rewritten effort. A best buy.

THE REST

All of the titles that follow would make an honors list, if they were readily available. The quality is high throughout these publications, but they are rather inaccessible. Some are not published in this country and others are out of print.

7.15   ATLAS OF ISRAEL. Cartography, Physical Geography, Human and Economic Geography, History
Amsterdam: Elsevier Publishing Co./Jerusalem: Ministry of Labour [State of Israel] (1970)

A contemporary atlas offering an extensive and sophisticated survey of some biblical lands as they appear today, this tool is definitive in its class. Five maps. Prohibitively expensive for individuals.

7.16   [Bayerische Schulbuch-Verlag, Hrsg.]
GROSSER HISTORISCHEN WELTATLAS
Teil 1. Vorgeschichte und Altertum
Munich: Bayerische Schulbuch-Verlag (Bavarian Textbook Publishers). 3rd ed. (1958)

This slender volume is the first part of one of the finest historical atlases ever produced. Although the maps are old-fashioned looking, they are of superior quality and detail and are easy to read because of the broad spectrum of colors used. There are more than seventy maps in this volume, some with transparent overlays to illustrate changes in successive historical periods. Hard to find, but an outstanding book.

7.17   Meer, F. van der, and C. Mohrmann
ATLAS OF THE EARLY CHRISTIAN WORLD
New York: Nelson (1958)

Currently not available, this is one of a series of lavish atlases produced by Nelson in the fifties (as were 7.9 and 7.18). This volume begins with the New Testament, but it is devoted mainly to the period immediately after that.

7.18   Heyden, A. A. M. van der, and H. H. Scullard
ATLAS OF THE CLASSICAL WORLD
New York: Nelson (1959)

This is another in the Nelson series and a companion to Grollenberg (7.9). Although it is not currently available, a revised shorter version can be found in 7.14.

D. The Geography of New Testament Lands

A map can tell a lot, but it cannot tell everything about the everyday life of biblical Palestine. To understand the New Testament more fully, one has to know the landscape on which its story is played out, the terrain that sheltered thieves and brigands and nourished sheep and wheat. The books listed here seek to fill in the geographical picture. None is restricted to the New Testament alone.

THE BEST

7.19   Aharoni, Y.
         THE LAND OF THE BIBLE. A Historical Geography
         Rev. and enlarged ed., trans. by A. F. Rainey
         Philadelphia: Westminster (1980)

This is a considerably enlarged and revised edition of a book that first appeared in English in 1967. The term "Bible" refers to the Jewish scriptures, and events and places exclusively of interest to readers of the New Testament are not covered. The work is authoritative and, thanks to Rainey's skillful editing, readable, with footnotes in a separate section. Designed as a textbook, it is best suited to the very serious, even technical, reader. The classic contemporary work in its field.

7.20   Avi-Yonah, M.
         THE HOLY LAND, FROM THE PERSIAN TO THE ARAB
         CONQUESTS
         (536 B.C. TO A.D. 640)
         Trans. by A. F. Rainey
         Grand Rapids: Baker. Rev. ed. (n.d.)

A very economical text, this work pays closer attention to New Testament times than most such books.

7.21   Baly, D.
         THE GEOGRAPHY OF THE BIBLE
         San Francisco: Harper & Row. 2nd ed. (1974)

Long a standard in the field, Baly's book was first published in 1957 and was revised in 1974. The information is reliable, and the format handy. Photographs and drawings or maps are all black-and-white. The text makes slightly dry reading, but it is an authoritative guide for the nonspecialist and the best on New Testament matters in this trio.

THE REST

7.22   Berrett, L. C.
DISCOVERING THE WORLD OF THE BIBLE
Nashville: Nelson (1973/1979)

This is a guide to the ancient world of the Bible and to the modern world the visitor finds today. It is divided into major sections on Cyprus, Egypt, Greece, Iraq, Israel, Italy, Jordan, Lebanon, Syria, and Turkey. In an appendix is a map of Paul's missionary journeys, a chronological chart covering the world from "Adam, c. 4000–3700" down to "Pope Paul VI (1963–)," a very brief glossary, and a short list of further readings.

The author is a Mormon. In some places the book refers to nonbiblical materials familiar mostly to Mormons, and the views of the Latter Day Saints sometimes come through. But that does not mar the book's usefulness for others or its attractiveness. It is an excellent if compressed guidebook for modern travelers visiting the biblical world, and it is particularly refreshing in its attention to places outside biblical Palestine. Included in the volume are some fine local maps and illustrations, a few stunning color photographs of no particular relevance, and some reproductions of what must be the worst religious art that could be found— all of that in seven hundred pages.

7.23   Pfeiffer, C. F., and H. F. Vos
WYCLIFFE HISTORICAL GEOGRAPHY OF BIBLE LANDS
Chicago: Moody (1967)

Modern, lavish in illustrations, and evangelical in perspective.

E. Archaeology

New Testament archaeology is not as well publicized as Old Testament archaeology; nor is it put to the same purposes— attempting to "confirm" historical events not reported outside the Bible. In fact, New Testament archaeology is really part of a larger enterprise, the excavation of classical antiquity. Books on archaeology, however, tend to segregate biblical interests from others. To compensate, the list that follows includes works that cover much more than the New Testament.

THE BEST

7.24	Avi-Yonah, M., and E. Stern
7.25	ENCYCLOPEDIA OF ARCHAEOLOGICAL EXCAVATIONS
7.26	IN THE HOLY LAND. 4 vols.
7.27	Englewood Cliffs (NJ): Prentice-Hall (1975)

An outstanding encyclopedia first published in Hebrew (Jerusalem, 1970) is here made available in English. It brings together data otherwise scattered throughout hundreds of technical publications, putting these in a form that the general reader can use. The articles are written by experts, often those who supervised the excavations; but a fine editorial hand has kept the English plain and clear.

The "geographical limits represented are the historic borders of the Holy Land on both sides of the Jordan, from the Ladder of Tyre and Dan in the north to the Gulf of Elath in the South." Chronologically, the limits are set by prehistory on the one end and the period of the Crusades on the other. In addition to basic entries on each significant site, there are numerous general entries that are wonderfully comprehensive—for example, on synagogues, or the Jordan Valley, or monasteries. There is a chronological table at the end of each volume (although these are not quite internally consistent). An index is found in Vol. IV. Avi-Yonah died before Vol. I appeared, having edited Vols. I and II. Stern shared in the editing of the remaining portions.

It is rare that a work genuinely suits both the needs of the expert and the curiosity of the novice, as this one does. Unparalleled.

7.28	Finegan, J.
	THE ARCHAEOLOGY OF THE NEW TESTAMENT
	The Life of Jesus and the Beginning of the Early Church
	Princeton: Princeton University Press (1970)

A smooth blend of good scholarship and good storytelling, this book takes the reader on a tour of the Holy Land starting with the life of John the Baptist and following the career of Jesus to its climax in Jerusalem. The arrangement, then, is historical rather than geographical. An interesting final chapter deals with tombs, catacombs, and the "sign of the cross." Hundreds of black-and-white photographs and line drawings are used. Finegan cleverly combines ancient written sources and the results of modern excavations, directing those who want to know more to the scholarly publications. A reliable and interesting work, especially suited to the general reader who is serious but just beginning.

7.28p	*Same:* paperback

7.29   Finegan, J.
THE ARCHAEOLOGY OF THE NEW TESTAMENT
The Mediterranean World of the Early Christian Apostles
Boulder (CO): Westview Press (1981)

A companion to Finegan's work on the gospels (7.28) and an extension of it to the rest of the New Testament, this volume follows Paul through fifteen thousand miles of travel, inserting what is known about Peter and John as well. The description of the preceding work fits this one as well.

7.30   Stilwell, R. (ed.)
THE PRINCETON ENCYCLOPEDIA OF CLASSICAL SITES
Princeton: Princeton University Press (1976)

This is a superb single volume covering major excavations from the classical period, with excellent maps. The book spans the period from 750 B.C. to A.D. 500, but Christian sites from the fourth and fifth centuries have not been included. The "Pauline cities" are well represented. Concise and authoritative.

THE REST

7.31   Aharoni, Y.
THE ARCHAEOLOGY OF THE LAND OF ISRAEL
Ed. by M. Aharoni and trans. by A. F. Rainey
Philadelphia: Westminster (1982)

This is of limited use to the reader of the New Testament since it covers sites only up to the period of the exile.

7.31p   *Same:* paperback

7.32   Blaiklock, E. M.
THE ARCHAEOLOGY OF THE NEW TESTAMENT
Grand Rapids: Zondervan (1970)

As the title indicates, this is one of the very few books that concentrate on the New Testament. In it a former professor of classics (New Zealand) takes a leisurely walk through the New Testament using archaeological data to shed light on the text. It is a *very* leisurely walk. Little is new and nothing is very systematic. Still, this is an enjoyable way to learn dozens of bits of interesting background information. Much of this is not archaeology at all but a primer in Roman history.

7.33   Cornfeld, G., and D. N. Freedman (eds.)
ARCHAEOLOGY OF THE BIBLE. Book by Book
San Francisco: Harper & Row (1976)

This is an excellent place to begin the study of biblical archaeology, because the editors have followed the biblical text rather than pursuing a topical or geographical arrangement. There is good coverage of the intertestamental period as well as of the New Testament itself.

7.33p   *Same:* paperback

7.34   Dever, W. G., and D. Lance
            A MANUAL OF FIELD EXCAVATION
            Handbook for Field Archaeologists
            New York: Ktav (1979)

One of the few books that carefully and patiently explain the theory and method of archaeological field work. While it focuses on the results obtained at Gezer, it can stand as an introduction to archaeology as such. Demanding; best for the very serious reader.

7.35   Kenyon, K.
            THE BIBLE AND RECENT ARCHAEOLOGY
            Atlanta: John Knox (1979)

Kenyon carries on a famous name in archaeology. This essay includes only a small amount of material on the New Testament period.

7.36   Moorey, P. R. S.
            BIBLICAL LANDS
            New York: Elsevier-Phaidon (1975)

Lavish pictures with a focus on archaeology.

7.37   Pfeiffer, C. F.
            THE BIBLICAL WORLD. A Dictionary of
            Biblical Archaeology
            Grand Rapids: Baker (1966)

In this volume, brief readable accounts of archaeological evidence significant for Bible study are arranged in dictionary form. The book is popular, not technical, and the format is handy for quick reference.

7.38   Schoville, K. N.
            BIBLICAL ARCHAEOLOGY IN FOCUS
            Grand Rapids: Baker (1981)

7.39   Shanks, H.
            JUDAISM IN STONE. The Archaeology of
            Ancient Synagogues
            San Francisco: Harper & Row (1979)

This work is limited in scope, especially when compared with Levine (7.40), but Shanks does offer a good introduction to the fascinating world of synagogues. The photographs are outstanding. The general reader who starts here can go on to more challenge and more substance in the next entry.

7.40   Levine, L. E.
              ANCIENT SYNAGOGUES REVEALED
              Detroit: Wayne State University Press (1981)

The New Testament shows that the synagogue played an important role in Jesus' teaching, in the life of the apostles, and in early Christianity. Thus, recovering ancient synagogues is an archaeological opportunity of great interest to students of the New Testament. This volume is a solid introduction to what is now known. It is technical but not beyond the resources of a serious reader. Well illustrated.

7.41   Thompson, J. A.
              THE BIBLE AND ARCHAEOLOGY
              Grand Rapids: Eerdmans (1981)

Elementary and nontechnical, this volume contains more than 175 photographs and illustrations plus charts, indexes, and bibliographies.

7.42   Unger, M. F.
              ARCHAEOLOGY AND THE NEW TESTAMENT
              Grand Rapids: Zondervan (1962)

7.43   Vos, H. F.
              ARCHAEOLOGY IN BIBLE LANDS
              Chicago: Moody (1977)

This is a nontechnical introduction to biblical archaeology and a survey of its results—for example, in Mesopotamia, Palestine, Egypt, Phoenicia, Syria, Iran, Cyprus, Asia Minor, and Greece. The discussion of each area starts with general remarks and then considers individual excavations. Useful for the arm-chair historian and the real-life traveler as well.

7.44   Yamauchi, E.
              THE ARCHAEOLOGY OF NEW TESTAMENT CITIES
              IN WESTERN ASIA MINOR
              Grand Rapids: Baker (1980)

Yamauchi focuses on twelve major cities of ancient Asia Minor, offering a primer of archaeological information about each: Assos, Pergamum, Thyatira, Smyrna, Sardis, Philadelphia, Ephesus, Miletus, Didyma, Laodicea, Hieropolis, and Colossae. Clearly written, generously illustrated. Paperback.

7.45   Wiseman, D. J., and E. Yamauchi
              ARCHAEOLOGY AND THE BIBLE
              Grand Rapids: Zondervan (1979)

This inexpensive paperback offers the introductory articles on biblical archaeology that appear in the initial volume of a major new commentary series, *The Expositor's Bible Commentary* (see Chapter 9, section B, EBC; note also 1.59).

7.46   Wright, G. E.
              BIBLICAL ARCHAEOLOGY
              Philadelphia: Westminster. Rev. and expanded ed. (1963)

An old standby, perhaps the most frequently read introduction and survey on the subject, this work has been kept reasonably up-to-date in this revision. Later chapters refer to the New Testament.

BEST BUYS

Perhaps the best value today in a Bible atlas is May (7.1), although some will prefer the slightly larger maps in Wright and Filson (7.2). For Palestine alone nothing rivals Monson (7.4), but it takes some time to learn to use this book effectively. Those interested primarily in the geographical spread of New Testament history and literature will find nothing more complete and up-to-date than Hammond (7.13).

Baly (7.21) is perhaps not the finest treatment of biblical geography, but it does offer much on the New Testament. In archaeology Avi-Yonah and Stern (7.24–7.27) offers the most complete coverage of Palestinian sites, but that leaves out much of the New Testament territory. For that, Finegan (7.28, 7.29) is the most comprehensive.

8

HANDBOOKS AND ALMANACS

Bible "handbooks" have long been popular. First-aid kits for church-school teachers, they pack a lot of basic information into a small space. The backbone of such books is usually a summary analysis of each biblical book, plus the sort of information that can be put into lists and charts and easily memorized. Some of the newer handbooks are a bit more sophisticated. An "almanac," as its name suggests, emphasizes people, the land, and the background of the Bible—with a little less attention to the literary aspects.

Handbooks and almanacs aim at providing the most general information and support for biblical study and teaching. Since they contain a variety of material, handbooks and almanacs overlap occasionally with other works—atlases, geographies, concordances, commentaries, dictionaries, and encyclopedias. Moreover, since there are no clear standards about what should be included in a handbook or an almanac, each takes its own path and the result is something of a jumble.

THE BEST

8.1   Blair, E. P. (ed.)
           ABINGDON BIBLE HANDBOOK
           Nashville/New York: Abingdon (1975)

Perhaps the best of the lot, this handbook includes articles introducing the Bible as a whole and each book individually. The writing is clear, and the appeal to general readers is enhanced by the extensive use of illustrations.

8.1p   *Same:* paperback

8.2   Alexander, D., and P. Alexander (eds.)
            EERDMAN'S HANDBOOK TO THE BIBLE
            Grand Rapids: Eerdmans (1973)

A very elementary book in style and content, this makes no heavy demands on the reader. A team of editors and thirty-one contributors have assembled a thin variety of information, charts, illustrations, tables, etc. The diagrams are good and sometimes clever. The illustrations are acceptable but can get garish. The Old Testament is valued mainly for illuminating the New Testament. Part 1 treats the nature of the Bible, its setting, and translation; part 2 offers an introduction to each Old Testament book; part 3 to the New Testament books; part 4 consists of lists, charts, etc.

8.3   Packer, J. I., M. C. Tenney, and W. White
            THE BIBLE ALMANAC
            Nashville: Nelson (1980)

Here the main focus is on the people of the Bible and the surrounding areas, their history and especially their daily life. Valuable for the beginner.

THE REST

8.4   Blaiklock, E. M.
            BLAIKLOCK'S HANDBOOK TO THE BIBLE
            Old Tappan (NJ): Revell (1981)

Essentially a brief, book-by-book introduction with background information.

8.5   Blunt, A. W. F., et al.
            HELPS TO THE STUDY OF THE BIBLE
            New York: Oxford University Press (1951)

Summaries, historic and geographic data, a dictionary of proper names, illustrations, a subject index, a concordance, and some maps.

8.6   Coleman, W. L.
            WHO, WHAT, WHEN, WHERE BOOK ABOUT THE BIBLE
            Chicago: Chariot/Cook (1980)

"Quizzes, puzzles, pictures and clear prose *for children in grades 1–6.*"

8.7   Alexander, D., and P. Alexander (eds.)
            EERDMAN'S CONCISE BIBLE HANDBOOK
            Grand Rapids: Eerdmans (1981)

A one-volume paperback revision of the *Handbook to the Bible* (8.2), without most of the illustrations. *Not* an improvement.

8.8   Foulkes, F.
    POCKET GUIDE TO THE NEW TESTAMENT
    Downers Grove (IL): InterVarsity (1978)

8.9   Bennett, B. M.
    BENNETT'S GUIDE TO THE BIBLE
    Graphic Aids and Outlines
    New York: Seabury (1982)

Part 1 outlines and summarizes each book of the Bible. Part 2 gives a time-line history with graphics. Part 3 deals with the text of the Bible and the role of archaeology.

8.10   Halley, H. H.
    HALLEY'S BIBLE HANDBOOK
    Grand Rapids: Zondervan (1927)

The popular old favorite. A venerable but rickety guide, book by book. Nothing significant has changed here in decades.

8.11   *Same:* large print edition with cloth binding

8.12   *Same:* large print edition with Kivar binding

8.13   Wilson, E. V.
    THE WESTMINSTER CONCISE HANDBOOK FOR THE
    BIBLE
    Philadelphia: Westminster (1979)

Very concise. One-half page summaries of all biblical books, twelve pages of introductory material, the standard Westminster maps (7.10), and two chronological charts. Brevity is a virtue, but this is a bit too little.

8.14   Unger, M. F.
    UNGER'S BIBLE HANDBOOK
    Chicago: Moody (1966)

A more recent competitor designed to be as much like *Halley's Bible Handbook* (8.10) as possible. It succeeds.

8.15   Jones, C. M.
    NEW TESTAMENT ILLUSTRATIONS
    New York: Cambridge University Press (1966)

A rich, well-chosen collection of black-and-white photographs (and some line drawings) illustrating the geography, historical background, archaeology, and manuscript tradition of the New Testament. Published as part of the Cambridge Commentary on the New English Bible.

8.15p   *Same:* paperback

8.16   Westermann, C.
          HANDBOOK TO THE NEW TESTAMENT
          Trans. and ed. by R. H. Boyd
          Minneapolis: Augsburg (1982)

A brief review of the message of every New Testament book, concentrating on major themes and the relationships among various sections of the books. Several charts and tables help clarify the material.

BEST BUYS

Blair (8.1) and Packer (8.3) are the most useful and certainly the best for the money. They make a complementary combination.

9

NEW TESTAMENT COMMENTARIES

Here the term "commentary" is used rather strictly to refer to close analysis and elucidation of biblical texts. There are some bench marks by which a true commentary may be measured. First, it follows the text in sequence and uniformly. A good resource does not comment only on what is most conspicuous or most arresting or what happens to appeal to the writer; it takes the whole text seriously and serves as a detailed guide for the reader. Next, a commentary seeks to make the text comprehensible, to clarify it. That may be done at a very technical level by concentrating on words and grammar, or it can be done at a more expository level by trying to locate the author's interests and intentions and to restate them. Finally, a commentary recognizes that the biblical texts, as we read them today, stand in traditions of interpretation. There are ecclesiastical traditions and scholarly traditions. Some commentaries pay more attention to the one than to the other, but no commentary deserving of the name simply records individual opinions without reference to these larger contexts.

In the listings below, availability is an important consideration. Some fine but older volumes are now hard to locate and are of interest almost exclusively to scholars who are interested in the history of interpretation. From time to time in what follows a truly classic older title will be included, but only because it is still so influential.

Another consideration is the version used in a commentary. Those represented here range from the Greek New Testament through the KJV up to the most recent versions. Today more good commentaries use the RSV than any other version, but the value of a commentary does not depend on the translation that is used.

Commentaries can appeal to different levels of interest. Some are very technical and analytical, of interest almost exclusively to scholars. Others are largely expositional, perhaps even homiletical. Confessional allegiance and theological taste are not wholly irrelevant matters to many readers (and authors), but most of the selections here have been made without regard to such questions. Where emphasis is placed on church affiliation (e.g., Roman Catholic, Brethren, Lutheran) or beliefs (e.g., inspiration of scripture) that is likely to be noted. Similarly, the term "evangelical" is used when it is a self-designation of an author or a reasonable inference. The term "traditional" refers to works in which it is important that the Bible be presented as confirming the classic beliefs of orthodox Christianity. But many authors who regard themselves as no less orthodox place no particular stress on this issue.

Finally, one must consider the format. Is a one-volume commentary that covers the entire Bible, or perhaps just the New Testament, the best choice? What about individual volumes? What about sets or series, sometimes sold collectively at a great saving over the cost of individual titles?

The breadth and convenience of a one-volume commentary are obvious, and some multi-volume sets may look more attractive than they are. Although some of the finest individual commentaries ever produced have come out of such series, they stand side by side with some of the worst volumes ever produced. A good commentary volume is one that is written by someone who has mastered the text and has something genuinely worth saying. Since series are planned and assigned far in advance of the publication of the volumes, the assignments often go to the best-known scholars— who may or may not be truly interested in the text assigned. Deadlines, alas, draw near whether the Spirit helps or not. As a result, the commentary series often produces humdrum work alongside very good work.

This survey looks first at one-volume commentaries (section A), the handiest and the best for beginners and for all-around utility. The next section (B) describes the current major series, and the final section (C) offers a review of the very best major commentaries arranged according to the order of the New Testament books. Some individual volumes from series are included where that is appropriate.

A. One-Volume Commentaries

THE BEST

9.1   Brown, R. E., J. A. Fitzmyer, and R. E. Murphy (eds.)
THE JEROME BIBLICAL COMMENTARY
Englewood Cliffs (NJ): Prentice-Hall (1968)

Two volumes published as one (in more than 1,500 pages), this is possibly the finest "compact" comprehensive commentary available. It is written and edited exclusively by Roman Catholic scholars, but it is neither narrow nor parochial. Here and there one may find a theme or idea of particular interest to ecclesiastical traditions, but for the most part the difference between good Roman Catholic and good Protestant biblical scholarship is negligible.

In addition to verse-by-verse commentary there are more than two dozen topical articles. Among the best are those on inspiration, interpretation, and hermeneutics. Generous cross-referencing and good indexing bind the whole together. The writing is clear, intended for the nonspecialist, but the references to contemporary scholarship are so ample that the specialist too will find this a useful resource. No single English translation is used. Coverage includes the Apocrypha.

9.2   Black, M., and H. H. Rowley (eds.)
PEAKE'S COMMENTARY ON THE BIBLE
Nashville/New York: Nelson (1962)

In 1920, A. S. Peake described the original edition in these words: "The present work is designed to put before the reader in a simple form, without technicalities, the generally accepted results of Biblical Criticism, Interpretation, History, and Theology. It is not intended to be homiletic or devotional, but to convey with precision, and yet in a popular and interesting way, the meaning of the original writers, and reconstruct the conditions in which they worked and of which they wrote."

"Peake" caught on and became *the* commentary of its day, at least in England. This complete revision brings it up to date and serves the same purposes and aspires to the same goals as the original. Like the JBC (9.1), it is meant for the nonspecialist but will be found on a scholar's shelf too. It is less extensive than the JBC in its appeal to scholarly literature and does not cover the Apocrypha. General articles are solid. The RSV text is used. Perhaps the only negative comment would concern the format: it sometimes takes a moment to get one's bearings on a page and locate the comments on a particular passage.

9.3   Guthrie, D., and J. A. Motyer (eds.)
               THE NEW BIBLE COMMENTARY. REVISED
               Grand Rapids: Eerdmans (1970)

This is the most recent of the three, but it is still more than a decade old now.
This popular commentary has been favored by evangelicals. Almost fifty contributors
have revised the first edition of 1953. The text used is *now* the RSV, but the
earlier commitment remains: to the Bible's "divine inspiration, essential historical
trustworthiness and positive Christian usefulness."

THE REST

9.4   Howley, G. C. D., F. F. Bruce, and H. L. Ellison (eds.)
               THE LAYMAN'S BIBLE COMMENTARY
               Grand Rapids: Zondervan (1978)

Published in England under the title *A Bible Commentary for Today,* this one-
volume effort represents primarily the recent work of Plymouth Brethren interpreters.
The position is that of knowledgeable traditionalism. The New Testament portion
appeared earlier under the title *A New Testament Commentary.*

9.5   Clarke, W. K. L.
               CONCISE BIBLE COMMENTARY
               New York: Macmillan (1953)

An old standby using the KJV, this volume offers a solid general introduction and
brief book-by-book analysis. Very compact but complete, including the Apocrypha.

9.6   Laymon, C. M.
               INTERPRETER'S ONE-VOLUME COMMENTARY
               Nashville/New York: Abingdon (1971)

This should not be confused with the much older, multi-volume *Interpreter's Bible*
(see section B below); it is not a revision of that set. This more recent and far
more compact commentary includes the Apocrypha and offers topical articles
along with brief commentary. Most of the contributors are Protestant, but Roman
Catholic and Jewish scholars are also represented. The material is aimed at the
general reader. Good cross-referencing and indexing.

9.7   *Same:* thumb-indexed

9.8   Pfeiffer, C. F., and E. F. Harrison (eds.)
               THE WYCLIFFE BIBLE COMMENTARY
               Chicago: Moody (1962)

Enormously popular (twelve printings in the first fourteen years), this commentary
was written by dozens of Protestant biblical scholars. The stance is clearly
conservative to fundamentalist. Fifteen denominations are represented, and the

writers "manifest their unflinching belief in the divine inspiration of Holy Scripture." The KJV is the text used.

9.9   Fuller, R. C., L. Johnston, and C. Kearns (eds.)
     A NEW CATHOLIC COMMENTARY ON HOLY SCRIPTURE
     London: Nelson (1969)

In this revision of a 1953 classic, the Bible is commented on paragraph by paragraph rather than verse by verse. The aim is "to unfold the genuine sense of Scripture while making the fullest use of modern Biblical research." The word "Catholic" in the title is not narrowly used. The articles are by dozens of scholars and are useful to a wide audience. The Apocrypha is included.

9.10   Blaiklock, E. M.
     COMMENTARY ON THE NEW TESTAMENT
     Old Tappan (NJ): Revell (1978)

Conservative, one-volume, confined to the New Testament.

9.11   Franzmann, M. H., and W. R. Roehrs (eds.)
     CONCORDIA SELF-STUDY COMMENTARY. An
     Authoritative In-Home Resource for Students of the Bible
     St. Louis: Concordia Publishing House (1978)

The New Testament portion was published earlier but now joins with more recent Old Testament exposition to make a handy one-volume commentary, traditional and Lutheran. Not strong on introductory material and less useful overall than many others of its size, it is elementary and a bit thin in comparison with others listed here.

9.12   Neill, W.
     HARPER'S BIBLE COMMENTARY
     San Francisco: Harper & Row (1962)

Neill *almost* overcomes the inevitable tendency of any commentary to read more like a reference manual than like a book. He offers a "running commentary" on the entire Bible, based on the assumption that the Old and New Testaments make the best sense when understood as serving one purpose. Although it is not as strong on background material as others, it is well written and enjoyable to read.

B. Commentaries in Series or Sets

Commentaries in series or sets are arranged here in alphabetical order according to the standard abbreviation (found to the left of the entry in place of the usual reference number). This is used for subsequent references. Some individual volumes are listed in section C, along with other commentaries not belonging to a series.

AB   Albright, W. F., and D. N. Freedman (gen. eds.)
            THE ANCHOR BIBLE
            Garden City: Doubleday

In its New Testament volumes (not necessarily in the Old Testament volumes), the AB must be regarded as a disappointment. Some would go so far as to say a failure, but four excellent volumes and the promise of at least one more make that judgment a bit harsh. Still, a wonderful publishing opportunity that could have meant much to scholars and general readers alike has been all but squandered in this case. But the exceptions are outstanding: R. E. Brown's two volumes on the Gospel of John (9.57, 9.58) and one on John's epistles (9.205); and J. A. Fitzmyer's volumes on Luke (Vol. 1 on chaps. 1–9 [9.42]; and the second volume forthcoming).

Apart from these, what has appeared thus far is of too little value to either the scholar or the general reader, and some of it is embarrassingly bad. Many other volumes, now several years overdue, have been reassigned to new writers, which keeps alive a flicker of hope for the final outcome. AB is generous in the space it allows its authors, who provide their own translations from the Greek text. However, the reader who does not know Greek is not at any real disadvantage, since the technical notes and the general commentary are usually separate. (See 9.85, 9.121, 9.152, 9.197, 9.224, 9.241, 9.261.)

ACNT   AUGSBURG COMMENTARY ON THE NEW TESTAMENT
            Minneapolis: Augsburg (1982–)

Two volumes (Romans [9.110] and 1 Peter, 2 Peter, James, and Jude [9.234, 9.254]) inaugurate a new series that will offer fourteen volumes in all. The scholarship is sound, the size and the price modest, and the aim is to present theologically sophisticated exposition in nontechnical language suitable for use by clergy, teachers, and lay readers.

AGT   Alford, H.
            ALFORD'S GREEK TESTAMENT
            An Exegetical and Critical Commentary
            Grand Rapids: Baker

Even older than the EGNT (below), Alford's four-volume work first appeared from 1849 to 1860. These volumes are of more than passing historical significance, since in their pages many learned American readers of the nineteenth century were first introduced to the results and perspectives of German New Testament scholarship. It was, in part, the sharp reaction to this "critical" feature of the AGT that called forth the EGNT, a blander expositional commentary.

Today the AGT looks tame, not radical, but it is still useful in a modest way. Those who want to work with a Greek text and need an analytical aid would do better with the AGT than with the EGNT. And for its scope and compact size there are few alternatives. Still, its age is a great handicap. The CGTC (below) would be the reasonable and contemporary alternative, but it is far from complete.

BBC   Allen, C. J. (gen. ed.)
      THE BROADMAN BIBLE COMMENTARY
      Nashville: Broadman

Five volumes cover the New Testament, including introductory and general articles. The concern is expository; the commentary is a paragraph-by-paragraph interpretation of the RSV text.

BNNT   Barnes, A.
      BARNES NOTES ON THE NEW TESTAMENT
      Grand Rapids: Baker

Eleven volumes of practical exposition from the early nineteenth century, designed for Bible classes and Sunday schools. The reprinting of this old work indicates that it is still used in such settings. An English translation of the text at the top of the page is followed by double columns of "notes," just as the title says. It sounds very old-fashioned at times; but that is not surprising, since the comments on Acts, for example, were in their tenth edition by 1850. Traditional, and so badly out-of-date that the word "obsolete" is not too strong.

CBCNT   CAMBRIDGE BIBLE COMMENTARY ON THE NEW
      ENGLISH BIBLE, NEW TESTAMENT
      New York: Cambridge University Press

Designed for general use and based on the NEB, this compact set of fifteen volumes (available in cloth and paper) provides basic exposition and discussion of major points of interpretation. It is excellent for the general reader. (See 9.26, 9.36, 9.53, 9.73, 9.86, 9.102, 9.118, 9.130, 9.139, 9.163, 9.164, 9.177, 9.190, 9.201, 9.212, 9.226, 9.248, 9.249, 9.262.)

CBSC   Perowne, J. J. S., and A. F. Kilpatrick (gen. eds.)
      THE CAMBRIDGE BIBLE FOR SCHOOLS AND COLLEGES
      Grand Rapids: Kregel

Originally published by Cambridge University Press (between 1877 and 1925) in fifty-six volumes, this is an older work that once had enormous influence. Because it was so widely used in the British system of education, it became a standard point of reference. Concise and aimed at the general reader, individual volumes were updated with frequent revisions, but the last of these was made long ago. In the meantime Cambridge University Press has moved on to new ventures such as the CBCNT (above) and the CGTC (below).

CGTC   Moule, C. F. D. (gen. ed.)
            THE CAMBRIDGE GREEK TESTAMENT COMMENTARY
            New York: Cambridge University Press

Thus far only two volumes in this promising series have appeared. One is on the
Gospel of Mark (9.27), the other on Colossians and Philemon (9.150). Authors
use the Greek text, and the style is analytical and concise. Both volumes are
models of how to pack a great amount of detailed exegetical information into a
small space, and both are available in cloth or paper. Of primary interest to the
advanced reader and the scholar.

CNT(L)   Lenski, R. C. H.
            COMMENTARY ON THE NEW TESTAMENT
            Minneapolis: Augsburg

Lenski's volumes are a Lutheran (and slightly older) counterpart of the Reformed
theological tradition reflected in NTC(H). Twelve volumes comprising ten thousand
pages blanket the Greek New Testament from beginning to end—from a very
conservative perspective. Note the caution in the section on "Best Buys" at the
end of this chapter.

CNTTH   Lightfoot, J.
            COMMENTARY ON THE NEW TESTAMENT FROM THE
            TALMUD AND HEBRAICA. Matthew–I Corinthians
            Grand Rapids: Baker

The reprinting of this four-volume work must be something of a publishing record:
it is over three hundred years old. Serious scholars will find nothing here that they
cannot find in more recent German works. But this work can help students of the
New Testament to become more familiar with postbiblical Jewish writings. While
there are real limits to the approach taken in these four volumes—and conceding
that this work is for the intrepid among general readers—it is interesting to have
material like this in print. If it does nothing else, reprinting Lightfoot shows how
little has been done in three centuries to make available the Jewish texts that help
to illuminate the background of the New Testament.

EB   Nicoll, W. R. (ed.)
            THE EXPOSITOR'S BIBLE
            Grand Rapids: Baker (1887–1896/1982)

These volumes (there are six in this current reprint, containing the original forty-
nine volumes) cover the entire Bible. The focus is expository and homiletical,
featuring as authors some of the great British scholars and preachers of the late
nineteenth century. Of less utility than the EGNT, the series is still attractive to
those who revel in the bygone glories of what was a great expositional age.

EBC   Gaebelein, F. E. (gen. ed.)
THE EXPOSITOR'S BIBLE COMMENTARY
Grand Rapids: Zondervan

Designed for clergy and serious general readers, this *new* series emphasizes exposition of the text rather than close analysis. The text used is the NIV, and the style suggests that, when the twelve volumes are completed, the EBC will become a staple in the libraries of many, perhaps especially evangelicals. Vol. 1 provides general introductory articles (some of which can be obtained elsewhere; see 1.59 and 7.45). The publishing schedule thus far has favored the New Testament exclusively, and only the synoptic gospels remain to be completed. Vols. 9–12 (9.80, 9.90, 9.105, 9.120, 9.129, 9.142, 9.173, 9.182, 9.216, 9.231, 9.250, 9.266) in the series cover everything from the Gospel of John to Revelation.

In addition to the exposition of the text, each volume offers a basic introduction to major analytical issues such as authorship and date, an outline of the New Testament document itself, and a very basic bibliography for further reading.

EGNT   Nicoll, W. R. (ed.)
THE EXPOSITOR'S GREEK NEW TESTAMENT
Grand Rapids: Eerdmans

An old series (1897–1910), *The Expositor's Greek Bible* is available still in a reprint with a slightly altered title. Designed to replace something even older (see AGT above) this series has never entirely lost its appeal. The New Testament is covered in five volumes, many portions of which were written by the leading scholars of the time, working from the Greek text. The exposition can be understood by those who do not know Greek—or at least one's knowledge need not be very extensive. Although badly out-of-date, the work still contains some sound scholarship, and for a modest price.

Reading these volumes one senses how much greater authors' expectations once were of a well-informed general readership. In any event, general readers will find more—and more that is up-to-date and presented in a congenial way—in other volumes or series. EGNT is not to be confused with EB, a closely related series.

HERME-   Koester, H. (chmn., ed. board)
NEIA   HERMENEIA
Philadelphia: Fortress

Under the direction of an academic editorial board, Fortress Press has for some time been publishing serious and scholarly analytical commentaries on both the Old and the New Testament. In the latter division six volumes have now appeared, all based on the Greek text. A working knowledge of Greek is presupposed, although passages of nonbiblical Greek (and Latin) are offered in both the original and in translation.

Thus far only one volume is original to the series (9.134); all others are translations of standard German scholarly commentaries (9.112, 9.148, 9.186, 9.206, 9.239). The standards are high and the volumes translated are examples of the best of Continental biblical scholarship from the leading exponents of the most sophisticated analytical techniques. There is, inevitably, a certain backward direction in all of this, accompanied by the implicit assumption that American scholars and general readers will be delighted with older work just because it is now available in English. Scholars, however, do not need English translations, and original work would have been more desirable. But the new volumes that have been commissioned have been slow in coming, and the series, unfortunately, is left with a "deflated" aura. If new volumes are as provocative as the one example to date (Betz on Galatians [9.134]), they may yet prove worth the wait.

In the meantime there is the minor issue of design and format. The publisher points with pride to the design, but it is pretentious, overdone, and makes these volumes needlessly difficult to use on a day-to-day basis.

HNTC   HARPER'S NEW TESTAMENT COMMENTARIES
        San Francisco: Harper & Row

Although volumes have been appearing for more than twenty-five years, not all the works planned for this outstanding series are yet available. In the meantime, alas, some have been allowed to go out of print. What is available, however, is excellent. The series rivals NCBC and NWPC for breadth, reliability, and responsible scholarship packaged so that the nonspecialist can understand and profit from the book.

The biblical text is the author's own English translation in each case, and reference to the biblical words is made by the judicious use of boldface type, leaving more room for the commentary itself. Bibliographical and purely scholarly references are kept to a minimum. Without question, the outstanding volumes in this series are three by C. K. Barrett—on Romans (9.99) and 1 and 2 Corinthians (9.113, 9.125)—but the entire series is excellent. It is available in England as BLACK'S New Testament Commentaries. (See 9.213, 9.242, 9.260.)

IB   Buttrick, G. A.
        THE INTERPRETER'S BIBLE
        Nashville: Abingdon

Numbering twelve volumes in all, the IB offers five large volumes of introduction and commentary on the New Testament. General articles comprise a virtual introduction to the New Testament. Thereafter, each book is analyzed in sequence. The book offers the KJV and RSV texts at the top of the page in parallel columns, followed by exegesis, which is in turn followed by exposition designed especially for the preacher. The exegesis is sound without being overly technical, and it is brief. Introductions are often outstanding. The final volume in the series adds introductory materials that were not included at the outset, one sign that the IB was born at a time of intense historical and theological activity. It was the period of the discovery and the initial investigation of the Dead Sea Scrolls, which coincided with the high-water mark of neo-orthodox thought and "biblical theology." Out of this mainstream and nonevangelical scholarly "biblicism" emerged IB. The passage of time has had less of an effect on the exegesis than on the exposition, but these volumes are still useful to the general reader.

ICC   Driver, S. R., A. Plummer, and C. A. Briggs (orig. eds.)
Emerton, J. A., and C. E. B. Cranfield (gen. eds.)
THE INTERNATIONAL CRITICAL COMMENTARY ON
THE HOLY SCRIPTURES OF THE OLD AND NEW
TESTAMENTS
New York: Seabury (for T. & T. Clark, Edinburgh)

ICC is the most extensive and scholarly series of commentaries on the Greek New Testament available today. Begun in 1895 by a team of American and British scholars, it was completed only in 1951. Thus, some volumes are relatively recent, but others are old and now faded. Only recently a revision has been undertaken, and now two volumes on Romans (9.95, 9.96) by Cranfield (one of the general editors) replace the earliest New Testament commentary in the series, written by Sanday and Headlam (9.97) in 1895. (That earlier volume on Romans is still rich and is not rendered entirely obsolete by its replacement.)

The ICC is known and valued as a work of scholarship; it is particularly prized for philological insight and exegetical detail. Some volumes can boast appended "notes" that are small masterpieces in their own right (Burton on Galatians [9.135], for example). Because of the heavy emphasis on philology and other matters of enduring analytical interest, even the older volumes retain considerable usefulness today for the most serious readers of the Greek text. But the revisions will be welcome as they bring more modern concerns and bibliography into the discussion. Authors in the ICC series traditionally have not been enamored of European and especially German scholarship, so that this series and HERMENEIA, for example, at present complement one another more than they compete. (See 9.13, 9.30, 9.43, 9.59, 9.60, 9.111, 9.124, 9.146, 9.147, 9.175, 9.187, 9.195, 9.207, 9.221, 9.235, 9.236, 9.255, 9.256.)

LBC   Kelly, B. H. (ed.)
THE LAYMAN'S BIBLE COMMENTARY
Atlanta: John Knox

In twenty-five volumes the whole of the Bible is covered at a level designed to appeal to the general reader. Based on the RSV and published between 1959 and 1962, these slender volumes are elementary. To a great extent they reflect the same theological currents noted in reference to the IB above, but these volumes are far more compact and designed to be read quickly rather than consulted frequently.

NCB   NEW CLARENDON BIBLE
New York: Oxford University Press (for the Clarendon Press, Oxford)

Since 1963 the Oxford University Press has been updating and completing an older series of small and useful commentaries once known as The Clarendon Bible. The RSV text is printed at the top of the page, and below is the succinct commentary reflecting scholarly consensus. (In early volumes the new series used the NEB but subsequently dropped it in favor of the RSV.) This series offers solid general exposition and interpretation but little detail and little scholarship at first hand. In the new series will be found commentaries on Matthew, John, Ephesians, Philippians, Colossians, and the letters to the Thessalonians, along with an introduction to Judaism between the Testaments. Reliable, readable, rewarding.

NCBC   Clements, R. E., and M. Black (eds.)
            NEW CENTURY BIBLE COMMENTARY
            Grand Rapids: Eerdmans

A complete, serious, and first-rate set of commentaries offering exegesis in a framework accessible to the general reader but attractive enough for the specialist too. More uniform than other series such as NWPC or even HNTC, this set is in many other ways comparable to those. In general, it is weightier and more impressive than TNTC (with which it shares many authors), but it is still lean and to the point.

Verse-by-verse commentary offers a balance of exposition and analytical detail. While the text used is the RSV, it is not reprinted in the commentary. This is one of the best series available, because often the authors have succeeded in using solid scholarship to make sense of a text in terms important to the general reader. Available only in paperback. (See 9.14, 9.33, 9.50, 9.67, 8.88, 9.103, 9.115, 9.127, 9.140, 9.160, 9.161, 9.162, 9.191, 9.227, 9.228, 9.246, 9.264.)

NICNT   Bruce, F. F. (ed.)
            THE NEW INTERNATIONAL COMMENTARY ON THE
            NEW TESTAMENT
            Grand Rapids: Eerdmans

F. F. Bruce is now the chief editor of this series, which is designed for the serious general reader rather than for the specialist. The text is the RV (1881), and the commentary is divided by units of thought rather than by individual verses. The emphasis is on exposition, and grammatical points and other exegetical details are handled unobtrusively only as needed. There will be eighteen volumes in the series; fifteen are now available. Volumes covering Matthew, Peter and Titus, and Timothy and Jude have *not* yet appeared. (See 9.35, 9.51, 9.70, 9.84, 9.104, 9.114, 9.126, 9.138, 9.165, 9.166, 9.179, 9.200, 9.214, 9.247, 9.263.)

NIGTC   Gasque, W. W., and I. H. Marshall (eds.)
            THE NEW INTERNATIONAL GREEK TESTAMENT
            COMMENTARY
            Grand Rapids: Eerdmans

Three volumes have been published in this major new series. Commentaries on the Greek text are always a formidable publishing project and a welcome prospect, and in this case the early returns suggest a very promising future. Judging from the evidence thus far, the emphasis will be more on literary and theological problems than on historical ones. While the reader is regularly directed to current issues in scholarly interpretation, the practical values of the text are not ignored. For the advanced reader and the specialist. (See 9.44, 9.137, 9.240.)

NTC(H)   Hendricksen, W.
          NEW TESTAMENT COMMENTARY
          Grand Rapids: Baker

Eight volumes cover the gospels, Romans, Galatians, Ephesians, Colossians, and Philemon, along with 1 and 2 Thessalonians and the three Pastoral epistles. The perspective is unmistakably that of contemporary Reformed theology, traditional in judgments and expositional in tastes. Note the caution expressed in the section on "Best Buys" at the end of this chapter.

NTM   Harrington, W. J., and D. Senior (eds.)
          THE NEW TESTAMENT MESSAGE
          Wilmington (DE): M. Glazier

Nineteen concise volumes provide commentary on the entire New Testament. These are supplemented by three more that offer introductory or general information (see 1.54, for example). Most of the editors and authors are Roman Catholic, but the books do not reflect a noticeably sectarian point of view. They were written for those who are serious about studying and understanding the Bible but who are not scholars. Designed in a handy format as small and compact volumes for general readers (not unlike the format of LBC), this series outstrips anything else available at that level, converting what the preface calls "an avalanche of Biblical scholarship" into understandable and relevant textual commentary. The text is usually the RSV. There is emphasis on some of the smaller and often slighted New Testament books (such as Colossians [9.169], James and Jude [9.251], and the Petrine and Pastoral letters [9.192]). All the more impressive because individual volumes or the entire set can be purchased in either cloth or paper, this new series sets something of a standard among the compact commentaries designed for a general audience. Certainly no other is so complete and up-to-date. (See 9.25, 9.34, 9.74, 9.89, 9.119, 9.131, 9.143, 9.167, 9.168, 9.184, 9.203, 9.218, 9.233, 9.269.)

NTSR   McKenzie, J. L. (ed.)
          THE NEW TESTAMENT FOR SPIRITUAL READING
          New York: Crossroad

Twenty-five volumes are devoted to a commentary designed for general readers and especially those interested in the New Testament as spiritual literature. McKenzie presides over the translation of work originally written by European Roman Catholic scholars and writers. (See 9.27, 9.28, 9.40, 9.41, 9.54, 9.55, 9.75, 9.76, 9.77, 9.91, 9.92, 9.107, 9.123, 9.132, 9.144, 9.170, 9.171, 9.172, 9.183, 9.193, 9.194, 9.202, 9.219, 9.232, 9.252, 9.253, 9.267, 9.268.)

NWPC   Nineham, D. E. (gen. ed.)
        THE NEW WESTMINSTER PELICAN COMMENTARIES
        Philadelphia: Westminster

These volumes, which constitute a "series" more in name than in fact, display only modest uniformity; but they offer outstanding writing and scholarship. Nineham's commentary on Mark (9.37), for example, may well be the best example of a New Testament commentary in print today. If the others are not quite up to that high standard, most are good to excellent. As a result, both general readers and those with more professional or scholarly interests will find these commentaries valuable.

To date only seven volumes have appeared, covering ten New Testament books: the four gospels (9.23, 9.37, 9.46, 9.68); 1 Corinthians (9.117); Philippians, Colossians, Philemon, and Ephesians (9.151); and Revelation (9.259). Each volume uses the New Testament in the author's own translation. Each strives for a balance between technical detail and clear exposition—and most succeed.

TNTC   Tasker, R. V. G. (ed.)
        TYNDALE NEW TESTAMENT COMMENTARIES
        Grand Rapids: Eerdmans

A rather remarkable series for its scope (now complete in twenty volumes) and its modest price (in paperback). The TNTC is a verse-by-verse commentary based on the KJV and (in the background, where it remains rather inconspicuous) the Greek New Testament. But those without Greek need have no fear of using this set, since it was designed with the general reader in mind. The authors are well-known evangelical and conservative writers and scholars. Although "traditional" in most views, this series does not have the "Reformed" cast of the NICNT. Here the predominantly British group of authors is more nearly "evangelical." The format of the TNTC is "handy," like the LBC and the NTM. Certainly more conservative, it is in most ways also more interesting and informative than the LBC. It is less arresting and original than the NTM, however. (See 9.22, 9.32, 9.52, 9.71, 9.87, 9.106, 9.116, 9.128, 9.141, 9.157, 9.158, 9.159, 9.178, 9.188, 9.199, 9.215, 9.229, 9.230, 9.244, 9.245, 9.265.)

WBC   Hubbard, D., and G. W. Barker (gen. eds.)
        Watts, J. D. W. (OT ed.) and R. P. Martin (NT ed.)
        THE WORD BIBLICAL COMMENTARY
        Waco (TX): Word Books

Called by the publisher "a harvest of Biblical scholarship from the evangelical renaissance," this mammoth undertaking will eventually produce fifty-two volumes of commentary on the Bible designed to be definitive. The project began in 1977, and one volume, on Colossians and Philemon (9.149), is now ready. Twenty volumes will be devoted to the New Testament, and prospective authors have been announced. The authors will provide their own translations of the Greek text, and in the commentary they will follow a strict format designed to be unusually comprehensive. The editors promise rich and scholarly bibliographical citations separated from the rest of the material for easy use (which also allows those not interested to skip over such details). Along with the standard features of "comment" (exegesis) and "explanation" (exposition), there is a separate section devoted to details of philological analysis and other analytical concerns. In addition, important issues are given separate treatment as detached notes, and there is a section dealing with the overall "structure" of the New Testament material. All of this makes a formidable and unusually full agenda for a single commentary.

In short, this is offered as a serious entry among the major commentary series such as the AB and HERMENEIA. Since the list of proposed authors is certainly respectable and since the AB has proved so disappointing, WBC could well emerge as a major resource for the general reader interested in serious scholarship. It will not likely rival HERMENEIA in scholarly sophistication, but it will probably be more up-to-date bibliographically. Right now WBC is only a promise, but it is one worth watching.

C. Notable Commentaries on Individual New Testament Books

Only the most noteworthy commentaries have been listed here. These make up but a fraction of what is available, especially since the term "commentary" is used rather loosely by some authors and publishers. Nor do these listings include any of the myriad "studies" of New Testament books, some of which are quite good.

Basic criteria for inclusion here include availability and usefulness for either the serious general reader or the more advanced student. Most important, however, is the *scope* of the commentary. For whatever level it wishes to reach, a good commentary will be sufficiently basic that it discusses the major issues and provides a solid foundation for any further study. As different as these volumes are, they do that. In general, these are the best of what is available.

The Gospel According to Matthew

9.13   ICC   Allen, W. C.
                             A CRITICAL AND EXEGETICAL COMMEN-
                             TARY ON THE GOSPEL ACCORDING TO
                             ST. MATTHEW
                             New York: Seabury (for T. & T. Clark, Edin-
                             burgh). 3rd ed. (1912)

9.14   NCBC   Hill, D.
                     THE GOSPEL OF MATTHEW
                     Grand Rapids: Eerdmans. Rev. ed. (1981)

9.15   McNeile, A. H.
                     THE GOSPEL ACCORDING TO ST. MAT-
                     THEW. The Greek Text with Introduction,
                     Notes and Indices Grand Rapids: Baker (1915/
                     1980)

A recent paperback reprint of an old classic, this is one of the few commentaries
on Matthew in Greek available to English readers.

9.16   Schweizer, E.
                     THE GOOD NEWS ACCORDING TO
                     MATTHEW
                     Atlanta: John Knox (1975)

9.17   Senior, D.
                     INVITATION TO MATTHEW. A Commentary
                     on the Gospel of Matthew with Complete Text
                     from the Jerusalem Bible
                     Garden City: Doubleday (1977)

This brief paperback original is designed for the nonspecialist.

9.18   Obach, R. E., and A. Kirk
                     A COMMENTARY ON THE GOSPEL OF
                     MATTHEW
                     Ramsey (NJ): Paulist (1978)

This volume serves the same purpose and the same audience as the preceding
item.

9.19   Plummer, A.
                     AN EXEGETICAL COMMENTARY ON THE
                     GOSPEL ACCORDING TO ST. MATTHEW
                     Grand Rapids: Baker (1909/1982)

Technical, analytical, and old, this commentary is nevertheless still attractive
because of its predominantly theological approach to Matthew. Plummer wrote
in an era when it was fashionable to play off Matthew's "legalism" against Paul's
"law-free" gospel. Concentrating on the theological meaning of the text, Plummer
plays down Matthew's particular views and emphasizes instead the historical
portrait of Jesus that emerges. The commentary presumes a knowledge of Greek,
but, while technical, it concentrates more on structure and continuity in the gospel
than on philological or historical details.

9.20   Kingsbury, J. D.
MATTHEW
Philadelphia: Fortress (1977)

Part of a series (Proclamation Commentaries) designed to focus on the significance of the book for preaching purposes, this is not a commentary in the classic mold but a systematic treatment in inexpensive format. It is particularly appealing to preachers and teachers.

9.21   Brown, R. E.
THE BIRTH OF THE MESSIAH. A Commentary on the Infancy Narratives in Matthew and Luke
Garden City: Doubleday (1977)

As the title indicates, this is a commentary on only a portion of Matthew and the similar material found in Luke. It is very detailed.

9.21p   *Same:* paperback

9.22   TNTC   Tasker, R. V. G.
MATTHEW
Grand Rapids: Eerdmans (1962)

9.23   NWPC   Fenton, J.
ST. MATTHEW
Philadelphia: Westminster (1978)

9.24   Fenton, J.
THE GOSPEL OF ST. MATTHEW
Baltimore: Penguin (1964)

This paperback edition is virtually the same as the cloth edition (9.23), which is more recent; the paperback is available at a fraction of the cost.

9.25   NTM   Meier, J. P.
MATTHEW
Wilmington (DE): M. Glazier (1979)

9.25p   *Same:* paperback

9.26   CBCNT   Argyle, A. W. (ed.)
THE GOSPEL ACCORDING TO MATTHEW
New York: Cambridge University Press (1963)

9.26p   *Same:* paperback

9.27   NTSR   Trilling, W.
THE GOSPEL ACCORDING TO ST. MAT-THEW, Vol. 1
New York: Crossroad (1969/1981)

9.27p		*Same:* paperback
9.28	NTSR	Trilling, W. THE GOSPEL ACCORDING TO ST. MAT- THEW, Vol. 2 New York: Crossroad (1969/1981)
9.28p		*Same:* paperback

The Gospel According to Mark

9.29	CGTC	Cranfield, C. E. B. THE GOSPEL ACCORDING TO ST. MARK. An Introduction and Commentary New York: Cambridge University Press (1959)
9.29p		*Same:* paperback
9.30	ICC	Gould, E. P. A CRITICAL AND EXEGETICAL COMMENTARY ON THE GOSPEL ACCORDING TO ST. MARK New York: Seabury (for T. & T. Clark, Edinburgh) (1896)
9.31		Taylor, V. THE GOSPEL ACCORDING TO ST. MARK. The Greek Text with Introduction Grand Rapids: Baker (1966/1981)

This paperback reprint of the second edition of a classic commentary on Mark, like the preceding two entries, is based on the Greek text.

9.32	TNTC	Cole, A. MARK Grand Rapids: Eerdmans (1962)
9.33	NCBC	Anderson, H. THE GOSPEL OF MARK Grand Rapids: Eerdmans. Rev. ed. (1981)
9.34	NTM	Harrington, W. MARK Wilmington (DE): M. Glazier (1979)
9.34p		*Same:* paperback

The Bible Book

| 9.35 | NICNT | Lane, W.
MARK
Grand Rapids: Eerdmans (1973) |

| 9.36 | CBCNT | Moule, C. F. D.
THE GOSPEL ACCORDING TO MARK
New York: Cambridge University Press (1965) |
| 9.36p | | *Same:* paperback |

| 9.37 | NWPC | Nineham, D. E.
ST. MARK
Philadelphia: Westminster (1964/1978) |

| 9.38 | | Nineham, D. E.
THE GOSPEL OF ST. MARK
Baltimore: Penguin (1964) |

This is the paperback original of an outstanding and perceptive commentary on Mark, one of the finest commentaries written. The preceding entry (9.37) is the same in hardback, not substantially revised.

| 9.39 | | Schweizer, E.
THE GOOD NEWS ACCORDING TO MARK
Atlanta: John Knox (1970) |

| 9.40 | NTSR | Schnackenburg, R.
THE GOSPEL ACCORDING TO ST. MARK,
Vol. 1
New York: Crossroad (1971/1981) |
| 9.40p | | *Same:* paperback |

| 9.41 | NTSR | Schnackenburg, R.
THE GOSPEL ACCORDING TO ST. MARK,
Vol. 2
New York: Crossroad (1971/1981) |
| 9.41p | | *Same:* paperback |

The Gospel According to Luke

| 9.42 | AB | Fitzmyer, J. A.
THE GOSPEL ACCORDING TO LUKE, Vol.
1: I–IX
Garden City: Doubleday (1981) |

The very best and the very latest, this volume covers only a scant half of the gospel. The second volume should appear soon. This detailed commentary is designed for scholars, but the more casual reader can also profit from it. Fitzmyer and Marshall (9.44) offer the most substantial recent commentaries available.

9.43	ICC	Plummer, A. A CRITICAL AND EXEGETICAL COMMEN- TARY ON THE GOSPEL ACCORDING TO ST. LUKE New York: Seabury (for T. & T. Clark, Edin- burgh). 5th ed. (1922)
9.44	NIGTC	Marshall, I. H. THE GOSPEL OF LUKE Grand Rapids: Eerdmans (1978)

This massive and detailed study of the Greek text launches a promising new series. A major contribution.

9.45		Creed, J. M. THE GOSPEL ACCORDING TO ST. LUKE. The Greek Text, with Introduction, Notes and Indices London: Macmillan (1930)

Older and not readily available in this country, this is still a good commentary on the Greek text and one of modest size and scope.

9.46	NWPC	Caird, G. B. ST. LUKE Philadelphia: Westminster (1964/1978)
9.47		Caird, G. B. THE GOSPEL OF ST. LUKE Baltimore: Penguin (1964)

These two entries are scarcely different except for the binding—hard cover (9.46) and paperback (9.47). This is a serious commentary on the English text at the intermediate level that is useful to general readers and scholars alike.

9.48		Karris, R. J. INVITATION TO LUKE. A Commentary on the Gospel of Luke with Complete Text from the Jerusalem Bible Garden City: Doubleday (1977)

Elementary and brief; see 9.17.

The Bible Book

9.49		Danker, F. W. JESUS AND THE NEW AGE ACCORDING TO ST. LUKE St. Louis: Clayton Publishing House (1980)
9.50	NCBC	Ellis, E. E. THE GOSPEL OF LUKE Grand Rapids: Eerdmans (1966)
9.51	NICNT	Geldenhuys, N. LUKE Grand Rapids: Eerdmans (1950)
9.52	TNTC	Morris, L. THE GOSPEL ACCORDING TO ST. LUKE Grand Rapids: Eerdmans (1974)
9.53	CBCNT	Tinsley, E. J. (ed.) THE GOSPEL ACCORDING TO LUKE New York: Cambridge University Press (1965)
9.53p		*Same:* paperback
9.54	NTSR	Stöger, A. THE GOSPEL ACCORDING TO ST. LUKE, Vol. 1 New York: Crossroad (1969/1981)
9.54p		*Same:* paperback
9.55	NTSR	Stöger, A. THE GOSPEL ACCORDING TO ST. LUKE, Vol. 2 New York: Crossroad (1969/1981)
9.55p		*Same:* paperback

The Gospel According to John

9.56	Barrett, C. K. THE GOSPEL ACCORDING TO SAINT JOHN Philadelphia: Westminster. 2nd ed. (1978)

Based on the Greek text and completely revised from the first edition, this is an outstanding commentary on John—probably the best in one volume that can be found today in English.

9.57	AB	Brown, R. E. THE GOSPEL ACCORDING TO JOHN, Vol. 1: I–XII Garden City: Doubleday. 2nd ed. (1979)
9.58	AB	Brown, R. E. THE GOSPEL ACCORDING TO JOHN, Vol. 2: XIII–XXI Garden City: Doubleday (1970)

A superior piece of work on every count. Specialists regard Brown as indispensable, but readers with more general interests will be no less pleased, because these volumes distinguish between commentary and detailed notes. One need not know Greek to benefit from this very impressive work.

9.59 9.60	ICC	Bernard, J. H. (ed. by A. H. McNeile) A CRITICAL AND EXEGETICAL COMMENTARY ON THE GOSPEL ACCORDING TO ST. JOHN. 2 vols. New York: Seabury (for T. & T. Clark, Edinburgh) (1928)
9.61		Bultmann, R. THE GOSPEL OF JOHN. A Commentary Philadelphia: Westminster (1971)

This is an English translation (barely adequate) of a very stimulating, influential, and controversial German commentary. Greek is presupposed, and the casual reader will find this a hard volume for quick consultation because it is ordered according to the author's reconstruction of the original gospel. Idiosyncratic and brilliant.

9.62		Schnackenburg, R. THE GOSPEL ACCORDING TO ST. JOHN, Vol. 1 New York: Crossroad (1968/1980)
9.63		Schnackenburg, R. THE GOSPEL ACCORDING TO ST. JOHN, Vol. 2 New York: Crossroad (1979/1981)

9.64

Schnackenburg, R.
THE GOSPEL ACCORDING TO ST. JOHN,
Vol. 3
New York: Crossroad (1982)

These three volumes constitute the English translation of a German Roman Catholic commentary that is monumental in scope and rich in detail. The Greek text is used throughout, and the author has been given ample room to discuss every range of interest—historical, theological, and literary. The generous bibliography includes many European studies. Theologically rich.

9.65

Plummer, A.
THE GOSPEL ACCORDING TO SAINT JOHN
Grand Rapids: Baker (1881/1981)

This is a recent reprint of a much older commentary, which uses the Greek text and first appeared in the Cambridge Bible for Schools and Colleges. It is no match for more modern commentaries on the Greek text.

9.66

Westcott, B. F. (ed. by A. Westcott)
THE GOSPEL ACCORDING TO ST. JOHN.
The Greek Text, with Introduction and Notes
Grand Rapids: Baker (1903/1919)

Another recent reprint offering an old commentary on the Greek text.

9.67   NCBC

Lindars, B.
THE GOSPEL OF JOHN
Grand Rapids: Eerdmans (1972)

Barnabas Lindars's commentary on John is one of the finest in this series and an excellent choice for those without Greek who want to know how the gospel is read by scholars today. Nor does Lindars lose sight of more practical concerns.

9.68   NWPC

Marsh, J.
ST. JOHN
Philadelphia: Westminster (1978)

9.69

Marsh, J.
THE GOSPEL ACCORDING TO ST. JOHN
Baltimore: Penguin (1968)

Again, the commentary is available in hard cover (9.68) or paperback (9.69); otherwise, there is little difference between the editions, save price.

9.70   NICTC

Morris, L.
THE GOSPEL OF JOHN
Grand Rapids: Eerdmans (1970)

9.71   TNTC   Tasker, R. V. G.
                THE GOSPEL ACCORDING TO ST. JOHN
                Grand Rapids: Eerdmans (1960)

9.72   Smith, D. M., Jr.
                JOHN
                Philadelphia: Fortress (1976)

This small introduction falls somewhere between a conventional commentary and a study of John. As part of the Proclamation Commentaries series, it is designed primarily for preachers.

9.73   CBCNT   Hunter, A. M.
                THE GOSPEL ACCORDING TO JOHN
                New York: Cambridge University Press (1965)

9.73p   *Same:* paperback

9.74   NTM   McPolin, J.
                JOHN
                Wilmington (DE): M. Glazier (1979)

9.74p   *Same:* paperback

9.75   NTSR   Huckle, J., and P. Visokay
                THE GOSPEL ACCORDING TO ST. JOHN,
                Vol. 1
                New York: Crossroad (1981)

9.75p   *Same:* paperback

9.76   NTSR   Blank, J.
                THE GOSPEL ACCORDING TO ST. JOHN,
                Vol. 2
                New York: Crossroad (1981)

9.76p   *Same:* paperback

9.77   NTSR   Blank, J.
                THE GOSPEL ACCORDING TO ST. JOHN,
                Vol. 3
                New York: Crossroad (1981)

9.77p   *Same:* paperback

9.78   Lightfoot, R. H.
                ST. JOHN'S GOSPEL. A Commentary
                New York: Oxford University Press (1956)

9.79   Westcott, B. F.
                          THE GOSPEL ACCORDING TO ST. JOHN.
                          English Text
                          Grand Rapids: Eerdmans (1880/1950)

Introduction and notes to the KJV text. See also 9.66.

9.80   EBC   Gaebelein, F. E. (ed.)
                          THE EXPOSITOR'S BIBLE COMMENTARY,
                          Vol. 9
                          Grand Rapids: Zondervan (1981)

This commentary on John, by M. C. Tenney, is in the same volume with that of R. N. Longenecker on Acts.

The Acts of the Apostles

9.81   Foakes Jackson, F. J., and K. Lake (eds.)
                          THE BEGINNINGS OF CHRISTIANITY
                          Part I: The Acts of the Apostles
                          Grand Rapids: Baker (1920–1933/1979)

This work consists of five volumes, originally published from 1920 to 1933. It is the most important resource for serious study of the Acts of the Apostles that has ever been published. Its significance extends beyond the interpretation of a single book, however, to the whole of early church life and history.

Originally published to inaugurate a large project, these five volumes now stand alone (hence the somewhat misleading phrase "Part I" in the title). Vol. 1 (*Prolegomena I,* 1920) offers introductory essays on the Jewish, Gentile, and Christian backgrounds of the New Testament. Vol. 2 (*Prolegomena II,* 1922) continues with a major treatment of the composition and purpose of Acts, the identity of its author, and the history of critical research on its problems. Vol. 3 (*The Text of Acts,* 1926) was written by J. H. Ropes and remains today the most detailed analysis we have of the textual traditions, although it is clearly outdated. Vol. 4 (*English Translation and Commentary,* 1933), by H. J. Cadbury, will likely get the most use since it offers an independent English translation at the top of the page and double columns of detailed exegetical notes beneath the text. One does not have to know Greek to profit from the commentary, although without that knowledge some portions will have to be skipped. Vol. 5 (*Additional Notes to the Commentary,* 1933) was edited by Lake and Cadbury and is still frequently used today because it offers masterful essays on perennial problems of interpretation within Acts and on background materials.

The reprint, in soft cover, is available only as a unit, but it is a bargain. The work itself is without peer.

9.82   Haenchen, E.
                            THE ACTS OF THE APOSTLES. A Commentary
                            Philadelphia: Westminster (1971)

A fine English translation of a scholarly German commentary, Haenchen presupposes Greek throughout, although the text of Acts is given in English translation. Some readers will regard the historical conclusions as somewhat radical, but the comprehensiveness of this commentary is undeniable. Its attention to the history of previous interpretation makes it all the more valuable.

9.83   Bruce, F. F.
                            THE ACTS OF THE APOSTLES
                            Grand Rapids: Eerdmans (1953)

This is the best one-volume commentary that is available on the Greek text of Acts. It is compact but thorough, well informed about the historical setting of Acts, and attentive to questions of textual criticism. Bruce is not long on theological discussions and remains traditional in his approach to the standard interpretive problems. Few commentaries—certainly none on Acts—say so much in so short a space. This is a commentary on the Greek text; the title that follows, by the same author, is on the English text.

9.84   NICNT   Bruce, F. F.
                            THE BOOK OF THE ACTS
                            Grand Rapids: Eerdmans (1954)

It would be nice to be able to report that this volume does for the English-text reader what the preceding entry does for the Greek-text reader, but that is not quite the case. Here Bruce offers more exposition and, of course, fewer remarks on textual readings. In general, the observations are less acute, and the whole lacks the energy so evident in his other commentary on Acts. Nevertheless, for the general reader this is a reliable commentary by a skilled interpreter.

9.85   AB   Munck, J.
                            THE ACTS OF THE APOSTLES
                            Garden City: Doubleday (1967)

One of the most disappointing volumes in the AB series, this is worth mentioning only because of the relative dearth of up-to-date commentaries for the serious reader. As in all AB volumes, the reader here finds it easy to separate general commentary from detailed analysis.

9.86   CBCNT   Packer, J. W. (ed.)
                            THE ACTS OF THE APOSTLES
                            New York: Cambridge University Press (1966)

9.86p   *Same:* paperback

9.87	TNTC	Marshall, I. H. THE ACTS OF THE APOSTLES Grand Rapids: Eerdmans (1980)
9.88	NCBC	Neill, W. THE ACTS OF THE APOSTLES Grand Rapids: Eerdmans. Rev. ed. (1981)
9.89	NTM	Crowe, J. THE ACTS Wilmington (DE): M. Glazier (1980)
9.89p		*Same:* paperback
9.90	EBC	Gaebelein, F. E. (ed.) THE EXPOSITOR'S BIBLE COMMENTARY, Vol. 9 Grand Rapids: Zondervan (1981)

R. N. Longenecker on Acts, in the same volume with M. C. Tenney on John (see 9.80 above).

9.91	NTSR	Kürzinger, J. THE ACTS OF THE APOSTLES, Vol. 1 New York: Crossroad (1961/1981)
9.91p		*Same:* paperback
9.92	NTSR	Kürzinger, J. THE ACTS OF THE APOSTLES, Vol. 2 New York: Crossroad (1971/1981)
9.92p		*Same:* paperback
9.93		Krodel, G. ACTS Philadelphia: Fortress (1981)

This is one of the Proclamation Commentaries, designed first of all for preachers. Krodel has a very good command of the material in this brief and readable volume.

9.94		Karris, R. J. INVITATION TO ACTS. A Commentary on the Acts of the Apostles with Complete Text from the Jerusalem Bible Garden City: Doubleday (1978)

Romans

9.95	ICC	Cranfield, C. E. B.
9.96		A CRITICAL AND EXEGETICAL COMMEN-
		TARY ON THE EPISTLE TO THE ROMANS

Vol. 1: Commentary on Romans i–viii; Vol. 2:
Commentary on Romans ix–xvi, Essays
New York: Seabury (for T. & T. Clark, Edin-
burgh). Vol. 1 (1975); Vol. 2 (1979)

The inaugural volumes of the *new* ICC, these are more detailed and up-to-date than any other commentary on the Greek text now available. These two volumes have replaced the one that follows.

| 9.97 | ICC | Sanday, W., and A. C. Headlam |

A CRITICAL AND EXEGETICAL COMMEN-
TARY ON THE EPISTLE TO THE ROMANS
New York: Seabury (for T. & T. Clark, Edin-
burgh). 5th ed. (1902)

From 1895 until 1975 Sanday and Headlam was the ICC on Romans. It set the overall tone of the entire series with a strong emphasis on historical and philological matters. Such interests wear well, and this volume remains useful. It is still in print, although it is now being phased out in favor of its successor above.

| 9.98 | | Käsemann, E. |

COMMENTARY ON ROMANS
Grand Rapids: Eerdmans (1980)

One of the most brilliant, provocative, and radical interpreters of the New Testament turns his attention to the most brilliant, provocative, and radical of Paul's letters. Käsemann is a theologian to the core, but he is also a meticulous New Testament exegete. The combination is powerful and makes for a dense book, which is not helped by an inadequate translation. The work is dauntingly serious but very rewarding. The text is cited in English, but the author does at times assume knowledge of the Greek New Testament in the comments.

| 9.99 | HNTC | Barrett, C. K. |

A COMMENTARY ON THE EPISTLE TO
THE ROMANS
San Francisco: Harper & Row (1958)

The serious student of Paul who wants a reasonably compact but complete commentary that covers the highlights and moves easily through both historical and theological issues will welcome Barrett's excellent commentary on Romans. The translation of the epistle is Barrett's own. The writing is clear, the scope adequate for all but the most dedicated. For those without Greek this is the best.

9.100   Barth, K.
EPISTLE TO THE ROMANS
New York: Oxford University Press. 6th ed.
(1968)

An unusual volume, this document marked the beginning of the neo-orthodox movement among Continental theologians, and it has exercised enormous influence in theology, though not much in New Testament study. A powerful theological meditation, for serious readers.

9.101   [Pauck, W. (ed.)]
LUTHER: LECTURES ON ROMANS
Philadelphia: Westminster (1961)

Romans was the seedbed of Luther's vision of Christian truth, and it was while he was lecturing on this epistle that he realized the meaning of what became for him *the* secret of the relationship between God and humanity—justification by faith alone. These lectures, excellently translated here, still have power and energy and are still worth reading as *one* kind of commentary on the letter.

9.102   CBCNT   Best, E.
THE LETTER OF PAUL TO THE ROMANS
New York: Cambridge University Press (1967)

9.102p   *Same:* paperback

9.103   NCBC   Black, M.
ROMANS
Grand Rapids: Eerdmans. Rev. ed. (1981)

9.104   NICNT   Murray, J.
ROMANS
Grand Rapids: Eerdmans (1960)

9.105   EBC   Gaebelein, F. E. (ed.)
THE EXPOSITOR'S BIBLE COMMENTARY,
Vol. 10
Grand Rapids: Zondervan (1976)

This volume covers Romans, 1 and 2 Corinthians, and Galatians. The commentary on Romans is by E. F. Harrison (see also 9.120, 9.129, and 9.142).

9.106   TNTC   Bruce, F. F.
ROMANS
Grand Rapids: Eerdmans (1963)

9.107   NTSR   Kertelge, K.
THE EPISTLE TO THE ROMANS
New York: Crossroad (1972/1981)

9.107p   *Same:* paperback

Kertelge is an unusually acute interpreter of Paul.

9.108   NTM   Maly, E.
                                ROMANS
                                Wilmington (DE): M. Glazier (1980)

9.108p   *Same:* paperback

9.109   Getty, M.
                                AN INVITATION TO THE NEW TESTA-
                                MENT EPISTLES, I
                                A Commentary on Galatians and Romans with
                                Complete Text from the Jerusalem Bible
                                Garden City: Doubleday (1982)

9.110   ACNT   Harrisville, R. A.
                                AUGSBURG COMMENTARY ON THE NEW
                                TESTAMENT—ROMANS
                                Minneapolis: Augsburg (1980)

The inaugural volume in a new series of succinct commentaries on the New
Testament designed for general readers.

1 Corinthians

9.111   ICC   Robertson, A., and A. Plummer
                                A CRITICAL AND EXEGETICAL COMMEN-
                                TARY ON THE FIRST EPISTLE OF ST. PAUL
                                TO THE CORINTHIANS
                                New York: Seabury (for T. & T. Clark, Edin-
                                burgh). 2nd ed. (1914/1978)

This volume in the ICC series is old and badly in need of revision, but it is also
one of the few available on the Greek text.

9.112   HERMENEIA   Conzelmann, H.
                                A COMMENTARY ON THE FIRST EPISTLE
                                TO THE CORINTHIANS
                                Philadelphia: Fortress (1975)

This is a translation of an earlier (1969) German commentary of the most technical
sort. The letter is cited in an English translation, but the author presumes familiarity
with Greek. This is the best technical commentary currently available, but it is
definitely for advanced students.

| 9.113 | HNTC | Barrett, C. K.
A COMMENTARY ON THE FIRST EPISTLE
TO THE CORINTHIANS
San Francisco: Harper & Row (1968) |

One of three volumes in this series by Barrett (Romans [9.99] and 2 Corinthians [9.125] are the others). The commentary uses Barrett's own English translation of the letter. Informed, reliable, of interest to more than just the specialist, this is the best general commentary for all-around use, and it is reasonable in its size and scope.

| 9.114 | NICNT | Grosheide, F. W.
COMMENTARY ON FIRST CORINTHIANS
Grand Rapids: Eerdmans (1953) |

| 9.115 | NCBC | Bruce, F. F.
COMMENTARY ON FIRST AND SECOND
CORINTHIANS
Grand Rapids: Eerdmans. Rev. ed. (1981) |

| 9.116 | TNTC | Morris, L.
THE FIRST EPISTLE OF PAUL TO THE COR-
INTHIANS
Grand Rapids: Eerdmans (1958) |

| 9.117 | NWPC | Ruef, J.
PAUL'S FIRST LETTER TO CORINTH
Philadelphia: Westminster (1978) |

Available in hard cover and paperback, this commentary is not overly technical and is somewhat bland.

| 9.117p | | *Same:* paperback |

| 9.118 | CBCNT | Thrall, M. E. (ed.)
THE FIRST AND SECOND LETTERS OF PAUL
TO THE CORINTHIANS
New York: Cambridge University Press (1965) |

| 9.118p | | *Same:* paperback |

| 9.119 | NTM | Murphy-O'Connor, J.
FIRST CORINTHIANS
Wilmington (DE): M. Glazier (1980) |

| 9.119p | | *Same:* paperback |

| 9.120 | EBC | Gaebelein, F. E. (ed.)
THE EXPOSITOR'S BIBLE COMMENTARY,
Vol. 10
Grand Rapids: Zondervan (1976) |

W. H. Mare has written the commentary on 1 Corinthians; the commentaries on Romans, 2 Corinthians, and Galatians are in the same volume (see 9.105, 9.129, and 9.142).

9.121	AB	Orr, W. F., and J. A. Walther I CORINTHIANS. A NEW TRANSLATION Introduction, With a Study of the Life of Paul, Notes and Commentary Garden City: Doubleday (1976)

This volume takes a curious form. Apparently it was thought that a long essay on the career and chronology of Paul would be a useful substitute for the usual introductory materials on 1 Corinthians. Within the commentary itself (only about 250 pages), many of the observations are of an elementary nature and concern Greek grammar. The book holds little appeal for scholars or advanced students. General readers, however, will appreciate the easy style and relatively compact sections devoted to expositional commentary. Somehow the whole thing looks like a rope that has been made by knotting together dozens of short pieces of twine.

9.122		LaVerdiere, E. INVITATION TO THE NEW TESTAMENT EPISTLES, II A Commentary on I Thessalonians, II Thessalonians, I Corinthians, II Corinthians, Philippians, and Philemon with Complete Text from the Jerusalem Bible Garden City: Doubleday (1980)
9.123	NTSR	Walter, E. THE FIRST EPISTLE TO THE CORINTHIANS New York: Crossroad (1971/1981)
9.123p		*Same:* paperback

2 Corinthians

9.124	ICC	Plummer, A. A CRITICAL AND EXEGETICAL COMMENTARY ON THE SECOND EPISTLE OF ST. PAUL TO THE CORINTHIANS New York: Seabury (for T. & T. Clark, Edinburgh) (1915/1978)

The situation here is much the same as with the ICC commentary on 1 Corinthians (see 9.111) except that the alternative resources are even slimmer. This is the only twentieth-century commentary currently available in the English language based on the Greek text of 2 Corinthians.

| 9.125 | HNTC | Barrett, C. K.
A COMMENTARY ON THE SECOND EPISTLE
TO THE CORINTHIANS
San Francisco: Harper & Row (1974) |

What has been said above about Barrett's work on 1 Corinthians (see 9.113) applies to this work as well. It is the best commentary now available for serious readers who are not specialists.

| 9.126 | NICNT | Hughes, P. E.
COMMENTARY ON THE SECOND EPISTLE
TO THE CORINTHIANS
Grand Rapids: Eerdmans (1962) |

| 9.127 | NCBC | Bruce, F. F.
COMMENTARY ON FIRST AND SECOND
CORINTHIANS
Grand Rapids: Eerdmans. Rev. ed. (1981) |

| 9.128 | TNTC | Tasker, R. V. G.
THE SECOND EPISTLE OF PAUL TO THE
CORINTHIANS
Grand Rapids: Eerdmans (1958) |

| 9.129 | EBC | Gaebelein, F. E. (ed.)
THE EXPOSITOR'S BIBLE COMMENTARY,
Vol. 10
Grand Rapids: Zondervan (1976) |

The commentary on 2 Corinthians in this composite volume is by M. J. Harris (see also 9.105, 9.120, and 9.142).

| 9.130 | CBCNT | Thrall, M. E. (ed.)
THE FIRST AND SECOND LETTERS OF PAUL
TO THE CORINTHIANS
New York: Cambridge University Press (1965) |
| 9.130p | | *Same:* paperback |

| 9.131 | NTM | Fallon, F. T.
SECOND CORINTHIANS
Wilmington (DE): M. Glazier (n.d.) |

9.131p		*Same:* paperback

9.132   NTSR   Schelkle, K.
                           THE SECOND EPISTLE TO THE CORIN-
                           THIANS
                           New York: Crossroad (1969/1981)

9.132p   *Same:* paperback

9.133   LaVerdiere, E.
                           INVITATION TO THE NEW TESTAMENT
                           EPISTLES, II
                           A Commentary on I Thessalonians, II Thessa-
                           lonians, I Corinthians, II Corinthians, Philippi-
                           ans, and Philemon with Complete Text from the
                           Jerusalem Bible
                           Garden City: Doubleday (1980)

Galatians

9.134   HERMENEIA   Betz, H. D.
                           A COMMENTARY ON PAUL'S LETTER TO
                           THE CHURCHES OF GALATIA
                           Philadelphia: Fortress (1979)

Betz has written the first original volume in this series, an unusual commentary that places particular emphasis on understanding the letter in its literary and rhetorical form. As always in this series, the work is for advanced readers who want solid scholarship and can handle basic Greek. This is the only modern commentary on this level in English.

9.135   ICC   Burton, E. DeW.
                           A CRITICAL AND EXEGETICAL COMMEN-
                           TARY ON THE EPISTLE TO THE GALA-
                           TIANS
                           New York: Seabury (for T. & T. Clark, Edin-
                           burgh) (1921/1977)

This is one of the finest volumes in the ICC, not quite as ancient as some in that series and still well worth consulting for exegesis. Burton's extended notes on critical issues are still basic reading for serious research.

9.136   Lightfoot, J. B.
                           THE EPISTLE OF PAUL TO THE GALATIANS.
                           With Introduction, Notes and Dissertations
                           Grand Rapids: Zondervan (1865/1957)

This is an old work that is well worth keeping in print, for Lightfoot stands up to modern scrutiny. He was leagues ahead of most of his colleagues; and the "dissertations" of the subtitle, long appended notes on difficult historical or literary issues, are still basic. Technical, but never dense and never dull.

| 9.137 | NIGTC | Bruce, F. F.
GALATIANS
Grand Rapids: Eerdmans (1982) |

This is a welcome addition to the volumes thus far published in a promising new series and to the small number of commentaries on the Greek text of Galatians.

| 9.138 | NICNT | Ridderbos, H. N.
THE EPISTLE OF PAUL TO THE CHURCHES
OF GALATIA
Grand Rapids: Eerdmans (1953) |

| 9.139 | CBCNT | Neill, W. (ed.)
THE LETTER OF PAUL TO THE GALATIANS
New York: Cambridge University Press (1967) |
| 9.139p | | *Same:* paperback |

| 9.140 | NCBC | Guthrie, D.
GALATIANS
Grand Rapids: Eerdmans. Rev. ed. (1981) |

| 9.141 | TNTC | Cole, A.
THE EPISTLE OF PAUL TO THE
GALATIANS
Grand Rapids: Eerdmans (1964) |

| 9.142 | EBC | Gaebelein, F. E. (ed.)
THE EXPOSITOR'S BIBLE COMMENTARY,
Vol. 10
Grand Rapids: Zondervan (1976) |

J. M. Boice handles Galatians in this composite work (see also 9.105, 9.120, and 9.129).

| 9.143 | NTM | Osiek, C.
GALATIANS
Wilmington (DE): M. Glazier (n.d.) |
| 9.143p | | *Same:* paperback |

| 9.144 | NTSR | Schneider, G.
THE EPISTLE TO THE GALATIANS
New York: Crossroad (1969/1981) |

9.144p   *Same:* paperback

9.145   Getty, M. A.
                                INVITATION TO THE NEW TESTAMENT
                                EPISTLES, I
                                A Commentary on Galatians and Romans with
                                Complete Text from the Jerusalem Bible
                                Garden City: Doubleday (1981)

Ephesians, Philippians, Colossians, and Philemon

9.146   ICC   Abbott, T. K.
                                A CRITICAL AND EXEGETICAL COMMEN-
                                TARY ON THE EPISTLES TO THE EPHE-
                                SIANS AND TO THE COLOSSIANS
                                New York: Seabury (for T. and T. Clark, Edin-
                                burgh) (1897)

There has never been more than one edition of this commentary on the Greek
text, but it has been reprinted regularly. Short and less than adequate, now largely
replaced by Lohse (9.148).

9.147   ICC   Vincent, M. R.
                                A CRITICAL AND EXEGETICAL COMMEN-
                                TARY ON THE EPISTLES TO THE PHILIP-
                                PIANS AND TO PHILEMON
                                New York: Seabury (for T. & T. Clark, Edin-
                                burgh) (1897)

Like the preceding entry, this commentary is old and has appeared in only one
edition, but there are really no adequate substitutes for a commentary in English
on the Greek text of these epistles. The HNTC volume is out of print, and other
commentaries, such as those by Lightfoot (9.153, 9.154) are even older.

9.148   HERMENEIA   Lohse, E.
                                A COMMENTARY ON THE EPISTLES TO
                                THE COLOSSIANS AND TO PHILEMON
                                Philadelphia: Fortress (1971)

An early and strong entry in this series, translated from German.

9.149   WBC   O'Brien, P. T.
                                COLOSSIANS–PHILEMON
                                Waco (TX): Word Books (1982)

For what is known about this new series, see the comments in Section A about
the WBC.

9.150   CGTC   Moule, C. F. D.
THE EPISTLES OF PAUL TO THE COLOS-
SIANS AND TO PHILEMON
New York: Cambridge University Press (1957)

This brief commentary is a superb analysis of the Greek text with excellent notes and good bibliography. The compact size is achieved by not printing the actual text but only those words or phrases commented on in the notes. Outstanding.

9.150p   *Same:* paperback

9.151   NWPC   Houlden, J. L. (ed.)
PAUL'S LETTERS FROM PRISON: PHILIP-
PIANS, COLOSSIANS, PHILEMON, AND
EPHESIANS
Philadelphia: Westminster (1978)

This middle-of-the-road commentary offers a good balance between detail and exposition. It is available in both hard cover and paperback.

9.151p   *Same:* paperback

9.152   AB   Barth, M.
EPHESIANS
Vol. 1: Introduction, Translation and Commen-
tary on chaps. 1–3; Vol. 2: Translation and
Commentary on chaps. 4–6
Garden City: Doubleday (1974)

Ephesians has never been treated to so much attention. Less could have been more.

9.153   Lightfoot, J. B.
ST. PAUL'S EPISTLE TO THE PHILIPPIANS.
A Revised Text with Introduction, Notes and
Dissertations
Grand Rapids: Zondervan (1879/1953)

This volume is still worthwhile. Like Lightfoot's commentary on Galatians (9.136), the notes are quite useful.

9.154   Lightfoot, J. B.
ST. PAUL'S EPISTLES TO THE COLOSSIANS
AND TO PHILEMON
Grand Rapids: Zondervan (1865/1957)

9.155   Robinson, J. A.
COMMENTARY ON EPHESIANS
Grand Rapids: Kregel (1909/1979)

A reprinting of an old classic, *St. Paul's Epistle to the Ephesians: A Revised Text and Translation with Exposition and Notes.*

9.156   Westcott, B. F.
ST. PAUL'S EPISTLE TO THE EPHESIANS
The Greek Text with Notes and Addenda
Grand Rapids: Baker (1906/1979)

The great age of this volume and the evidence that it is still in demand indicates how important Ephesians is and how limited our resources are in English for working with the Greek text.

9.157   TNTC   Foulkes, F.
THE EPISTLE OF PAUL TO THE EPHESIANS
Grand Rapids: Eerdmans (1963)

9.158   TNTC   Carson, H. M.
THE EPISTLES OF PAUL TO THE COLOS-
SIANS AND TO PHILEMON
Grand Rapids: Eerdmans (1960)

9.159   TNTC   Martin, R. P.
THE EPISTLE OF PAUL TO THE PHILIPPI-
ANS
Grand Rapids: Eerdmans (1960)

9.160   NCBC   Martin, R. P.
COMMENTARY ON PHILIPPIANS
Grand Rapids: Eerdmans (1980)

9.161   NCBC   Martin, R. P.
COMMENTARY ON COLOSSIANS AND
PHILEMON
Grand Rapids: Eerdmans. Rev. ed. (1981)

9.162   NCBC   Mitton, C. L.
COMMENTARY ON EPHESIANS
Grand Rapids: Eerdmans (1981)

9.163   CBCNT   Grayston, K. (ed.)
THE LETTERS OF PAUL TO THE PHILIPPI-
ANS AND TO THE THESSALONIANS
New York: Cambridge University Press (1967)

9.163p   *Same:* paperback

9.164	CBCNT	Thompson, G. H. P. (ed.) THE LETTERS OF PAUL TO THE EPHE- SIANS, TO THE COLOSSIANS AND TO PHI- LEMON New York: Cambridge University Press (1967)
9.164p		*Same:* paperback
9.165	NICNT	Simpson, E. K., and F. F. Bruce THE EPISTLES TO THE EPHESIANS AND COLOSSIANS Grand Rapids: Eerdmans (1958)
9.166	NICNT	Muller, J. J. THE EPISTLES OF PAUL TO THE PHILIPPI- ANS AND TO PHILEMON Grand Rapids: Eerdmans (1955)
9.167	NTM	Swain, L. EPHESIANS Wilmington (DE): M. Glazier (n.d.)
9.167p		*Same:* paperback
9.168	NTM	Getty, M. A. PHILIPPIANS AND PHILEMON Wilmington (DE): M. Glazier (n.d.)
9.168p		*Same:* paperback
9.169	NTM	Rogers, P. V. COLOSSIANS Wilmington (DE): M. Glazier (n.d.)
9.169p		*Same:* paperback
9.170	NTSR	Zerwick, M. THE EPISTLE TO THE EPHESIANS New York: Crossroad (1969/1981)
9.170p		*Same:* paperback
9.171	NTSR	Reuss, J., and A. Stöger THE EPISTLE TO TITUS; THE EPISTLE TO PHILEMON New York: Crossroad (1971/1981)
9.171p		*Same:* paperback

9.172   NTSR   Gnilka, J., and F. Mussner
THE EPISTLE TO THE PHILIPPIANS; THE
EPISTLE TO THE COLOSSIANS
New York: Crossroad (1971/1981)

9.172p   *Same:* paperback

9.173   EBC   Gaebelein, F. E. (ed.)
THE EXPOSITOR'S BIBLE COMMENTARY,
Vol. 11
Grand Rapids: Zondervan (1978)

Commentary on Ephesians by A. Skevington Wood; on Philippians by H. A. Kent, Jr.; on Colossians by C. Vaughn; on Philemon by A. A. Ruprecht (see also 9.182).

9.174   LaVerdiere, E.
INVITATION TO THE NEW TESTAMENT
EPISTLES, II
A Commentary on I Thessalonians, II Thessa-
lonians, I Corinthians, II Corinthians, Philippi-
ans and Philemon with Complete Text from the
Jerusalem Bible
Garden City: Doubleday (1980)

1 and 2 Thessalonians

9.175   ICC   Frame, J. E.
A CRITICAL AND EXEGETICAL COMMEN-
TARY ON THE EPISTLES OF ST. PAUL TO
THE THESSALONIANS
New York: Seabury (for T. & T. Clark, Edin-
burgh) (1912)

The two most useful commentaries on the Greek text of these letters, this and the next one, are both quite old and badly in need of updating or replacement. In fact, the choices available to the reader, at whatever level, are distressingly few. (For example, there is not yet a volume on the Thessalonian letters in NCBC.)

9.176   Milligan, G.
ST. PAUL'S EPISTLES TO THE THESSALON-
IANS
The Greek Text with Introduction and Notes
Minneapolis: Klock & Klock (1908/1980)

Milligan on Thessalonians was one of the best commentaries from the turn of the century. Since resources for these letters are few, this volume is especially welcome as a recent reprint. But it would merit consideration even in a crowded field.

9.177	CBCNT	Grayston, K. THE LETTERS OF PAUL TO THE PHILIPPIANS AND TO THE THESSALONIANS New York: Cambridge University Press (1967)
9.177p		*Same:* paperback
9.178	TNTC	Morris, L. THE EPISTLES OF PAUL TO THE THESSALONIANS Grand Rapids: Eerdmans (1957)
9.179	NICNT	Morris, L. THE FIRST AND SECOND EPISTLES TO THE THESSALONIANS Grand Rapids: Eerdmans (1959)
9.180		Whiteley, D. E. THESSALONIANS New York: Oxford University Press (1969)

This entry in Oxford's New Century Bible is more up-to-date than most brief commentaries available on the Thessalonian letters. It is also somewhat sturdier than any of the remaining entries below, except for the next, which is considerably more traditional and expositional.

| 9.181 | | Draper, J.
FIRST AND SECOND THESSALONIANS
Wheaton (IL): Tyndale (1979) |

This commentary, of conservative cast and recent vintage, is noticeably more traditional and expositional than most of what has been described above.

| 9.182 | EBC | Gaebelein, F. E. (ed.)
THE EXPOSITOR'S BIBLE COMMENTARY, Vol. 11
Grand Rapids: Zondervan (1978) |

The commentary on 1 and 2 Thessalonians in this volume was written by R. L. Thomas (see also 9.173).

9.183	NTSR	Schürmann, H., and H. A. Egenolf THE FIRST EPISTLE TO THE THESSALON- IANS; THE SECOND EPISTLE TO THE THES- SALONIANS New York: Crossroad (1969/1981)

9.183p   *Same:* paperback

9.184	NTM	Reese, J. M. 1 AND 2 THESSALONIANS Wilmington (DE): M. Glazier (n.d.)

9.184p   *Same:* paperback

9.185   LaVerdiere, E.
INVITATION TO THE NEW TESTAMENT
EPISTLES, II
A Commentary on I Thessalonians; II Thessa-
lonians; I Corinthians; II Corinthians; Philip-
pians; and Philemon with Complete Text from
the Jerusalem Bible
Garden City: Doubleday (1980)

The Pastoral Letters:
1 Timothy, 2 Timothy, and Titus

9.186   HERMENEIA   Dibelius, M.
THE PASTORAL EPISTLES
Philadelphia: Fortress (1972)

Regardless of one's views about the authenticity of the Pastoral letters (Dibelius doubts that they are Pauline), this is the richest commentary available and a mine of valuable insights drawn from the ancient world. Like all volumes in this series, it comments on an English text printed at the head of each section, but it presupposes familiarity with Greek. Greek and Latin quotations from outside the New Testament are furnished with translations. The finest analytical commentary on the Pastorals now in print.

9.187   ICC   Lock, W.
A CRITICAL AND EXEGETICAL COMMEN-
TARY ON THE PASTORAL EPISTLES (I AND
II TIMOTHY AND TITUS)
New York: Seabury (for T. & T. Clark, Edin-
burgh) (1924/1978)

A concise and still quite good commentary, this volume is particularly noteworthy for its introductory material (Lock cannot decide on the issue of authorship) and some detached notes along the way.

9.188   TNTC   Guthrie, D.
                       THE PASTORAL EPISTLES
                       Grand Rapids: Eerdmans (1957)

The approach here and in the next volume is somewhat more traditional and expositional.

9.189   CBCNT   Hanson, A. T. (ed.)
                       THE PASTORAL LETTERS
                       New York: Cambridge University Press (1966)

9.189p   *Same:* paperback

9.190   Kelly, J. N. D.
                       A COMMENTARY ON THE PASTORAL
                       EPISTLES
                       Grand Rapids: Baker (1964/1981)

Originally part of the HNTC, this volume was allowed to go out of print by the original American publisher. It shares with the other volumes in that series the reputation of being well suited to both general readers and more advanced students. Since Kelly strikes a balance between thoroughness and concision and is still relatively up-to-date, this is more than welcome as a reprint.

9.191   NCBC   Hanson, A. T.
                       THE PASTORAL EPISTLES
                       Grand Rapids: Eerdmans (1982)

This author has also provided the commentary in CBCNT (9.189).

9.192   NTM   Karris, R. J.
                       PASTORAL EPISTLES
                       Wilmington (DE): M. Glazier (n.d.)

9.192p   *Same:* paperback

9.193   NTSR   Reuss, J.
                       THE FIRST EPISTLE TO TIMOTHY; THE
                       SECOND EPISTLE TO TIMOTHY
                       New York: Crossroad (1969/1981)

9.193p   *Same:* paperback

9.194   NTSR   Reuss, J., and A. Stöger
                              THE EPISTLE TO TITUS; THE EPISTLE TO
                              PHILEMON
                              New York: Crossroad (1971/1981)

9.194p   *Same:* paperback

The Epistle to the Hebrews

9.195   ICC   Moffatt, J.
                              A CRITICAL AND EXEGETICAL COMMEN-
                              TARY ON THE EPISTLE TO THE HEBREWS
                              New York: Seabury (for T. & T. Clark, Edin-
                              burgh) (1924)

9.196   Westcott, B. F.
                              A COMMENTARY ON THE EPISTLE TO
                              THE HEBREWS
                              Grand Rapids: Eerdmans (1920/1950)

Westcott's commentary on the Greek text first appeared in 1889. This is a reprint
of the third edition (1920).

9.197   AB   Buchanan, G. W.
                              TO THE HEBREWS
                              Garden City: Doubleday (1972)

Technical yet accessible to the nonspecialist, this thorough but somewhat idiosyncratic commentary provides its own translation. The format distinguishes between
technical notations and more general commentary.

9.198   Hughes, P. E.
                              A COMMENTARY ON THE EPISTLE TO
                              THE HEBREWS
                              Grand Rapids: Eerdmans (1977)

A substantial reading of Hebrews from the right wing of the Reformation, this
commentary is more theological and more expository than most. It is also recent.

9.199   TNTC   Hewitt, T.
                              THE EPISTLE TO THE HEBREWS
                              Grand Rapids: Eerdmans (1961)

9.200   NICNT   Bruce, F. F.
                              THE EPISTLE TO THE HEBREWS
                              Grand Rapids: Eerdmans (1964)

9.201	CBCNT	Davies, J. H. THE LETTER TO THE HEBREWS New York: Cambridge University Press (1967)
9.201p		*Same:* paperback
9.202	NTSR	Schierse, F. J., and O. Knoch THE EPISTLE TO THE HEBREWS; THE EPIS- TLE OF ST. JAMES New York: Crossroad (1969/1981)
9.202p		*Same:* paperback
9.203	NTM	Casey, J. HEBREWS Wilmington (DE): M. Glazier (n.d.)
9.203p		*Same:* paperback
9.204		Danker, F. W. INVITATION TO THE NEW TESTAMENT EPISTLES, IV A Commentary on Hebrews; James; 1 and 2 Peter; 1, 2, and 3 John; and Jude with Complete Text from the Jerusalem Bible Garden City: Doubleday (1980)

The Johannine Epistles: 1, 2, and 3 John

9.205	AB	Brown, R. E. THE EPISTLES OF JOHN Garden City: Doubleday (1982)

Once again Brown distinguishes himself and the AB series. It can be said without qualification that this is *the* commentary on the Johannine epistles, the newest and the finest available. Brown has also put the letters into a larger context that takes account of his own earlier work on the fourth gospel (9.57, 9.58). For the specialist and the general reader alike.

9.206	HERMENEIA	Bultmann, R. THE JOHANNINE EPISTLES Philadelphia: Fortress (1973)

Bultmann was a masterful scholar of the New Testament and was nowhere more at home than in the Johannine literature. This advanced commentary is for the specialist and the most serious student. It uses an English text but presupposes Greek throughout. Although compact in scope, it is somewhat intimidating as well.

9.207   ICC   Brooke, A. E.
                            A CRITICAL AND EXEGETICAL COMMEN-
                            TARY ON THE JOHANNINE EPISTLES
                            New York: Seabury (for T. & T. Clark, Edin-
                            burgh) (1912)

Brooke is especially strong on introductory materials and shows the characteristic ICC interest in philological matters. The bulk of his attention is given to 1 John, somewhat to the slighting of the other brief letters. An appendix conveniently offers the text in Old Latin. A dated but still useful work.

9.208   Plummer, A.
                            THE EPISTLES OF ST. JOHN
                            Grand Rapids: Baker (1886/1980)

One of Plummer's many contributions to the old *Cambridge Greek Testament* (for schools and colleges), this concise commentary on the Greek text is now reprinted. It is very old, of course, but it is inexpensive and an excellent place for a novice in Greek to begin without being overwhelmed.

9.209   Westcott, B. F.
                            THE EPISTLES OF ST. JOHN
                            Grand Rapids: Eerdmans (1902/1966)

A new introduction by F. F. Bruce bridges the distance to this old but still impressive commentary on the Greek text. The first edition appeared in 1883; this reprinting offers the third edition of 1902. At the end of his commentary Westcott added three long notes on special topics—one is on art and early Christianity—and these are still interesting. This reissue would serve the same purpose as Plummer (9.208).

9.210   Bruce, F. F.
                            THE EPISTLES OF ST. JOHN
                            Grand Rapids: Eerdmans (1978)

This general work is for the uninitiated but serious reader of the English text.

9.211   McKenzie, J. L.
                            LIGHT ON THE EPISTLES. A Reader's Guide
                            Chicago: Thomas More (1975)

This guide covers far more than the Johannine epistles, in a way that general readers will find informative and interesting. A bit expensive.

9.212   CBCNT   Williams, R. R. (ed.)
                         THE LETTER OF JOHN AND JAMES
                         New York: Cambridge University Press (1965)

9.212p   *Same:* paperback

9.213   HNTC   Houlden, J. L.
                         THE JOHANNINE EPISTLES
                         San Francisco: Harper & Row (1973)

Another entry in the Harper's New Testament Commentary series, this volume offers solid interpretation and a balance between analytical concerns and the needs of the more general reader. Good.

9.214   NICNT   Marshall, I. H.
                         THE EPISTLES OF JOHN
                         Grand Rapids: Eerdmans (1978)

9.215   TNTC   Stott, J. R. W.
                         THE EPISTLES OF JOHN
                         Grand Rapids: Eerdmans (1964)

Quite homiletical.

9.216   EBC   Gaebelein, F. E. (ed.)
                         THE EXPOSITOR'S BIBLE COMMENTARY,
                         Vol. 12
                         Grand Rapids: Zondervan (1981)

G. W. Barker writes on the Johannine epistles in a volume that covers also Hebrews, James, 1 and 2 Peter, Jude, and Revelation (see also 9.231, 9.250, 9.266).

9.217   Danker, F. W.
                         INVITATION TO THE NEW TESTAMENT,
                         IV
                         A Commentary on Hebrews; James; 1 and 2 Peter; 1, 2, and 3 John; and Jude with Complete Text from the Jerusalem Bible
                         Garden City: Doubleday (1980)

9.218   NTM   Perkins, P.
                         THE JOHANNINE EPISTLES
                         Wilmington (DE): M. Glazier (1980)

Good work in short space, this volume makes an excellent place for the beginner to start.

9.218p		*Same:* paperback

9.219	NTSR	Thüsing, W., and A. Stöger THE THREE EPISTLES OF ST. JOHN; THE EPISTLE OF ST. JUDE New York: Crossroad (1971/1981)

9.219p		*Same:* paperback

1 and 2 Peter

9.220		Selwyn, E. G. THE FIRST EPISTLE OF ST. PETER Grand Rapids: Baker. 2nd ed. (1947/1981)

This is a welcome reprint, because nothing has yet replaced Selwyn's careful and painstaking analysis of the Greek text of 1 Peter. Very full and very demanding, but a standard and classic volume.

9.221	ICC	Bigg, C. A CRITICAL AND EXEGETICAL COMMEN- TARY ON THE EPISTLES OF ST. PETER AND ST. JUDE New York: Seabury (for T. & T. Clark, Edin- burgh). 2nd ed. (1902)

9.222		Mayor, J. B. THE EPISTLES OF JUDE AND SECOND PETER The Greek Text with Introduction, Notes and Comments Grand Rapids: Baker (1907/1979)

This very old and comprehensive commentary on the Greek text is reprinted because it still has considerable appeal. The same volume with a slightly different title and in cloth binding is also available (9.223).

9.223		Mayor, J. B. THE EPISTLE OF ST. JUDE AND THE SECOND EPISTLE OF ST. PETER Minneapolis: Klock & Klock (1907/1978)

9.224	AB	Reicke, B. I. THE EPISTLES OF JAMES, PETER AND JUDE Garden City: Doubleday. 2nd ed. (1978)

Following the Anchor Bible format, Reicke provides an independent translation and distinguishes between more technical matters and general exposition.

9.225
> Kelly, J. N. D.
> A COMMENTARY ON THE EPISTLES OF PETER AND JUDE
> Grand Rapids: Baker (1969/1981)

Originally published as a commentary in the HNTC and then allowed to go out of print, Kelly's crisp commentary is an excellent place for the serious nontechnical reader to begin.

9.226 CBCNT
> Leaney, A. R. C.
> THE LETTERS OF PETER AND JUDE
> New York: Cambridge University Press (1967)

9.226p
> *Same:* paperback

9.227 NCBC
> Best, E.
> A COMMENTARY ON I PETER
> Grand Rapids: Eerdmans (1982)

9.228 NCBC
> Sidebottom, E. M.
> A COMMENTARY ON THE EPISTLES OF JAMES, JUDE, AND 2 PETER
> Grand Rapids: Eerdmans (1982)

9.229 TNTC
> Stibbs, A. M.
> THE FIRST EPISTLE OF PETER
> Grand Rapids: Eerdmans (1959)

9.230 TNTC
> Green, M.
> THE SECOND EPISTLE OF PETER AND THE EPISTLE OF JUDE
> Grand Rapids: Eerdmans (1968)

9.231 EBC
> Gaebelein, F. E. (ed.)
> THE EXPOSITOR'S BIBLE COMMENTARY, Vol. 12
> Grand Rapids: Zondervan (1981)

The commentary on the Petrine letters is by E. A. Blum (see also 9.216, 9.250, 9.266)

9.232 NTSR
> Schwank, B., and A. Stöger
> THE FIRST EPISTLE OF ST. PETER; THE SECOND EPISTLE OF ST. PETER
> New York: Crossroad (1971/1981)

9.232p   *Same:* paperback

9.233   NTM   Senior, D.
1 AND 2 PETER
Wilmington (DE): M. Glazier (n.d.)

9.233p   *Same:* paperback

9.234   ACNT   Martin, R. A., and J. H. Elliott
AUGSBURG COMMENTARY ON THE NEW
TESTAMENT—JAMES, I PETER, II PETER,
JUDE
Minneapolis: Augsburg (1982)

The Epistles of James and Jude

9.235   ICC   Ropes, J. H.
A CRITICAL AND EXEGETICAL COMMEN-
TARY ON THE EPISTLE OF ST. JAMES
New York: Seabury (for T. & T. Clark, Edin-
burgh) (1916/1978)

Although quite old, this is still a standard commentary on the Greek text of James.
The commentary by Mayor (9.237) is even older. Both are now eclipsed by the
Dibelius/Greeven commentary (9.239) and by Davids (9.240).

9.236   ICC   Bigg, C.
A CRITICAL AND EXEGETICAL COMMEN-
TARY ON THE EPISTLES OF ST. PETER AND
ST. JUDE
New York: Seabury (for T. & T. Clark, Edin-
burgh). 2nd ed. (1902/1978)

9.237   Mayor, J. B.
THE EPISTLE OF ST. JAMES. The Greek Text
with Introduction, Notes and Comments
Grand Rapids: Baker (1913/1978)

A paperback reprint of the third edition of a commentary on the Greek text of
James, which first appeared in 1892.

9.238   Mayor, J. B.
THE EPISTLE OF ST. JAMES
Minneapolis: Klock & Klock (1913/1977)

A cloth binding of the same commentary as 9.237, despite the slightly different title.

| 9.239 | HERMENEIA | Dibelius, M. (rev. by H. Greeven)
A COMMENTARY ON THE EPISTLE OF JAMES
Philadelphia: Fortress (1976) |

For the serious student of the New Testament this is the most comprehensive and up-to-date commentary available, the first and last word. Dibelius/Greeven presumes a knowledge of Greek.

| 9.240 | NIGTC | Davids, P.
A COMMENTARY ON JAMES
Grand Rapids: Eerdmans (1982) |

The most recent commentary available on the Greek text.

| 9.241 | AB | Reicke, B. I.
THE EPISTLES OF JAMES, PETER AND JUDE
Garden City: Doubleday. 2nd ed. (1978)
(*See 9.224.*) |

| 9.242 | HNTC | Laws, S.
A COMMENTARY ON THE EPISTLE OF JAMES
San Francisco: Harper & Row (1980) |

Not as technical as Dibelius/Greeven (9.239), this commentary is well suited to serious readers who are not interested in technicalities.

| 9.243 | | Kelly, J. N. D.
A COMMENTARY ON THE EPISTLES OF PETER AND JUDE
Grand Rapids: Baker (1969/1981)
(*See 9.225.*) |

| 9.244 | TNTC | Tasker, R. V. G.
THE GENERAL EPISTLE OF JAMES
Grand Rapids: Eerdmans (1957) |

| 9.245 | TNTC | Green, M.
THE SECOND EPISTLE OF PETER AND THE EPISTLE OF JUDE
Grand Rapids: Eerdmans (1968)
(*See 9.230.*) |

9.246   NCBC   Sidebottom, E. M.
A COMMENTARY ON THE EPISTLES OF
JAMES, JUDE AND 2 PETER
Grand Rapids: Eerdmans (1982)
(*See 9.228.*)

9.247   NICNT   Adamson, J.
A COMMENTARY ON THE EPISTLE OF
JAMES
Grand Rapids: Eerdmans (1976)

Substantial in scope, this is somewhat more expositional than Laws (9.242), but
in other ways it appeals to the same kind of reader.

9.248   CBCNT   Williams, R. R.
THE LETTERS OF JOHN AND JAMES
New York: Cambridge University Press (1965)
(*See 9.212.*)

9.248p   *Same:* paperback

9.249   CBCNT   Leaney, A. R. C.
THE LETTERS OF PETER AND JUDE
New York: Cambridge University Press (1967)
(*See 9.226.*)

9.249p   *Same:* paperback

9.250   EBC   Gaebelein, F. E. (ed.)
THE EXPOSITOR'S BIBLE COMMENTARY,
Vol. 12
Grand Rapids: Zondervan (1981)

The commentary on James is provided by D. W. Burdick and that on Jude by E.
A. Blum (see also 9.216, 9.231, 9.266).

9.251   NTM   Kugelman, R.
JAMES AND JUDE
Wilmington (DE): M. Glazier (n.d.)

9.251p   *Same:* paperback

9.252   NTSR   Schierse, F. J., and O. Knoch
THE EPISTLE TO THE HEBREWS; THE EPIS-
TLE OF JAMES
New York: Crossroad (1969/1981)

9.252p   *Same:* paperback

| 9.253 | NTSR | Thüsing, W., and A. Stöger
THE THREE EPISTLES OF ST. JOHN; THE EPISTLE OF ST. JUDE
New York: Crossroad (1971/1981) |

9.253p   *Same:* paperback

| 9.254 | ACNT | Martin, R. A., and J. H. Elliott
AUGSBURG COMMENTARY ON THE NEW TESTAMENT: JAMES, I PETER, II PETER, JUDE
Minneapolis: Augsburg (1982) |

Revelation

| 9.255
9.256 | ICC | Charles, R. H.
A CRITICAL AND EXEGETICAL COMMENTARY ON THE REVELATION OF ST. JOHN. 2 vols.
New York: Seabury (for T. & T. Clark, Edinburgh) (1920) |

This remains *the* standard commentary in English on the Greek text of Revelation.

| 9.257 | | Swete, H. B.
COMMENTARY ON REVELATION
Grand Rapids: Kregel (1911/1978) |

Swete's commentary (originally *The Apocalypse of John*) is older than that of Charles (9.255, 9.256) and has seldom been out of print. Swete was a master of the intersection of Hebrew and Greek in the Septuagint and in early Christianity, and his commentary remains worthwhile. This is a reprint of the third edition.

| 9.258 | | Beckwith, I. T.
THE APOCALYPSE OF JOHN. Studies in Introduction, with a Critical and Exegetical Commentary
Grand Rapids: Baker (1919/1967/1979) |

Once again an older commentary based on the Greek text seems to have remarkable appeal. Beckwith's strongest point is the critical analysis of the Greek text, which is sandwiched between an introduction and the actual commentary itself.

9.259   NWPC   Sweet, J. P. M.
                             REVELATION
                             Philadelphia: Westminster (1979)

An intermediate commentary that deals with the text in English and presupposes no special knowledge, this is a solid and recent contribution to the literature. It affords an excellent beginning point for the serious, nontechnical reader.

9.259p   *Same:* paperback

9.260   HNTC   Caird, G. B.
                             THE REVELATION OF ST. JOHN THE DI-VINE
                             San Francisco: Harper & Row (1966)

Like the commentary of Sweet (9.259), this is of intermediate scope and designed for the general audience. Fr reliable and clear exposition it is hard to beat. Caird is especially skillful at penetrating the symbolic imagination of one of the New Testament's more imaginative authors.

9.261   AB   Ford, J. M.
                             REVELATION
                             Garden City: Doubleday (1975)

This Anchor Bible offering is large and generally useful to the nonspecialist, but it does have some unusual interpretations, not all of which should be taken without critical sifting.

9.262   CBCNT   Glasson, T. F. (ed.)
                             THE REVELATION OF JOHN
                             New York: Cambridge University Press (1965)

9.262p   *Same:* paperback

9.263   NICNT   Mounce, R.
                             THE BOOK OF REVELATION
                             Grand Rapids: Eerdmans (1977)

9.264   NCBC   Beasley-Murray, G. R.
                             THE BOOK OF REVELATION
                             Grand Rapids: Eerdmans. Rev. ed. (1981)

9.265   TNTC   Morris, L.
                             THE REVELATION OF ST. JOHN
                             Grand Rapids: Eerdmans (1957)

9.266   EBC   Gaebelein, F. E. (ed.)
                             THE EXPOSITOR'S BIBLE COMMENTARY, Vol. 12
                             Grand Rapids: Zondervan (1981)

A. F. Johnson completes Vol. 12 with the commentary on Revelation (see also 9.216, 9.231, 9.250).

9.267	NTSR	Schick, E. THE REVELATION OF ST. JOHN, Vol. 1 New York: Crossroad (1971/1981)
9.267p		*Same:* paperback
9.268	NTSR	Schick, E. THE REVELATION OF ST. JOHN, Vol. 2 New York: Crossroad (1971/1981)
9.268p		*Same:* paperback
9.269	NTM	Collins, A. Y. THE APOCALYPSE Wilmington (DE): M. Glazier (1979)
9.269p		*Same:* paperback
9.270		Fiorenza, E. S. INVITATION TO THE BOOK OF REVELATION A Commentary with Complete Text from the Jerusalem Bible Garden City: Doubleday (1981)

BEST BUYS

It probably cannot be said too often: A *series* of commentaries is certain to be of uneven quality. But a series does set goals and standards to which its individual authors aspire, and knowing these can be of some help. The ICC, for example, will always stand for philological detail and working with the Greek text. If NIGTC, which is only now appearing, has less detail, it too represents careful attention to the Greek text—and a slightly less "critical" attitude than the older ICC. It remains to be seen what the tone of the new ICC volumes will be. HERMENEIA still has a very Continental air about it and offers the best access to contemporary and well-informed interpretation with an emphasis on analytical matters.

Those who want the results of scholarship without the scholarly paraphernalia will find NWPC attractive, but this series is by no means complete. The same can be said for HNTC, which unfortunately is not only not yet completed but is also riddled with omissions since earlier titles have been allowed to go out of print. Those that are available in reprints have been noted in the proper place in Section C above. The NCBC is not quite of the same order as these other two series, but it shares some similarities and offers compact but serious reading for the nonspecialist. More expositional commentary designed to help those who must expound the text will be found in TNTC, while a blend of interests is served by NICNT. Among the smaller, handy volumes designed for the easiest reading, NTM (complete, modern, concise) is a model. NTSR offers "spiritual" reading at an impressively high intellectual level.

Perhaps the best advice is to be eclectic in reading and to shop around among the very best commentaries, those listed here.

10

A WISE BUYER'S GUIDE

O f the thousands of books available for unlocking the New Testament—from the rarified level of scholarly investigation to the practical level of inspirational reading—the very best resources have been listed and described in the preceding chapters. Now that you know what is best, how do you get it? If you wish to purchase these books, how do you go about doing so?

The simple way is to walk into a bookstore and buy what you want. Unfortunately, that is too simple to be always practical. Not all Americans today live close to first-rate bookstores, and even the best such stores cannot be expected to stock more than a few of the titles listed here. If you have a store nearby that specializes in religious titles, your situation may be somewhat better, but you still should not expect an inventory that allows you to choose from among twenty commentaries or seven atlases. The rate of publication of titles in this field makes it difficult for most retailers to keep up with what is available, and it is virtually impossible for any small business to stock a complete inventory. Complicating matters further are two recent trends. One is the move toward retail discount stores in large cities; the other is a trend toward mail-order business, especially for "Christian" books, which usually means the very titles described here.

How to Get the Most out of Your Bookstore

Discount bookstores in large cities need not concern us save for this lament: while they are convenient places to buy best sellers, they do not shave the price without shaving the service, and a bookstore should be a resource for service as well as for books. In many instances you can still expect a retailer to special-order what you want and cannot find there, especially if the book is from a publisher with whom the bookseller regularly deals. Discounters find this impossible to do, and by skimming the cream off the top of the retail trade—customers who want to buy what is current and selling well—they drive out other retailers who wish to provide such service.

Let us suppose, however, that you have a book retailer who wants to meet your needs and is happy to take your special orders. In that case, all you need to convey to the retailer is the information found in the Quick Reference Chart at the end of this chapter. Each book described and listed in the preceding pages is indexed in the QRC by the reference number assigned to it earlier. Following this number is the information the bookseller will need in order to help you: the publisher; the ISBN (International Standard Book Number, assigned to every new book at the time of publication and used throughout the world); the current price; binding information (cloth and paper are distinguished when this is known); and, of course, the date of publication and the edition, if this can be known.

Every effort has been made to make the QRC accurate and as up-to-the-minute as possible, and it should save you and your retailer a great deal of time. Nevertheless, some details can change quickly—especially prices—and books do go out of print or out of stock and appear again with depressing frequency. This is especially true in the United States where tax laws make it less advantageous than it once was for publishers to keep an ample inventory of books that sell regularly but only modestly. The moral of all this is that your retailer may want to make a final check before placing the order. But you can be specific about what you want by using the QRC; and that will same time, save money, and avoid confusion.

Books by Mail?

Mentioning money brings us to the next point. What about the growing popularity of mail-order book retailing, especially in the field of religious books and particularly for books dealing with the Bible? It is not at all uncommon now to find advertisements promoting businesses that promise to deliver books at significant discount—sometimes as much as 50 to 60 percent on special items, and regularly 20 to 30 percent. Are such businesses legitimate? Are they worthwhile? Are they better than the local bookstore?

The answers depend on several factors. There are some large mail-order discounters that are entirely reputable. How useful they will be to you depends in part on how and when you do your buying. Here are a few factors to keep in mind.

First, you cannot browse by mail very easily. It is a way to purchase when you are certain what you want. Otherwise, try to find another way. Second, shipping and handling charges add up, right on your bill. Third, the discounts are far better for some volumes than for others, and you may want to stay with the high discount items when buying by mail. Fourth, the best and most reliable mail-order services charge a yearly membership fee. Although it is modest, usually three to five dollars, it is a consideration. Fifth, such mail-order houses do not always stock everything you may be interested in, even in the case of books about the Bible. Some have rather definite ideas about what is "proper" biblical interpretation and what is not, and while they will usually special-order for you, they have been known on occasion to decline to do so (for "doctrinal" reasons). In any case, the small discount that would apply to such orders is more than offset in most instances by shipping charges and the increased delay.

Those are all things to be cautious about. On the other hand, there are real savings to be had through such retailers and you should know who they are and how to get the most from their offerings.

A Strategy for Buying

The first thing to do is to decide which possibilities you want to investigate. There are five good avenues to explore.

1. Baker Book House regularly offers its own and competitors' wares by mail and will be glad to put your name on its mail-order catalogue list. The catalogues are printed and distributed irregularly and are rather haphazard in organization. Still, the savings are real:

Baker Book House
2768 East Paris, S.E.
P.O. Box 6287
Grand Rapids, MI 49506

As a publisher Baker specializes in books that appeal particularly to conservative and evangelical tastes. It is also responsible for keeping some old classics alive in reprint. The mail-order catalogues cover a much broader range, however, and include titles from dozens of other publishers. There is an unmistakable accent on the practical, the homiletic, the inspirational; but almost anything listed here can be obtained from Baker. The discounts vary, apply only to what is listed in each catalogue, and are not as generous as those of some large mail-order retailers. They will, however, set up a charge account for you if you make application. In any event, a card will get you on their mailing list, free.

   2. Scholars and buyers of serious books will want to know about:

Eisenbrauns
P.O.B. 275
Winona Lake, IN 46590

Eisenbrauns is a more specialized service, concentrating on scholarly books but carrying a full line of the most important publications on the Bible. It sells through printed catalogues, usually one each year supplemented several times. It sells all books at a discount, but the discounts vary. If you want an item not found there you may write an inquiry. They are usually glad to special-order. Service is excellent and the business is handled in a crisp, efficient, and friendly manner, with one exception: back orders. Do *not* ask for back-ordering (sending later a book that is not currently in stock); ask for a refund instead. At the present time the yearly catalogue fee is two dollars. Eisenbrauns' greatest service is in providing for American customers foreign books in the areas of biblical studies and the ancient Near East.

   3. One of the largest mail-order firms is:

Puritan-Reformed Discount Book Service
1319 Newport Gap Pike
Wilmington, DE 19804
Orders: 1-800-441-7596/Customer Service: 1-302-999-0595

PR publishes a monthly catalogue, which is sent to all subscribers. Membership costs five dollars a year. The catalogues are arranged so that the most recent three monthly catalogues constitute the whole of the firm's offerings. The emphasis on biblical materials is unmistakable, particularly on those slanted toward the Reformed tradition. While the management reserves the right not to carry books it considers inappropriate or out of keeping with its values, in fact the range of offerings is quite spectacular. That means that you can count on saving money on items regularly stocked—and at times the savings are enormous. You should probably stay away from special orders, however. Books can be charged (Mastercard or Visa), paid for by check, or sent C.O.D. The very best offers from PR come on books announced at special discount *prior* to publication. By paying a few weeks in advance of publication you can often save substantial amounts. Again, however, you have to know what you really want. Even with a fair-handed return policy such as PR's, the cost of postage makes browsing impractical.

4. There is a competitive service that publishes a smaller catalogue but regularly offers the wares of an even wider range of publishers than does PR.

Christian Book Distributors
Box 2687
Peabody, MA 01960-0687

Newer than PR, CBD strives to get a competitive edge. Its prices come within pennies of its competitor; its membership rate is a bit lower (three dollars a year). The catalogue is published about every two months and is complete in each issue. It is also easier to use than PR's, because it is arranged by publisher. In general, there is not much that helps one choose between these two mail-order firms, since both seem competent, reliable, and speedy. They will probably be willing to meet each other's prices.

5. Do not forget that books published or distributed in this country by the American Bible Society are least expensive when ordered directly from:

American Bible Society
P.O. Box 5656
Grand Central Station
New York, NY 10163

ABS asks for cash in advance but pays for postage. Their books listed above are: 2.7, 2.29, 2.30, 4.1, 4.2, 4.3, 4.4, 4.5, 4.6, 4.7, 4.8, 4.9, 4.10, 4.11, 4.13, 4.14, 4.24, 4.26, 4.31, 4.53, and 4.63.

But what is the best strategy? Some things are obvious. Larger orders and orders on featured items can be purchased at substantial savings through discount mail retailers. Using this book with their catalogues will take some of the guesswork out of ordering by mail and will reduce the chances of your being disappointed. Second, postage on small orders and the minimal discounts that can be allowed on special orders result in hardly any saving.

Finally, if you are more interested in convenience and speed than in hunting for bargains, you can always order directly from the publisher, at retail cost plus a charge for shipping and handling. The addresses and telephone numbers of all the publishers listed in this book may be found at the back of the "Titles" volumes of *Books in Print,* copies of which are readily available in most libraries and in all bookstores.

QUICK REFERENCE CHART

This chart contains the basic information needed for quick and precise identification of each item listed in *The Bible Book*. It is specifically designed to simplify the purchase of these books and to avoid confusion where many titles are similar.

Each book is identified by the number used for its entry in *The Bible Book*. In addition, the QRC gives the author, a short title, the publisher, and information about binding—paper (p), leather (L), or some form of plastic (K or v). The ISBN, the date, and the price are also included.

Some of this information will change quickly. Books go out of print, and prices change frequently. While every effort has been made to provide the most recent and accurate information, prices and availability may change. Nevertheless, if there are several editions of a single book, prices can be expected to remain relative to one another.

The Bible Book concentrates on books *currently* available. Nevertheless, a few very worthwhile older items that are not now in print have been included because one might wish to consult them in a library. An asterisk (*) following the serial number marks the few titles in the QRC that are out of print. In other cases, current information about ISBNs and prices is not available. The notation "n.a." suggests that the book is currently out of stock or off the publisher's list; but in most such instances new editions or new printings can be expected. The dates given are those known for the earliest and latest significant "editions" or printings. In some instances no date is available, and this is indicated by "n.d."

BB#	AUTHOR/EDITOR	SHORT TITLE	PUBLISHER	B	ISBN	DATE	PRICE
1.1	Kümmel	INTRO TO NT	Abingdon		0-687-119575-6	1975	15.95
1.2	Koester	INTRO TO NT, 1	Fortress		0-8006-6010-2	1982	24.95
1.3	Koester	INTRO TO NT, 2	Fortress		0-8006-6011-0	1982	22.95
1.4	Marxsen	INTRO TO NT	Fortress	p	0-8006-1181-0	1968	n.a.
1.5	Moffatt	INTRO TO LIT OF NT	Seabury		0-567-07213-4	1918/1961[3]	11.95
1.6	Zahn	INTRO TO NT (3 v.)	Klock & Klock		0-86524-975-X	1909/1977	48.00
1.7	Davies, W. D.	INVITATION TO NT	Doubleday	p	0-385-04767-3	1969	6.95
1.8	Grant	HISTRCL INTRO NT	Simon & Schuster	p	0-671-21406-3	1972	4.95
1.9	Metzger	NT: BCKGRD, GROWTH	Abingdon	p	0-687-27913-5	1965	9.95
1.10	Guthrie	NT INTRO	InterVarsity		0-87784-953-6	1971[r]	24.95
1.11	Gundry, R. H.	SURVEY OF NT	Zondervan		0-310-25410-8	1982[r]	16.95
1.12	Tenney	NT SURVEY	Eerdmans		0-8028-3251-2	1961[r]	13.95
1.13	Martin, R. P.	NT FOUNDATIONS, 1	Eerdmans		0-8028-3444-2	1975	9.95
1.14	Martin, R. P.	NT FOUNDATIONS, 2	Eerdmans		0-8028-3506-2	1978	11.95
1.15	Kee	UNDERSTANDING NT	Prentice-Hall		0-13-936591-5	1983[4]	21.95
1.16	Price, J.	INTERPRETING NT	Holt, Rnhrt & Winst		0-03-085261-7	1971	20.95
1.17	Spivey & Smith	ANATOMY OF NT	Macmillan		0-02-415300-1	1982[3]	21.95
1.18	Perrin & Duling	NT: AN INTRO	Harcrt Brace Jovan	p	0-15-565726-7	1982[2]	14.95
1.19	Juel, Ackerman	INTRO TO NT LIT	Abingdon		0-687-01360-7	1978	13.95
1.19p	(same)	(same)	(same)	p	0-687-01361-5	1978	9.50
1.20	Perkins	READING NT	Paulist	p	0-8091-9535-6	1978	3.50
1.21	Connick	NT: INTRO	Dickenson	p	0-8221-0205-6	1978[2]	19.95
1.22	Thompson, L. L.	INTRDCNG BIB LIT	Prentice-Hall		0-13-498824-8	1979	19.95
1.23	Beck	READING NT TODAY	John Knox	p	0-8042-0391-1	1978	4.95
1.24	Walton	BIB STUD SOURCEBK	John Knox	p	0-8042-0009-2	1970/1981	9.95
1.25	Briggs	INTERP NT TODAY	Abingdon	p	0-687-19327-3	1973	6.75
1.26	Efird	NT WRITINGS	John Knox	p	0-8042-0246-X	1980	5.50
1.27*	Harvey	SOMETHING OVERHRD	John Knox		n.a.	1979	n.a.
1.28	Hendricksen	LAYMAN'S GDE BIB	Zondervan	p	0-310-37701-3	1979	5.95

BB#	AUTHOR/EDITOR	SHORT TITLE	PUBLISHER	B	ISBN	DATE	PRICE
1.29	Ramsay	LAYMAN'S GDE NT	John Knox	p	0-8042-0322-9	1980	10.50
1.30	Barrett	NT BACKGROUND	Harper & Row	p	0-06-130086-1	1956	4.95
1.31	Kee	ORIGINS CHRISTNTY	Prentice-Hall	p	0-13-642553-4	1973	12.95
1.32	Theron	EVIDENCE	Baker	p	0-8010-8849-6	1957/1980	4.95
1.33	Bruce	NT HISTORY	Doubleday	p	0-385-02533-5	1969/1972	5.95
1.34*	Ellison, H. L.	BABYLON-BETHLEHEM	John Knox		n.a.	n.d.	n.a.
1.35	Filson	NT HISTORY	Westminster		0-664-20525-9	1964	10.00
1.36	Lohse	NT ENVIRONMENT	Abingdon		0-687-27945-3	1976	12.95
1.36p	(same)	(same)	(same)	p	0-687-27944-5	1976	6.95
1.37	Reicke	NT ERA	Fortress	p	n.a.	n.d.	n.a.
1.38	Freyne	GALILEE	Notre Dame/Glazier	p	0-268-01002-1	1980	27.50
1.39	Goppelt	APOSTLC . . . TIMES	Baker		0-8010-3712-3	1970/1977	5.95
1.40	Hengel	JUDAISM & HELLEN	Fortress	p	0-8006-1495-X	1974/1981	19.95
1.41	Rhoads	ISRAEL IN RVLTN	Fortress		0-8006-0442-3	1976	5.00
1.41p	(same)	(same)	(same)	p	0-8006-1142-9	1976	3.00
1.42	Schürer	HISTORY, 1	T & T Clark		0-567-02242-0	1973	38.00
1.43	Schürer	HISTORY, 2	T & T Clark		0-567-02243-9	1979	38.00
1.44	Simon	JEWISH SECTS	Fortress		0-8006-0183-1	1967/1980	5.95
1.45	Smallwood	JEWS UNDER ROMAN	Brill	p	90-04-06403-6	1976/1981	50.00
1.45p	(same)	(same)	(same)	p	n.a.	1976/1981	n.a.
1.46	Vermes	DSS IN ENGLISH	Penguin	p	0-14-020551-9	1975[2]	3.00
1.47	Gaster	DEAD SEA SCRIPT	Doubleday	p	0-385-08859-0	1976[3]	7.95
1.48	Vermes	DEAD SEA SCROLLS	Fortress	p	0-8006-1435-6	1978/1981	8.50
1.49	Burrows	BURROWS ON DSS	Baker	p	0-8010-0752-6	1956–1958	11.95
1.50	Cross, F. M.	ANCIENT LIBRARY	Baker	p	0-8010-2447-1	1958/1980	5.95
1.51	Wilson, E.	ISRAEL AND DSS	Farrar, Straus & Gir	p	0-374-51341-4	1978	8.95
1.52	LaSor	SCROLLS & NT	Eerdmans	p	0-8028-1114-0	1972	4.95
1.53	Fitzmyer	DSS: MAJOR PUBS	Scholars Press		0-88414-053-9	1975/1977[2]	10.50
1.54	Harrington, D. J.	INTERPRETING NT	Glazier		0-89453-124-7	1979	8.95

BB#	AUTHOR/EDITOR	SHORT TITLE	PUBLISHER	B	ISBN	DATE	PRICE
1.54p	(same)	(same)	(same)	p	0-89453-189-1	1979	4.95
1.55	Kaiser & Kümmel	EXEGET METHOD	Seabury	p	0-8164-2303-2	1981ʳ	5.95
1.56	Marshall, I. H.	NT INTERP	Eerdmans		0-8028-3503-1	1978	13.95
1.57	Ladd	NT AND CRIT	Eerdmans	p	0-8028-1680-0	1966	4.95
1.58	Soulen	HANDBK BIB CRIT	John Knox	p	0-8042-0045-9	1981ʳ	9.95
1.59	Harrison et al.	BIBLICAL CRIT	Zondervan	p	0-310-37351-4	1978	5.95
1.60	Henry	NEW DIRECTIONS	Westminster		0-664-21376-6	1979	19.95
1.60p	(same)	(same)	(same)	p	0-664-24283-9	1979	9.95
1.61	Turner	HANDBK BIB STUD	Westminster	p	0-664-24436-X	1982	6.95
1.62	Hooker	STUDYING NT	Augsburg	p	0-8066-19341	1982	7.95
1.63	Maas	CHURCH. . HANDBK	Abingdon	p	0-687-08146-7	1982	9.95
2.1		EIGHT-TRANSLT NT	Tyndale		0-8423-4690-2	1974	19.95
2.1p	(same)	(same)	(same)	K	0-8423-4691-0	1974	14.95
2.2	Vaughn	NT FROM 26 TRANS	Zondervan	K	0-310-95505-X	1967	11.95
2.3		LAYMAN'S PAR BIB	Zondervan	K	0-310-95005-8	1973	29.95
2.4		LAYMAN'S PAR NT	Zondervan		0-310-95070-8	1970	n.a.
2.4p	(same)	(same)	(same)	p	0-310-95055-4	1970	n.a.
2.5*	Weigle	NT OCTAPLA	Nelson		n.a.	1962	n.a.
2.6*		6 VERSION PAR NT	Creation House		n.a.	1974	n.a.
2.7	Aland	SYNOPSIS/ENGLISH	Amer Bib Soc		n.a.	1982	5.95
2.8	Throckmorton	GOSP PARALLELS	Nelson		0-8407-5150-8	1979⁴	7.95
2.9	Francis & Sampley	PAULINE PARALLELS	Fortress	p	n.a.	n.d.	n.a.
2.10	Swanson	HORIZ SYNOPSIS	Baker		0-8010-8164-5	1979	23.95
2.11	Thomas & Gundry	HARMONY OF GOSP	Moody		0-8024-3413-4	1978	11.95
2.12	Robertson	HARMONY OF GOSP	Harper & Row		0-06-066890-3	1932/1974	10.95
2.13	Finegan	ENCOUNTER NT MSS	Eerdmans		0-8028-1836-6	1974	8.95
2.14	Metzger	TEXT OF NT	Oxford	p	0-19-500391-8	1968²	9.95
2.15	Campenhausen	FORMATION CHN BIB	Fortress		0-8006-1263-9	1977	7.50
2.16	Ackroyd	CAMBRDG HIST, 1-3	Cambridge	p	0-521-08778-3	1963–1970	144.00

BB#	AUTHOR/EDITOR	SHORT TITLE	PUBLISHER	B	ISBN	DATE	PRICE
2.16p	(same)	(same)	(same)	p	0-521-29018-X	1963–1970	39.95
2.17	Ackroyd & Evans	CAMBRIDGE HIST, 1	Cambridge		0-521-07418-5	1970	57.00
2.17p	(same)	(same)	(same)	p	0-521-09973-0	1970	16.95
2.18	Lampe	CAMBRIDGE HIST, 2	Cambridge		0-521-04255-0	1969	57.50
2.18p	(same)	(same)	(same)	p	0-521-29017-1	1969	16.95
2.19	Greenslade	CAMBRIDGE HIST, 3	Cambridge		0-521-04254-2	1963	57.50
2.19p	(same)	(same)	(same)	p	0-521-29016-3	1963	16.95
2.20	Bruce	BKS & PARCHMENTS	Revell		0-8007-0032-5	1963[3]	11.95
2.21*	Kenyon, F. G.	BIBLE & MSS	Harper & Row		n.a.	1958[r]	n.a.
2.22	Greenlee	INTR NT TEXT CRIT	Eerdmans	p	0-8028-1724-6	1964	4.95
2.23*	Price, I.	ANCESTRY ENG BIB	Harper & Row		n.a.	1956[3]	n.a.
2.24	Metzger	VERSIONS	Oxford		0-19-82617-0	1977	19.95
2.25	Westcott	BIBLE IN CHURCH	Baker	p	0-8010-9627-8	1865/1980	6.95
2.26	Westcott	SURVEY. . .CANON	Baker	p	0-8010-9640-5	1855/1980	12.95
2.27	Bruce	HIST BIBLE ENG	Oxford		0-19-520087-X	1978[3]	13.95
2.27p	(same)	(same)	(same)	p	0-19-520088-8	1978[3]	5.95
2.28	Lewis	ENGLISH BIBLE	Baker		0-8010-5599-7	1981	16.95
2.29	Hills & Eisenhart	HIST ENG BIBL	Amer Bib Soc	p	n.a.	1979[6]	2.00
2.30	Nida	THOUSAND TONGUES	Amer Bib Soc		n.a.	1972[r]	n.a.
2.31	Kubo & Specht	SO MANY VERSIONS	Zondervan	p	0-310-26941-5	1975	4.95
2.32	Walden	GUIDE BIB TRANS	Livingbooks	p	n.a.	1979	1.50
2.33	Glassman	TRANSLAT DEBATE	InterVarsity		0-87784-467-4	1981	4.95
2.34	Beekman & Callow	TRANSLATING	Zondervan	K	0-310-20771-1	n.d.	8.95
2.35	Carson	KJV DEBATE	Baker	p	0-8010-2427-7	1978	3.95
3.1	Darton	MODERN CONCORD	Doubleday		0-385-07901-X	1977	12.95
3.2	Hartdegen	CONCORDANCE: NAB	Nelson		0-8407-4900-7	1977	39.95
3.3	Morrison	ANALYT CONC: RSV	Westminster		0-664-20773-1	1979	45.00
3.4	Strong	EXHAUST CONCORD	Abingdon		0-687-40030-9	1980[r]	21.95
3.5	Strong	(same; thumb-indexed)	Abingdon		0-687-40031-7	1980[r]	26.95

BB#	AUTHOR/EDITOR	SHORT TITLE	PUBLISHER	B	ISBN	DATE	PRICE
3.6	Young	ANALYT CONCORD	Nelson		0-8407-4985-6	1980ʳ	18.95
3.7	Young	ANALYT CONCORD	Eerdmans		0-8028-8084-3	1955	19.95
3.8	Young	(same; thumb-indexed)	Eerdmans		0-8028-8085-1	1955	22.95
3.9	Young	ANALYT CONCORD	Church History		0-686-12407-3	n.d.	18.50
3.10	Young	(same; thumb-indexed)	Church History		0-686-12408-1	n.d.	22.50
3.11	Cruden	UNABRIDGED CONC	Broadman		0-8054-1123-2	n.d.	14.95
3.12	Cruden	UNABRIDGED CONC	Baker		0-8010-2316-5	n.d.	12.95
3.13	Cruden	CRUDEN'S CONCORD	Warne		0-7232-0260-5	1872	15.00
3.14	Cruden	CRUDEN'S CONCORD	Zondervan		0-310-22921-9	1949	11.95
3.14p	(same)	(same)	(same)	p	0-310-22921-9	1976	6.95
3.15	Cruden	COMPACT CONCORD	Zondervan		0-310-22910-3	1968	7.95
3.16	Cruden	HANDY CONCORD	Zondervan	p	0-310-22931-6	n.d.	2.95
3.17	Cruden	CRUDEN'S CONCORD	Jove	p	0-515-04776-7	1970	1.75
3.18	Bullinger	CRIT LEX & CONC	Zondervan		0-310-20310-4	1975	24.95
3.19	Ellison, J. W.	NELSON'S CONC: RSV	Nelson		0-8407-5015-3	1957/1978	49.95
3.20	[Moody]	BIBLE CONCORDANCE	Moody	p	0-8024-0040-X	1959	2.25
3.21	Strong	EXHAUST CONCORD	Nelson		0-8407-4999-6	1977	18.95
3.22	Strong	(same; thumb-indexed)	Nelson		0-8407-4967-8	1977	22.95
3.23	Strong	EXHAUST CONCORD	Baker	p	0-8010-8108-4	n.d.	13.95
3.24	Strong	EXHAUST CONCORD	Broadman	p	0-8054-1134-8	1978	13.95
3.25	Strong	CONCORDANCE	Nelson		0-8407-4986-4	1980	9.95
3.26	Goodrick & Kohlenberger	NIV CONCORDANCE	Zondervan		0-310-43650-8	1981	19.95
3.27	Joy	HARPER'S TOP CONC	Harper & Row	p	0-06-064229-7	1976ʳ	11.95
3.28	Viening	ZONDERVAN TOP BIB	Zondervan		0-310-33710-0	1969	19.95
3.29	Griffith	NEW WORLD INDEX	World		n.a.	1972	n.a.
3.30	Nave	TOPICAL BIBLE	Nelson		0-8407-4992-9	1979	n.a.
3.31	Nave	TOPICAL BIBLE	Baker	p	0-8010-6684-0	n.d.	4.95
3.32	Nave	TOPIC BIB (Abrdgd)	Moody	p	0-8024-0030-2	n.d.	3.95
3.33	Nave & Coder	TOPIC BIB (Enlrgd)	Moody	p	0-8024-5861-0	1975	19.95

BB#	AUTHOR/EDITOR	SHORT TITLE	PUBLISHER	B	ISBN	DATE	PRICE
3.34	Monser	TOP INDEX/DIGEST	Baker	p	0-8010-6083-4	1979	4.95
3.35	Wharton	COMP TOPIC BIB	Zondervan		0-310-3431-0	1972	7.95
3.36	[Holman]	TOPICAL BIBLE	Holman		0-87981-019-X	1973	5.95
3.37	Miller	TOPIC BIB CONCORD	Abingdon	p	0-687-42390-2	1977	1.75
4.1	Aland et al.	GREEK NT	Amer Bib Soc	K	3-438-05110-9	1983[3]	7.75
4.2	Aland et al.	NOV TEST GRAECE	Amer Bib Soc		3-438-05100-1	1979	8.65
4.3	Aland et al.	GREEK NT/DICT	Amer Bib Soc		3-438-05113-3	1983[3]	9.75
4.4	Aland et al.	GREEK NT	Amer Bib Soc	L	3-438-05111-7	1983[3]	14.00
4.5	Aland et al.	GK NT (Span intro)	Amer Bib Soc		3-438-05112-5	1975[3]	7.50
4.6	Aland et al.	GK NT (Span int & dic)	Amer Bib Soc		3-438-05114-1	1975[3]	9.75
4.7	Aland et al.	NOV TEST GRAECE	Amer Bib Soc	L	3-438-05101-X	1979	16.35
4.8	Aland et al.	NOV TEST GRAECE	Amer Bib Soc		3-438-05102-8	1979	15.50
4.9	Kilpatrick	HĒ KAINĒ DIATHĒKĒ	Amer Bib Soc		n.a.	1958	5.50
4.10		HĒ KAINĒ DIATHĒKĒ	Amer Bib Soc		n.a.	1844/1967	4.00
4.11		HĒ KAINĒ DIATHĒKĒ	Amer Bib Soc		n.a.	1967/1970	4.00
4.12	Friberg & Friberg	ANALYT GRK NT	Baker		0-8010-3496-5	1981	19.95
4.13	Aland	SYNOPSIS QUAT EV	Amer Bib Soc		3-438-05130-3	1978[10]	20.00
4.14	Aland	SYNOPSIS FOUR GOSP	Amer Bib Soc		3-438-05405-1	1979[3]	20.00
4.15	Huck & Greeven	SYNOPSIS	Eerdmans		0-8028-3568-6	1981[13]	22.50
4.16		INTERLIN GK-ENG NT	Baker	p	0-8010-5034-0	n.d.	19.95
4.17	Berry	INTERLIN GK-ENG NT	Baker		0-8010-0700-3	n.d.	12.95
4.18	Berry	INTERLIN GK-ENG NT	Zondervan		0-310-21170-0	n.d.	16.95
4.19	Marshall, A.	INTERLIN GK-ENG NT	Broadman	p	0-8054-1372-3	1978	9.95
4.20	Marshall, A.	INTERLIN GK-ENG NT	Zondervan		0-310-20380-5	1958	19.95
4.21	Marshall, A.	INTERLIN GK-ENG NT	Zondervan		0-310-28680-8	1958/1976	19.95
4.22	Marshall, A.	INTERLIN GK-ENG NT	Zondervan		0-310-20410-0	1958/1968	19.95
4.23	Marshall, A.	ZON PAR NT GK-ENG	Zondervan		0-310-95070-8	1975	19.95
4.24		NT IN GK & ENG	Amer Bib Soc		n.a.	1966	n.a.
4.25	Newberry	ENGLISHMAN'S GK NT	Zondervan		0-310-20330-9	1877/1970	14.95

BB#	AUTHOR/EDITOR	SHORT TITLE	PUBLISHER	B	ISBN	DATE	PRICE
4.26	Rahlfs	SEPTUAGINTA	Amer Bib Soc		3-438-05120-6	1935/1979	15.50
4.27	Brenton	SEPTUAG: GK-ENG	Zondervan		0-310-20420-8	1844/1970	29.95
4.28	Brenton	SEPT/APOC GK-ENG	Zondervan		0-310-20430-5	1844–1851/1972	39.95
4.29	Abbott-Smith	MANUAL GK LEX	Attic		0-567-01001-5	1937/1977	20.95
4.30	Arndt & Gingrich	GK-ENG LEXICON	Chicago		0-226-03932-3	1979[2]	37.50
4.30	(same)	(same)	Zondervan	V	0-310-20570-0	1979[2]	37.50
4.31	Newman	CONC GK-ENG DICT	Amer Bib Soc		3-348-06008-6	1971	3.50
4.32	Berry	GK-ENG NT LEXICON	Baker	p	0-8010-0791-7	1980	5.95
4.33	Gingrich	SHORTER LEXICON	Chicago		0-226-29520-6	1957/1965	10.00
4.33	(same)	(same)	Zondervan		0-310-25030-7	1957/1965	12.00
4.34	Moulton & Milligan	VOCABUL GK NT	Eerdmans		0-8028-2178-2	1949	24.95
4.35	Sophocles	GREEK LEXICON	Scribner		n.a.	1887/1957	n.a.
4.36	Hickie	GK-ENG LEXICON	Baker	p	0-8010-4164-3	1977	4.95
4.37	Souter	POCKET LEXICON	Oxford		0-19-864203-2	1916	14.95
4.38	Thayer	GK-ENG LEXICON	Zondervan		0-310-36850-2	1889/1956	18.95
4.39	Thayer	GK-ENG LEXICON	Broadman	p	0-8054-1376-6	1889/1978	10.95
4.40	Thayer	GK-ENG LEXICON	Baker	p	0-8010-8838-0	1889/n.d.	14.95
4.41	Kubo	READ GK-ENG LEX	Zondervan		0-310-26920-2	1975	12.95
4.42	Moulton, H. K.	ANALYT GK-ENG LEX	Zondervan		0-310-20280-9	1978	15.95
4.43	Liddell & Scott	GK-ENG LEXICON	Oxford		0-19-864210-5	1968[9]	79.00
4.44	Liddell & Scott	INTERM GK-ENG LEX	Oxford		0-19-910206-6	1889/1957	29.00
4.45	Liddell & Scott	ABRIDG GK-ENG LEX	Oxford		0-19-910207-4	1953	24.95
4.46	Lampe	PATRISTIC GK LEX	Oxford		0-19-864213-X	1961/1968	185.00
4.47	Kittel & Friedrich	THEOL DICT NT	Eerdmans		0-8028-2324-6	1963–1976	279.95
4.48	Cremer	BIB THEO LEX NT	Seabury		0-567-01004-X	1895[4]	27.95
4.49		COMP KONKORDANZ	de Gruyter		3-11-007313-7	1980	70.50
4.50	Smith	GK-ENG CONCORD	Herald		0-8361-1368-3	1955	24.95
4.51	Moulton & Geden	CONCORD GK TEST	Attic		0-567-01021-X	1978[5]	51.95
4.52	(same)	(same)	Kregel		0-8254-3205-7	1978[5]	49.50

BB#	AUTHOR/EDITOR	SHORT TITLE	PUBLISHER	B	ISBN	DATE	PRICE
4.53	Schmoller	HANDKONKORDANZ	Amer Bib Soc		0-438-05131-1	1973[15]	12.85
4.54	Gall	LAYM ENG-GK CON	Baker		0-8010-3686-0	1974	5.95
4.55	Stegenga	GK-ENG ANALYT CON	Hellenes-English		0-910710-01-5	1963	14.95
4.56	Wigram	ENGLSHMNS GK CON	Zondervan		0-310-20320-1	1883–1889	29.95
4.57	Wigram	ENGLSHMNS GK CON	Baker	p	0-8018-3357-8	1883/1980	23.95
4.58	Wigram	ENGLSHMNS GK CON	Broadman	p	0-8054-1388-X	1883/1980	26.95
4.59	Winter	WORD-STUDY CON	Tyndale		0-8423-8390-5	1978	29.95
4.60	(same)	(same)	Wm. Carey Lib		0-87808-741-9	1978	34.95
4.61	Hatch & Redpath	CONCORD SEPTUAG	International		3-201-0058-2	1892–1906/1975	160.00
4.62	Morrish	CONCORD SEPTUAG	Zondervan		0-310-20300-7	1900/1976	15.95
4.63	Metzger	TEXTUAL COMMENT	Amer Bib Soc	V	3-438-06010-8	1971/1972	6.45
5.1	Hudson	TEACH YOURSELF	McKay	p	0-679-10191-8	1979	4.95
5.2	Wenham	ELEMENTS OF NT GK	Cambridge	p	0-521-09842-2	1965	7.95
5.3	Wenham	KEY TO ELEMENTS	Cambridge	p	0-521-06769-3	1965	2.50
5.4	Nunn	SHORT SYNTAX	Cambridge	p	0-521-09941-2	1938[5]	7.50
5.5	Powers	LEARN TO READ	Eerdmans		0-8028-3578-3	1982	19.95
5.6	Goodrick	DO IT YOURSELF	Zondervan	p	0-310-41741-4	1976/1980	9.95
5.7	Werner	GREEK READER (3 vols)	Presbyterian & Reformed		0-87552-532-6	n.d.	27.00
5.8	Jay	NT GREEK	Seabury	p	0-281-02806-0	1961	10.50
5.9	Jay	KEY TO NT GREEK	Seabury	p	0-281-00664-4	1961	5.25
5.10	Machen	NT GREEK	Macmillan		0-02-373480-9	1923	17.95
5.11	Colwell & Tune	BEGINNER'S NT GREEK	Harper & Row		0-06-061530-3	1965	11.00
5.12	Davis	BEGINNER'S GRAMMAR	Harper & Row		0-06-061710-1	1923	10.95
5.13	Goetchius	LANGUAGE OF NT	Scribner		0-684-41263-2	1966	14.95
5.14	Goetchius	LANGUAGE: WORKBOOK	Scribner		0-684-41264-0	1966	10.95
5.15	Moulton, J. H.	INTRO NT GREEK	Macmillan		n.a.	1955[5]	n.a.
5.16	Drumwright	INTRO GREEK NT	Broadman		0-8054-1368-5	1980	9.95
5.17	Greenlee	CONCISE GRAMMAR	Eerdmans		0-8028-1092-6	1963	1.95
5.18	LaSor	HDBK NT GREEK (2 vols)	Eerdmans	p	0-8028-2341-6	1973	10.95

BB#	AUTHOR/EDITOR	SHORT TITLE	PUBLISHER	B	ISBN	DATE	PRICE
5.19	Mare	MASTER NT GREEK	Baker		0-8010-6064-8	1979	12.95
5.20	Marshall, A.	NT GREEK PRIMER	Zondervan	p	0-310-20401-1	1981	5.95
5.21	Story & Story	GREEK TO ME	Harper & Row	p	0-06-067705-8	1979	8.95
5.22	Summers	ESSENTIALS NT GREEK	Broadman		0-8054-1309-X	1950	8.95
5.23	Argyle	INTRO GRAMM NT GREEK	Cornell		0-8014-0018-X	1966	14.50
5.24	Gignac	INTRO NT GREEK	Loyola		0-8294-0223-3	n.d.	4.20
5.25	Dana & Mantey	MAN GRAM GREEK NT	Macmillan		0-02-327070-5	1927/1957	15.95
5.26	Moule	IDIOM BOOK NT GREEK	Cambridge		0-521-05774-4	1959^2	36.00
5.26p	(same)	(same)	(same)	p	0-521-09237-X	1959^2	9.95
5.27	Chamberlain	EXEG GRAMM GREEK NT	Baker	p	0-8010-2438-2	1941/1975	7.95
5.28	Robertson & Davis	SHORT GRAMMAR	Baker	p	0-8010-7656-0	1933^{10}	10.95
5.29	Zerwick	BIBLICAL GREEK	Loyola	p	0-8294-0317-5	1963	8.00
5.30	Vaughn & Gideon	GREEK GRAMMAR NT	Broadman		0-8054-1378-2	1975/1979	9.95
5.31	Funk	GREEK GRAMMAR NT	Chicago		0-226-27110-2	1961	22.00
5.32	(same)	(same)	Zondervan		0-310-24780-2	1961	22.00
5.33	Burton	SYNTAX MOODS/TENSES	Seabury		0-567-01002-3	1898^3/1976	11.50
5.34	Moulton, J. H.	GRAMMAR, 1: PROLEG	Seabury		0-567-01011-2	1908^3/1978	14.50
5.35	Howard	GRAMMAR, 2: ACCIDENCE	Seabury		0-567-01012-0	1922/1979	16.50
5.36	Turner	GRAMMAR, 3: SYNTAX	Seabury		0-567-01013-9	1963/1978	16.50
5.37	Turner	GRAMMAR, 4: STYLE	Seabury		0-567-01018-X	1976	12.50
5.38	Moulton et al.	(4-volume set)	Seabury		0-567-00901-7	1898–1976/1979	60.00
5.39	Robertson	GRAMM HIST RESEARCH	Broadman		0-8054-1308-1	1923^4/1934	39.95
5.40	Owings	CUM INDEX GK GRAMM	Baker	p	0-8010-6702-2	1983	7.95
5.41	Chapman	NT GREEK NOTEBOOK	Baker		0-8010-2389-0	1978^2	9.95
5.42	Chapman	GREEK NT INSERT	Baker	p	0-8010-2405-6	1978	1.95
5.43	Chapman	CARD-GUIDE/EXEG	Baker		0-8010-2396-3	1977	2.95
5.44	Chapman	CARD-GUIDE/NT GREEK	Baker		0-8010-2388-2	1976	1.75
5.45	Mueller	GRAMM AIDS NT GREEK	Eerdmans	p	0-8028-1447-6	1972	2.45
5.46	Peterson	CONJUGATION CHART	Zondervan		0-310-31080-6	n.d.	3.95

BB#	AUTHOR/EDITOR	SHORT TITLE	PUBLISHER	B	ISBN	DATE	PRICE
5.47	Boyer	MANUAL OF GREEK FORMS	BMH	p	0-88469-007-5	n.d.	4.95
5.48	Metzger	LEXICAL AIDS	Allenson	p	0-8401-1618-7	1969[3]	4.95
5.49	Morrison & Barnes	NT WORD LISTS	Eerdmans		0-8028-1141-8	1964	3.95
5.50	Rogers	GREEK WORD ROOTS	Baker	p	0-8010-7707-9	1968	1.95
5.51	Berry	DICTIONARY SYNONYMS	Zondervan		0-310-21160-3	1897/1979	5.95
5.52	Zerwick	GRAMM ANALYSIS, 1	Loyola	V	0-8294-0316-7	1974	15.00
5.53	Zerwick	GRAMM ANALYSIS, 2	Loyola	V	n.a.	1979	n.a.
5.54	Rienecker	LINGUISTIC KEY, 1	Zondervan		0-310-32020-8	[1970] 1976	15.95
5.55	Rienecker	LINGUISTIC KEY, 2	Zondervan		0-310-32030-5	[1970] 1980	17.95
5.56	(same)	(same, one vol)	(same)	V	0-310-32050-X	1980	27.95
5.57	(same)	(same, two-vol set)	(same)		0-310-32148-8	1980	31.90
5.58	Holly	CATEGORIZED NT VOCAB	Attic		0-85150-119-2	1978	12.50
5.59	(same)	(same)	Baker		0-8010-4224-0	1978/1980	6.95
5.60	Alsop	INDEX TO BAUER	Zondervan	p	0-310-44031-9	1981[r]	11.95
5.61	Han	PARSING GUIDE	Herald	p	0-8361-1653-4	1971	14.95
5.62*	Crosby & Schaeffer	INTRO TO GREEK	Allyn & Bacon		n.a.	1928	n.a.
5.63	Goodwin	GREEK GRAMMAR	St. Martin		0-312-34825-8	1879[2]	18.95
5.64	Goodwin & Gulick	GREEK GRAMMAR	Caratzas		0-89241-118-X	1958	22.50
5.64p	(same)	(same)	(same)	p	0-89241-332-8	1958	12.50
5.65	Smyth/[Messing]	GREEK GRAMMAR	Harvard		0-674-3625-0	1920/1956[r]	18.50
5.66	Conybeare & Stock	SEPTUAGINT GREEK	Zondervan	p	0-310-43001-1	1909/1980	5.95
6.1	Douglas	NEW BIBLE DICTIONARY	Eerdmans		0-8423-4667-8	1982[2]	24.95
6.2	McKenzie	DICTIONARY OF BIBLE	Macmillan		0-685-07628-8	1965	17.95
6.2p	(same)	(same)	(same)	p	0-685-07629-6	1965	10.95
6.3	Miller & Miller	HARPER'S DICT BIBLE	Harper & Row		0-06-065676-X	1973[r]/1978	16.95
6.4	(same)	(same; thumb-indexed)	(same)		0-06-065674-3	1973[r]/1978	21.95
6.5	Gehman	NEW WESTMINSTER DICT	Westminster		0-664-21277-8	1970	18.95
6.6	(same)	(same; thumb-indexed)	(same)		0-664-21388-X	1970	21.95
6.7	Alexander	EERDMANS' FAM ENCYC	Eerdmans		0-8028-3517-1	1978	18.95

BB#	AUTHOR/EDITOR	SHORT TITLE	PUBLISHER	B	ISBN	DATE	PRICE
6.8	Alexander	EERDMANS' CONC ENCYC	Eerdmans	p	0-8028-1876-5	1981	9.95
6.9	Davis	DICTIONARY OF BIBLE	Baker		0-8010-2805-1	1954[4]	18.95
6.10	Davis	DAVIS' DICTIONARY	Revell		0-8007-0061-9	1972[5]	18.95
6.11	Davis	DAVIS' DICTIONARY	Broadman		0-8054-1124-0	1973	14.95
6.12	Davis	DAVIS' DICTIONARY	Church History		0-686-12413-8	n.d.	18.00
6.13	Smith/Lemmons	NEW SMITH'S BIB DICT	Doubleday		0-385-04872-6	1966	8.95
6.13p	(same)	(same)	(same)	p	0-385-14652-3	1979[r]	6.95
6.14	(same)	(same; thumb-indexed)	(same)		0-385-04869-6	1966	9.95
6.15	Peloubet & Peloubet	SMITH'S BIBLE DICT	Nelson		0-8407-5170-2	1979	8.95
6.15p	(same)	(same)	(same)	p	0-8407-5700-X	1979	6.95
6.16		SMITH'S BIBLE DICT	Holman		0-87981-033-5	n.d.	8.50
6.17		(same; thumb-indexed)	(same)		0-87981-035-1	n.d.	10.95
6.18		SMITH'S BIBLE DICT	Jove	p	0-515-06182-4	1967	3.50
6.19		SMITH'S BIBLE DICT	Revell	p	0-8007-8039-6	n.d.	2.95
6.20		SMITH'S BIBLE DICT	Zondervan		0-310-32870-5	1955	9.95
6.21	Unger	UNGER'S BIBLE DICT	Moody		0-8024-9035-2	1961[3]	21.95
6.22	(same)	(same; thumb-indexed)	(same)		0-8024-9036-0	1961[3]	24.95
6.23	Smith	WESTM CONCISE DICT	Westminster	p	0-664-24363-0	1981	5.95
6.24	Hastings	DICTIONARY OF BIBLE	Scribner		0-684-15556-7	1963[r]	45.00
6.25	Tenney	ZOND PICTORIAL DICT	Zondervan		0-310-33160-9	1963/1967[r]	21.95
6.26	(same)	(same; thumb-index)	(same)		0-310-33170-6	1963/1967[r]	24.95
6.27	Bryant	NEW COMPACT DICT	Zondervan		0-310-22080-7	1967	8.95
6.27p	(same)	(same)	(same)	p	0-310-22061-0	1967	4.95
6.28	Boyd	BOYD'S BIBLE DICT	Holman	p	0-87981-087-4	n.d.	2.95
6.29	Buttrick & Crim	INTERPRETER'S DICT	Abingdon		0-687-19268-4	1976	84.95
6.30	Hillyer	ILLUS BIBLE DICT	InterVarsity		0-8423-7575-2	1980	99.50
6.31	Bromiley	INTERNAT BIB ENC, 1	Eerdmans		0-8028-8161-0	1939/1979[r]	32.50
6.32	Bromiley	INTERNAT BIB ENC, 2	Eerdmans		0-8028-8162-9	1939/1982[r]	35.00
6.33	Bromiley	INT BIB ENC (2 vol)	Eerdmans		0-8028-8160-2	n.a.	n.a.

BB#	AUTHOR/EDITOR	SHORT TITLE	PUBLISHER	B	ISBN	DATE	PRICE
6.34	Tenney	ZOND ENC BIB (5 vols)	Zondervan		0-310-33188-9	1975	119.95
6.35	Pfeiffer et al.	WYCL BIB ENC (2 vols)	Moody		0-8024-9697-0	1975	40.00
6.36	Orr et al.	INT BIB ENC, 1-4	Eerdmans		0-8028-8045-2	1939/1957	75.00
6.37	Cheyne & Black	ENCYC BIB (4 v)	Gordon		0-8490-1764-5	1899–1903/1977	425.95
6.38	Smith, W.	SMITH BIB DIC (4 vols)	Baker		0-8010-8211-0	1870/1981	95.00
6.39	Brown, C.	NEW INT DICT NT, 1	Zondervan		0-310-21890-X	1975	29.95
6.40	(same)	NEW INT DICT NT, 2	Zondervan		0-310-21900-0	1976	31.95
6.41	(same)	NEW INT DICT NT, 3	Zondervan		0-310-21910-8	1978	44.95
6.42	(same)	NEW INT DICT NT, set	Zondervan		0-310-21928-0	1975–1978	100.00
6.43	Bauer, J. B.	ENCYC BIB THEOL	Crossroad		0-8245-0042-3	1970/1981	32.50
6.44	Rahner	ENCYC THEOLOGY	Crossroad		0-8245-0303-1	1975	39.50
6.45	Leon-Dufour	DICT BIB THEOL	Seabury		0-8164-1146-8	1973ʳ	27.50
6.46	Leon-Dufour	DICT OF NT	Harper & Row		0-06-062100-1	1980	21.95
6.47	Vine	EXP DICT NT WORDS	Nelson		0-8407-5138-9	1978	14.95
6.48	Vine	EXP DICT OT/NT WDS	Revell		0-8007-1282-X	1981	17.95
6.49	Cruden	CRUDEN PCKT DICT	Baker	p	0-8010-2380-7	1976	3.95
6.50	Miller & Miller	HARP ENC BIB LIFE	Harper & Row		0-06-065676-X	1978ʳ	16.95
6.51	Cross & Livingstone	OXFORD DIC CHRCH	Oxford		0-19-211545-6	1974²	49.95
6.52	Douglas & Cairns	NEW INT DIC CHRCH	Zondervan		0-310-23830-7	1974/1978ʳ	29.95
6.53	Livingstone	CONC OX DIC CHRCH	Oxford		0-19-211549-9	1978	18.95
6.53p	(same)	(same)	(same)	p	0-19-283014-7	1978	8.95
6.54	Brauer	WESTM DICT CHURCH	Westminster		0-664-21285-9	1971	19.95
6.55	Dowley	EERD HDBK HIS CHNTY	Eerdmans		0-8028-3450-7	1977	24.95
6.56*	Roth	ENC JUDAICA (16 vols)	Macmillan		n.a.	1971–1972	n.a.
6.57	Singer	JEWISH ENC (12 vols)	Ktav		0-87068-104-4	1901–1906/1964	250.00
6.58	(same	(same)	Gordon		0-8490-2101-4	1901–1906/1976	998.95
6.59	Hastings	ENC REL & ETH (13 v)	Scribner		0-684-13857-3	1908–1927	250.00
7.1	May	OXFORD BIB ATLAS	Oxford		0-19-211556-1	1974²	13.95
7.1p	(same)	(same)	(same)	p	0-19-211557-X	1974²	6.95

BB#	AUTHOR/EDITOR	SHORT TITLE	PUBLISHER	B	ISBN	DATE	PRICE
7.2	Wright & Filson	WESTM HIST ATLAS	Westminster		0-664-20535-6	1956[r]	16.95
7.3	Grollenberg	PENG SHORT ATLAS	Penguin		0-14-051056-7	1978	4.95
7.4	Monson	STUDENT MAP MANUAL	Zondervan		0-310-42980-3	1979	34.95
7.5	Aharoni & Avi-Yonah	MACMILL BIB ATLAS	Macmillan		0-02-500590-1	1977[t]	24.95
7.6	Bruce	BIBLE HIST ATLAS	Crossroad		0-8245-0418-6	1982	14.95
7.7	Blaiklock	ZOND PICT ATLAS	Zondervan		0-310-21240-5	1969	19.95
7.8	Pfeiffer	BAKER'S BIBLE ATLAS	Baker		0-8010-6930-0	1961[r]	15.95
7.9*		ATLAS OF BIBLE	Nelson		n.a.	1956	n.a.
7.10	Grollenberg	WESTM HIST MAPS	Westminster	p	0-664-29077-9	n.d.	1.85
7.11	Wright & Filson	ATLAS BIBLE LANDS	Hammond	p	0-8437-7055-4	1977[t]	3.95
7.12	Frank	COMPACT BIB ATLAS	Baker	p	0-8010-2432-3	1979	3.95
7.13		ATLAS GK ROM WORLD	Noyes		0-8155-5060-X	1981	48.00
7.14	Hammond	SHORT ATLAS CLASSIC	Dutton	p	n.a.	1962/1967	n.a.
7.15	Scullard & v d Heyden	ATLAS OF ISRAEL	Elsevier		0-444-40740-5	1970	256.00
7.16*		GRSS HIST WELTATL, 1	Bayerische Schulbuch	p	n.a.	1958[3]	n.a.
7.17*	v d Meer & Mohrman	ATL EARLY CHRSTNY	Nelson		n.a.	1958	n.a.
7.18*	v d Heyden & Scullard	ATLAS CLASS WRLD	Nelson	p	n.a.	1959	n.a.
7.19	Aharoni	LAND OF BIBLE	Westminster		0-664-242669-9	1980[r]	19.95
7.20	Avi-Yonah	HOLY LAND	Baker		0-8010-0010-6	n.d.	4.95
7.21	Baly	GEOGRAPHY	Harper & Row		0-06-060371-2	1974[2]	16.95
7.22	Berrett	DISC WRLD OF BIB	Nelson		0-8407-5182-6	1973/1979	14.95
7.23	Pfeiffer & Vos	WYCLIF HIST GEOG	Moody		0-8024-9699-7	1967	15.95
7.24	Avi-Yonah & Stern	ENC ARCH EXCAV, 1	Prentice-Hall		0-13-275115-1	1975	25.00
7.25	(same)	ENC ARCH EXCAV, 2	Prentice-Hall		0-13-275123-2	1975	25.00
7.26	(same)	ENC ARCH EXCAV, 3	Prentice-Hall		0-13-275131-3	1975	25.00
7.27	(same)	ENC ARCH EXCAV, 4	Prentice-Hall		0-13-275149-6	1975	25.00
7.28	Finegan	ARCH NT: JESUS	Princeton		0-691-03534-2	1970	45.00
7.28p	(same)	(same)	(same)	p	0-691-02000-0	1970	8.95
7.29	Finegan	ARCH NT: APOSTLES	Westview		0-86531-064-5	1981	36.50

BB#	AUTHOR/EDITOR	SHORT TITLE	PUBLISHER	B	ISBN	DATE	PRICE
7.30	Stilwell	ENCYC CLASS SITES	Princeton		0-691-03542-3	1976	165.00
7.31	Aharoni	ARCHAEOL ISRAEL	Westminster		0-664-21384-7	1982	27.50
7.31p	(same)	(same)	(same)	p	0-664-24430-0	1982	18.95
7.32*	Blaiklock	ARCHAEOL NT	Zondervan		n.a.	1970	n.a.
7.33	Cornfeld & Freedman	ARCHAEOL BIBLE	Harper & Row		0-06-061584-2	1976	19.95
7.33p	(same)	(same)	(same)	p	0-06-061587-7	1976/1982	12.95
7.34	Dever & Lance	MANUAL FIELD EXC	Ktav		0-87820-303-6	1979	12.50
7.35	Kenyon, K.	BIB RECENT ARCH	John Knox	p	0-8042-0010-6	1979	6.95
7.36*	Moorey	BIBLICAL LANDS	Elsevier		n.a.	1975	n.a.
7.37	Pfeiffer	BIBLICAL WORLD	Baker		0-8010-6915-7	1966	18.95
7.38	Schoville	BIB ARCH FOCUS	Baker		0-8010-8112-2	1981	15.95
7.39	Shanks	JUDAISM IN STONE	Harper & Row		n.a.	1979	n.a.
7.40	Levine	ANC SYNAGOGUES	Wayne State		0-8143-1706-5	1981	24.00
7.41	Thompson	BIB AND ARCHAEOL	Eerdmans		0-8028-3545-7	1981	15.95
7.42	Unger	ARCH AND NT	Zondervan		0-310-33380-6	1962	13.95
7.43	Vos	ARCH BIB LANDS	Moody		0-8024-0293-3	1978	11.95
7.44	Yamauchi	NT CITIES ASIA MIN	Baker	p	0-8010-9915-3	1980	7.95
7.45	Wiseman & Yamauchi	ARCHAEOL AND BIB	Zondervan	p	0-310-36831-5	1979	3.95
7.46	Wright	BIBLIC ARCHAEOL	Westminster	p	0-664-20420-1	1963r	24.95
8.1*	Blair	ABINGDON BIB HDBK	Abingdon		n.a.	1975	n.a.
8.1p	(same	(same)	(same)	p	n.a.	1975	n.a.
8.2	Alexander & Alexander	EERDMANS HANDBOOK	Eerdmans		0-8028-3436-1	1973	24.95
8.3	Packer et al.	BIBLE ALMANAC	Nelson		0-8407-5162-1	1980	16.95
8.4	Blaiklock	HANDBOOK TO BIBLE	Revell	p	0-8007-5055-1	1981	5.95
8.5	Blunt et al.	HELPS TO STUDY	Oxford		0-19-122402-2	1951	n.a.
8.6	Coleman	WHO, WHAT, WHERE	Chariot/Cook		0-89191-291-6	1980	10.95
8.7	Alexander & Alexander	EERD CONCISE HDBK	Eerdmans	p	0-8028-1875-7	1981	9.95
8.8	Foulkes	POCKET GUIDE	InterVarsity	p	0-87784-580-8	1978	2.95
8.9	Bennett	BENNETT'S GUIDE	Seabury	p	0-8164-2397-0	1982	9.95

BB#	AUTHOR/EDITOR	SHORT TITLE	PUBLISHER	B	ISBN	DATE	PRICE
8.10	Halley	HALLEY'S HANDBOOK	Zondervan		0-310-25720-4	1927	8.95
8.11	(same)	(same: large print)	(same)	V	0-310-41390-7	1927	17.95
8.12	(same)	(same: large print)	(same)	p	0-310-25727-1	1927	12.95
8.13	Wilson	WESTM CONC HDBK	Westminster		0-664-24272-3	1979	3.95
8.14	Unger	UNGER'S BIB HDBK	Moody		0-8024-9039-5	1966	9.95
8.15	Jones	NT ILLUSTRATIONS	Cambridge		0-521-05446-X	1966	24.50
8.15p	(same)	(same)	(same)	p	0-521-09376-9	1966	9.95
8.16	Westermann	HANDBOOK TO NT	Augsburg	p	0-8066-1600-8	1982	7.50
9.1	Brown, R. E., et al.	JEROME COMMENTARY	Prentice-Hall		0-13-509612-X	1968	43.95
9.2	Black & Rowley	PEAKE'S COMMENTARY	Nelson		0-8407-5019-6	1962	34.95
9.3	Guthrie & Motyer	NEW BIBLE COMM	Eerdmans		0-8028-2281-9	1970	24.95
9.4	Howley et al.	LAYMAN'S COMM	Zondervan		0-310-22010-6	1978	27.95
9.5*	Clarke	CONCISE BIBLE COMM	Macmillan		n.a.	1953	n.a.
9.6	Laymon	INTER ONE-VOL COMM	Abingdon		0-687-19299-4	1971	22.95
9.7	(same)	(same; thumb-index)	(same)		0-687-19300-1	1971	27.95
9.8	Pfeiffer & Harrison	WYCLIFFE BIB COMM	Moody		0-8024-9695-4	1962	21.95
9.9	Fuller et al.	NEW CATHOLIC COMM	Nelson (England)		17-122010-2	1969	50.00
9.10*	Blaiklock	COMMENTARY ON NT	Revell		n.a.	1978	n.a.
9.11	Franzmann & Roehrs	CONCORD SELF-STUDY	Concordia	p	n.a.	1978	5.95
9.12	Neill	HARP BIBLE COMM	Harper & Row		0-06-066090-2	1962	15.95
9.13	Allen	MATTHEW—ICC	Seabury		0-567-05021-1	1912³	8.95
9.14	Hill	MATTHEW—NCBC	Eerdmans	p	0-8028-1886-2	1981ʳ	8.95
9.15	McNeile	MATTHEW	Baker	p	0-8010-6099-0	1915/1980	17.95
9.16	Schweizer	MATTHEW	John Knox		0-8042-0257-6	1975	4.50
9.17	Senior	INVITATION TO MATT	Doubleday	p	0-385-12211-X	1977	4.95
9.18	Obach & Kirk	MATTHEW	Paulist	p	0-8091-2173-5	1978	12.95
9.19	Plummer	MATTHEW	Baker	p	0-8010-7078-3	1909/1982	3.50
9.20	Kingsbury	MATTHEW	Fortress	p	0-8006-0586-1	1977	14.95
9.21	Brown, R. E.	BIRTH OF MESSIAH	Doubleday	p	0-385-05907-3	1977	14.95

BB#	AUTHOR/EDITOR	SHORT TITLE	PUBLISHER	B	ISBN	DATE	PRICE
9.21p	(same)	(same)	(same)	p	0-385-05405-X	1979	7.95
9.22	Tasker	MATTHEW—TNTC	Eerdmans	p	0-8028-1400-X	1962	4.95
9.23	Fenton	MATTHEW	Westminster		0-664-21343-X	1978	12.95
9.24	Fenton	MATTHEW	Penguin	p	0-14-020488-1	1964	6.95
9.25	Meier	MATTHEW—NTM	Glazier		0-89453-126-3	1979	12.95
9.25p	(same)	(same)	(same)	p	0-89453-191-3	1979	9.95
9.26	Argyle	MATTHEW—CBCNT	Cambridge		0-521-04197-X	1963	19.95
9.26p	(same)	(same)	(same)	p	0-521-09198-5	1963	7.50
9.27	Trilling	MATTHEW 1—NTSR	Crossroad		0-8245-0334-1	1969/1981	10.00
9.27p	(same)	(same)	(same)	p	0-8245-0110-1	1981	4.95
9.28	(same)	MATTHEW 2—NTSR	Crossroad		0-8245-0335-X	1969/1981	10.00
9.28p	(same)	(same)	(same)	p	0-8245-0111-X	1981	4.95
9.29	Cranfield	MARK—CGTC	Cambridge		0-521-04253-4	1959	56.00
9.29p	(same)	(same)	(same)	p	0-521-09204-3	1959	16.95
9.30	Gould	MARK—ICC	Seabury		0-567-05022-X	1896	15.95
9.31	Taylor	MARK	Baker	p	0-8010-8859-3	1966/1981	13.95
9.32	Cole	MARK—TNTC	Eerdmans	p	0-8028-1401-8	1962	4.95
9.33	Anderson	MARK—NCBC	Eerdmans	p	0-8028-1887-0	1981ʳ	8.95
9.34	Harrington, W.	MARK—NTM	Glazier		0-89453-127-1	1979	10.95
9.34p	(same)	(same)	(same)	p	0-89453-192-1	1979	7.95
9.35	Lane	MARK—NICNT	Eerdmans		0-8028-2340-8	1973	n.a.
9.36	Moule	MARK—CBCNT	Cambridge		0-521-04210-0	1965	13.95
9.36p	(same)	(same)	(same)		0-521-09288-4	1965	5.95
9.37	Nineham	MARK—NWPC	Westminster		0-664-21344-8	1964/1978	n.a.
9.38	Nineham	MARK	Penguin	p	0-14-020489-X	1964	4.95
9.39	Schweizer	MARK	John Knox		0-8042-0250-8	1970	16.95
9.40	Schnackenburg	MARK 1—NTSR	Crossroad		0-8245-0336-8	1971/1981	10.00
9.40p	(same)	(same)	(same)		0-8245-0112-8	1981	4.95
9.41	(same)	MARK 2—NTSR	(same)	p	0-8245-0113-6	1981	10.00

BB#	AUTHOR/EDITOR	SHORT TITLE	PUBLISHER	B	ISBN	DATE	PRICE
9.41p	(same)	(same)	(same)	p	0-686-85824-7	1981	4.95
9.42	Fitzmyer	LUKE 1:1-9—AB	Doubleday		0-385-00515-6	1981	18.00
9.43	Plummer	LUKE—ICC	Seabury		0-567-05023-8	1922[5]	17.95
9.44	Marshall	LUKE—NIGTC	Eerdmans		0-8028-3512-0	1978	24.95
9.45*		LUKE	Macmillan		n.a.	1930	n.a.
9.45*	Creed	LUKE	Westminster		0-664-21345-6	1964/1978	9.50
9.46	Caird	LUKE—NWPC	Penguin		0-14-020490-3	1964	3.95
9.47	Caird	LUKE	Doubleday		0-385-12209-8	1977	4.95
9.48	Karris	INVITATION TO LUKE	Clayton		0-915644-21-5	1980	12.00
9.49	Danker	JESUS ACC TO LUKE	Eerdmans	p	0-8028-1863-3	1966	7.95
9.50	Ellis	LUKE—NCBC	Eerdmans	p	0-8028-2184-7	1950	16.95
9.51	Geldenhuys	LUKE—NICNT	Eerdmans	p	0-8028-1402-6	1974	4.95
9.52	Morris	LUKE—TNTC	Cambridge		0-521-04200-3	1965	19.95
9.53	Tinsley	LUKE—CBCNT	(same)	p	0-521-09252-3	1965	7.50
9.53p	(same)	(same)	Crossroad		0-8245-0338-4	1969/1981	10.00
9.54	Stöger	LUKE 1—NTSR	(same)	p	0-8245-0114-4	1981	4.95
9.54p	(same)	(same)	(same)		0-8245-0339-2	1969/1981	10.00
9.55	(same)	LUKE 2—NTSR	(same)	p	0-8245-0115-2	1981	4.95
9.55p	(same)	(same)	Westminster		0-664-21364-2	1978[2]	27.95
9.56	Barrett	JOHN	Doubleday		0-385-01517-8	1979[2]	18.00
9.57	Brown, R. E.	JOHN, 1:i-xii—AB	Doubleday		0-385-03761-9	1970	18.00
9.58	Brown, R. E.	JOHN, 2:xiii-xxi—AB	Seabury		0-567-05024-6	1928	17.00
9.59	Bernard	JOHN 1:1-7—ICC	Seabury		0-567-05025-4	1928	17.00
9.60	Bernard	JOHN 2:8-21—ICC	Westminster		0-664-20893-2	1964/1971	21.50
9.61	Bultmann	JOHN	Crossroad		0-8245-0098-9	1968/1980	29.50
9.62	Schnackenburg	JOHN 1:1-4	Crossroad		0-8245-0311-2	1979/1981	29.50
9.63	Schnackenburg	JOHN 2:5-12	Crossroad		0-8245-0312-0	1982	29.50
9.64	Schnackenburg	JOHN 3:13-21	Baker	p	0-8010-7068-6	1881/1981	9.95
9.65	Plummer	JOHN	Baker		0-8010-9644-8	1903/1919	16.95
9.66	Westcott	JOHN					

BB#	AUTHOR/EDITOR	SHORT TITLE	PUBLISHER	B	ISBN	DATE	PRICE
9.67	Lindars	JOHN—NCBC	Eerdmans	p	0-8028-1864-1	1972	12.95
9.68	Marsh	JOHN—NWPC	Westminster		0-664-21346-4	1968/1978	17.50
9.69	Marsh	GOSP JOHN	Penguin	p	0-14-02049-1	1968	4.95
9.70	Morris	JOHN—NICTC	Eerdmans		0-8028-2296-7	1970	19.95
9.71	Tasker	JOHN—TNTC	Eerdmans	p	0-8028-1403-4	1960	3.95
9.72	Smith, D. M.	JOHN	Fortress	p	0-8006-0582-9	1976	3.50
9.73	Hunter	JOHN—CBCNT	Cambridge		0-521-04201-1	1965	18.95
9.73p	(same)	(same)	(same)	p	0-521-09255-8	1965	7.50
9.74	McPolin	JOHN—NTM	Glazier		0-89453-129-8	1979	9.95
9.74p	(same)	(same)	(same)	p	0-89453-194-8	1979	6.95
9.75	Huckle & Visokay	JOHN 1—NTSR	Crossroad		0-8245-0340-6	1981	10.00
9.75p	(same)	(same)	(same)	p	0-8245-0116-0	1981	4.95
9.76	Blank	JOHN 2—NTSR	Crossroad		0-686-85822-0	1981	10.00
9.76p	(same)	(same)	(same)	p	0-8245-0117-9	1981	4.95
9.77	Blank	JOHN 3—NTSR	Crossroad		n.a.	1981	10.00
9.77p	(same)	(same)	(same)	p	0-8245-0118-7	1981	4.95
9.78*	Lightfoot, R. H.	JOHN'S GOSPEL	Oxford	p	n.a.	1956	n.a.
9.79	Westcott	GOSP JOHN (ENG)	Eerdmans	p	0-8028-3288-1	1880/1950	n.a.
9.80	Gaebelein	EXP BIB COMM, 9	Zondervan		0-310-36510-4	1981	19.95
9.81	Foakes Jackson & Lake	BEGINNINGS (5-v set)	Baker	p	0-8010-5084-7	1920–1933/1979	49.50
9.82	Haenchen	ACTS	Westminster		0-664-20919-X	1965/1971	24.50
9.83	Bruce	ACTS	Eerdmans		0-8028-3056-0	1953	8.95
9.84	Bruce	ACTS—NICNT	Eerdmans		0-8028-2182-0	1954	14.95
9.85	Munck	ACTS—AB	Doubleday		0-385-00914-3	1967	16.00
9.86	Packer	ACTS—CBCNT	Cambridge		0-521-04221-6	1966	21.50
9.86p	(same)	(same)	(same)	p	0-521-09383-X	1966	7.50
9.87	Marshall, I. H.	ACTS—TNTC	Eerdmans	p	0-8028-1423-9	1980	6.95
9.88	Neill	ACTS—NCBC	Eerdmans	p	0-8028-1904-4	1981r	7.95
9.89	Crowe	ACTS—NTM	Glazier		0-89453-131-X	1980	9.95

BB#	AUTHOR/EDITOR	SHORT TITLE	PUBLISHER	B	ISBN	DATE	PRICE
9.89p	(same)	(same)	(same)	p	0-89453-196-4	1980	5.95
9.90	Gaebelein	EXPOS BIB COM, 9	Zondervan		0-310-36510-4	1981	19.95
9.91	Kürzinger	ACTS 1—NTSR	Crossroad	p	0-8245-0343-0	1961/1981	10.00
9.91p	(same)	(same)	(same)		0-8245-0119-5	1981	4.95
9.92	Kürzinger	ACTS 2—NTSR	Crossroad		0-8245-0344-9	1971/1981	10.00
9.92p	(same)	(same)	(same)	p	0-8245-0120-9	1981	4.95
9.93	Krodel	ACTS	Fortress	p	0-8006-0585-3	1981	3.95
9.94	Karris	INVITATION TO ACTS	Doubleday	p	0-385-12210-1	1978	4.95
9.95	Cranfield	ROMANS 1:1-8—ICC	Seabury		0-567-05040-8	1975	23.95
9.96	Cranfield	ROMANS 2:9-16—ICC	Seabury		0-567-05041-6	1979	23.95
9.97	Sanday & Headlam	ROMANS—ICC	Seabury		0-567-05026-2	1902[5]	n.a.
9.98	Käsemann	ROMANS	Eerdmans		0-8028-3499-X	1978/1980	22.50
9.99	Barrett	ROMANS—HNTC	Harper & Row		0-06-060550-2	1958	10.95
9.100	Barth, K.	ROMANS	Oxford	p	0-19-500294-6	1968[6]	8.95
9.101	Luther	LECT ON ROMANS	Westminster	K	0-664-24151-4	1961	8.95
9.102	Best	ROMANS—CBCNT	Cambridge		0-521-04197-X	1967	19.95
9.102p	(same)	(same)	(same)		0-521-09198-5	1967	6.95
9.103	Black	ROMANS—NCBC	Eerdmans	p	0-8028-1905-2	1981[1]	5.95
9.104	Murray	ROMANS—NICNT	Eerdmans	p	0-8028-2286-X	1960	16.95
9.105	Gaebelein	EXP BIB COM, 10	Zondervan		0-310-36520-1	1976	16.95
9.106	Bruce	ROMANS—TNTC	Eerdmans	p	0-8028-1405-0	1963	4.95
9.107	Kertelge	ROMANS—NTSR	Crossroad		0-8245-0345-7	1972/1981	10.00
9.107p	(same)	(same)	(same)	p	0-8245-0121-7	1981	4.95
9.108	Maly	ROMANS—NTM	Glazier		0-89453-132-8	1980	8.95
9.108p	(same)	(same)	(same)	p	0-09453-197-2	1980	4.95
9.109	Getty	INVITATION TO EP, 1	Doubleday	p	0-385-14796-1	1982	4.95
9.110	Harrisville	ROMANS—ACNT	Augsburg	K	0-8066-8864-5	1980	7.50
9.111	Robertson & Plummer	1 COR—ICC	Seabury		0-567-05027-0	1914/1978	17.95
9.112	Conzelmann	1 COR—HERMENEIA	Fortress		0-8006-6005-6	1975	21.95

BB#	AUTHOR/EDITOR	SHORT TITLE	PUBLISHER	B	ISBN	DATE	PRICE
9.113	Barrett	1 COR—HNTC	Harper & Row		0-06-060551-0	1968	16.95
9.114	Grosheide	1 COR—NICNT	Eerdmans		0-8028-2185-5	1953	12.95
9.115	Bruce	1 & 2 COR—NCBC	Eerdmans	p	0-8028-1839-0	1981ʳ	6.95
9.116	Morris	1 COR—TNTC	Eerdmans	p	0-8028-1406-9	1958	4.95
9.117	Ruef	1 COR—NWPC	Westminster		0-664-21348-0	1978	10.00
9.117p	(same)	(same)	(same)	p	0-664-24183-2	1978	5.45
9.118	Thrall	1 & 2 COR—CBCNT	Cambridge		0-521-04203-8	1965	18.95
9.118p	(same)	(same)	(same)	p	0-521-09251-5	1965	7.50
9.119	Murphy-O'Connor	1 COR—NTM	Glazier		0-89453-133-6	1980	8.95
9.119p	(same)	(same)	(same)	p	0-89453-198-0	1980	5.95
9.120	Gaebelein	EXP BIB COM, 10	Zondervan		0-310-36520-1	1976	16.95
9.121	Orr & Walther	1 COR—AB	Doubleday		0-385-02853-9	1976	16.00
9.122	LaVerdiere	INVITATION TO EP, 2	Doubleday	p	0-385-14797-X	1980	3.95
9.123	Walter	1 COR—NTSR	Crossroad		0-8245-0346-5	1971/1981	10.00
9.123p	(same)	(same)	(same)	p	0-8245-0122-5	1981	4.95
9.124	Plummer	2 COR—ICC	Seabury		0-567-05028-9	1915/1978	17.95
9.125	Barrett	2 COR—HNTC	Harper & Row		0-06-060552-9	1974	13.95
9.126	Hughes	2 COR—NICNT	Eerdmans		0-8028-2186-2	1962	11.95
9.127	Bruce	1 & 2 COR—NCBC	Eerdmans	p	0-8028-1839-0	1981ʳ	6.95
9.128	Tasker	2 COR—TNTC	Eerdmans	p	0-8028-1407-7	1958	3.95
9.129	Gaebelein	EXP BIB COM, 10	Zondervan		0-310-36520-1	1976	16.95
9.130	Thrall	1 & 2 COR—CBCNT	Cambridge		0-521-04203-2	1965	16.95
9.130p	(same)	(same)	(same)	p	0-521-09251-5	1965	7.50
9.131	Fallon	2 COR—NTM	Glazier		0-89453-134-4	n.d.	8.95
9.131p	(same)	(same)	(same)	p	0-89453-199-9	n.d.	4.95
9.132	Schelkle	2 COR—NTSR	Crossroad		0-8245-0347-3	1969/1981	10.00
9.132p	(same)	(same)	(same)	p	0-8245-0123-3	1981	4.95
9.133	LaVerdiere	INVITATION TO EP, 2	Doubleday	p	0-385-14797-X	1980	3.95
9.134	Betz	GALATIANS—HERM	Fortress	p	0-8006-6009-9	1979	27.95

BB#	AUTHOR/EDITOR	SHORT TITLE	PUBLISHER	B	ISBN	DATE	PRICE
9.135	Burton	GALATIANS—ICC	Seabury		0-567-05029-7	1921/1977	17.95
9.136	Lightfoot, J. B.	GALATIANS	Zondervan		0-8010-27640-3	1865/1957	15.95
9.137	Bruce	GALATIANS—NIGTC	Eerdmans		0-8028-2387-4	1982	15.95
9.138	Ridderbos	GALATIANS—NICNT	Eerdmans		0-8028-2191-X	1953	10.95
9.139	Neill	GALATIANS—CBCNT	Cambridge		0-521-04218-6	1967	12.50
9.139p	(same)	(same)	(same)	p	0-521-09402-X	1967	4.95
9.140	Guthrie	GALATIANS—NCBC	Eerdmans	p	0-8028-1906-0	1981r	5.95
9.141	Cole	GALATIANS—TNTC	Eerdmans	p	0-8028-1408-5	1964	3.95
9.142	Gaebelein	EXP BIB COM, 10	Zondervan		0-310-36520-1	1976	16.95
9.143	Osiek	GALATIANS—NTM	Glazier		0-89453-135-2	n.d.	8.95
9.143p	(same)	(same)	(same)	p	0-89453-200-6	n.d.	4.95
9.144	Schneider	GALATIANS	Crossroad		0-8245-0348-1	1969/1981	10.00
9.144p	(same)	(same)	(same)	p	0-8245-0124-1	1981	4.95
9.145	Getty	INVITATION TO EP, 1	Doubleday	p	0-385-147961-1	1981	4.95
9.146	Abbott	EPH & COL—ICC	Seabury		0-567-05030-0	1897	15.95
9.147	Vincent	PHIL & PHLMN—ICC	Seabury		0-567-05031-9	1897	13.95
9.148	Lohse	COL & PHLMN—HERM	Fortress		0-8006-6001-3	1971	14.95
9.149	O'Brien	COL & PHLMN—WBC	Word		0-8499-0243-6	1982	19.95
9.150	Moule	COL & PHLMN—CGTC	Cambridge		0-521-04252-6	1957	32.50
9.150p	(same)	(same)	(same)	p	0-521-09236-1	1957	10.95
9.151	Houlden	PHL COL PHLM EPH	Westminster		0-664-21347-2	1978	11.50
9.151p	(same)	(same)	(same)	p	0-664-24182-4	1978	5.95
9.152	Barth, M.	EPHESIANS—AB (2 vols)	Doubleday		0-385-04772-X	1974	32.00
9.153	Lightfoot, J. B.	PHILIPPIANS	Zondervan		0-310-27650-0	1879/1953	14.95
9.154	Lightfoot, J. B.	COL & PHILEMON	Zondervan		0-310-27630-6	1865/1957	13.95
9.155	Robinson	EPHESIANS	Kregel		0-8254-3612-5	1909/1979	12.95
9.156	Westcott	EPHESIANS	Baker	p	0-8010-9623-5	1906/1979	5.95
9.157	Foulkes	EPHESIANS—TNTC	Eerdmans	p	0-8028-1409-3	1963	3.95
9.158	Carson	COL & PHLMN—TNTC	Eerdmans	p	0-8028-1411-5	1960	2.95

BB#	AUTHOR/EDITOR	SHORT TITLE	PUBLISHER	B	ISBN	DATE	PRICE
9.159	Martin	PHILIPPIANS—TNTC	Eerdmans	p	0-8028-1410-7	1960	3.95
9.160	Martin	PHILIPPIANS—NCBC	Eerdmans	p	0-8028-1840-4	1980	5.95
9.161	Martin	COL & PHLMN—NCBC	Eerdmans	p	0-8028-1908-7	1981ʳ	5.95
9.162	Martin	EPHESIANS—NCBC	Eerdmans	p	0-8028-1907-9	1981ʳ	6.95
9.163	Grayston	PHIL & THESS—CBCNT	Cambridge		0-521-04224-0	1967	14.95
9.163p	(same)	(same)	(same)	p	0-521-09490-7	1967	6.50
9.164	Thompson	EPH COL PHLN—CBCNT	Cambridge		0-521-04227-5	1967	18.95
9.164p	(same)	(same)	(same)	p	0-521-09410-0	1967	7.50
9.165	Simpson & Bruce	EPH & COL—NICNT	Eerdmans		0-8028-2193-6	1958	12.95
9.166	Müller	PHIL & PHLMN—NICNT	Eerdmans		0-8028-2188-X	1955	10.95
9.167	Swain	EPHESIANS—NTM	Glazier		0-89453-136-0	n.d.	8.95
9.167p	(same)	(same)	(same)	p	0-89453-201-4	n.d.	4.95
9.168	Getty	PHIL & PHLMN—NTM	Glazier		0-89453-137-9	n.d.	8.95
9.168p	(same)	(same)	(same)	p	0-89453-202-2	n.d.	4.95
9.169	Rogers	COLOSSIANS—NTM	Glazier		0-89453-138-7	n.d.	8.95
9.169p	(same)	(same)	(same)	p	0-89453-203-0	n.d.	4.95
9.170	Zerwick	EPHESIANS—NTSR	Crossroad		0-8245-0349-X	1969/1981	10.00
9.170p	(same)	(same)	(same)	p	0-8245-0125-X	1981	4.95
9.171	Reuss & Stöger	TITUS & PHLMN—NTSR	Crossroad		n.a.	1971/1981	n.a.
9.171p	(same)	(same)	(same)	p	n.a.	1981	n.a.
9.172	Gnilka & Mussner	PHIL & COL—NTSR	Crossroad		0-8245-0351-1	1971/1981	10.00
9.172p	(same)	(same)	(same)	p	0-8245-0126-8	1981	4.95
9.173	Gaebelein	EXP BIB COM, 11	Zondervan		0-310-36530-9	1978	16.95
9.174	LaVerdiere	INVITATION TO EP, 2	Doubleday	p	0-385-14797-X	1980	3.95
9.175	Frame	1 & 2 THESS—ICC	Seabury		0-567-05032-7	1912	13.95
9.176	Milligan	THESSALONIANS	Klock & Klock		0-86524-022-1	1908/1980	12.00
9.177	Grayston	PHIL & THESS—CBCNT	Cambridge		0-521-04224-0	1967	14.95
9.177p	(same)	(same)	(same)	p	0-521-09409-7	1967	6.50
9.178	Morris	THESS—TNTC	Eerdmans	p	0-8028-1412-3	1957	3.95

BB#	AUTHOR/EDITOR	SHORT TITLE	PUBLISHER	B	ISBN	DATE	PRICE
9.179	Morris	1 & 2 THESS—NICNT	Eerdmans		0-8028-2187-1	1959	11.95
9.180	Whiteley	THESSALONIANS	Oxford	p	0-19-836906-0	1969	7.95
9.181	Draper	1 & 2 THESS	Tyndale		0-8423-7051-X	1979	4.95
9.182	Gaebelein	EXP BIB COM, 11	Zondervan		0-310-36530-9	1978	16.95
9.183	Schürmann & Egenolf	THESS—NTSR	Crossroad		0-8245-0352-X	1969/1981	10.00
9.183p	(same)	(same)	(same)	p	0-8245-0217-6	1981	4.95
9.184	Reese	1 & 2 THESS—NTM	Glazier		0-89453-139-5	n.d.	8.95
9.184p	(same)	(same)	(same)	p	0-89453-204-9	n.d.	4.95
9.185	LaVerdiere	INVITATION TO EP, 2	Doubleday	p	0-385-14797-X	1980	3.95
9.186	Dibelius	PASTORALS—HERM	Fortress	p	0-8006-6002-1	1972	19.95
9.187	Lock	PASTORALS—ICC	Seabury		0-567-05033-5	1924/1978	13.95
9.188	Guthrie	PASTORALS—TNTC	Eerdmans	p	0-8028-1413-1	1957	3.95
9.189	Hanson	PASTORALS—CBCNT	Cambridge		0-521-04214-3	1966	14.95
9.189p	(same)	(same)	(same)	p	0-521-09380-5	1966	6.50
9.190	Kelly	PASTORALS	Baker	p	0-8010-54281-1	1964/1981	6.95
9.191	Hanson	PASTORALS—NCBC	Eerdmans	p	0-8028-1924-9	1982	6.95
9.192	Karris	PASTORALS—NTM	Glazier		0-89453-140-9	n.d.	8.95
9.192p	(same)	(same)	(same)	p	0-89453-205-7	n.d.	4.95
9.193	Reuss	1 & 2 TIM—NTSR	Crossroad		0-8245-0353-8	1969/1981	10.00
9.193p	(same)	(same)	(same)	p	0-8245-0128-4	1981	4.95
9.194	Reuss & Stöger	TITUS & PHLMN—NTSR	Crossroad		n.a.	1971/1981	n.a.
9.194p	(same)	(same)	(same)	p	n.a.	1981	n.a.
9.195	Moffatt	HEBREWS—ICC	Seabury		0-567-05034-3	1924	13.95
9.196	Westcott	HEBREWS	Eerdmans		0-8028-3289-X	1920/1950	9.95
9.197	Buchanan	HEBREWS—ICC	Doubleday		0-385-02995-0	1972	14.00
9.198	Hughes	HEBREWS	Eerdmans		0-8028-3495-7	1977	15.95
9.199	Hewitt	HEBREWS—TNTC	Eerdmans		0-8028-1414-X	1961	3.95
9.200	Bruce	HEBREWS—NICNT	Eerdmans		0-8028-2183-9	1964	14.95
9.201	Davies, J. H.	HEBREWS—CBCNT	Cambridge		0-521-04222-4	1967	13.95

BB#	AUTHOR/EDITOR	SHORT TITLE	PUBLISHER	B	ISBN	DATE	PRICE
9.201p	(same)	(same)	(same)	p	0-521-09408-9	1967	6.50
9.202	Schierse & Knoch	HEBR & JMS—NTSR	Crossroad		0-8245-0355-4	1969/1981	10.00
9.202p	(same)	(same)	(same)	p	0-8245-0130-6	1981	4.95
9.203	Casey	HEBREWS—NTM	Glazier		0-89453-141-7	n.d.	8.95
9.203p	(same)	(same)	(same)	p	0-89453-206-5	n.d.	4.95
9.204	Danker	INVITATION TO EP, 4	Doubleday	p	0-385-14799-6	1980	3.95
9.205	Brown, R. E.	EPISTLES JOHN—AB	Doubleday	p	0-385-05686-9	1982	18.00
9.206	Bultmann	JOHANNINE EP—HERM	Fortress		0-8006-6003-X	1973	14.95
9.207	Brooke	JOHANNINE EP—ICC	Seabury		0-567-05037-8	1912	15.95
9.208	Plummer	EPISTLES JOHN	Baker	p	0-8010-7058-9	1886/1980	7.95
9.209	Westcott	EPISTLES JOHN	Eerdmans		0-8028-3290-3	1902/1966	7.95
9.210	Bruce	EPISTLES JOHN	Eerdmans	p	0-8028-1783-1	1978	4.95
9.211	McKenzie	LIGHT ON EPISTLES	More		0-88347-057-8	1975	12.95
9.212	Williams	LTRS JN & JS—CBCNT	Cambridge		0-521-04206-2	1965	14.95
9.212p	(same)	(same)	(same)	p	0-521-09250-7	1965	6.50
9.213	Houlden	JOHANNINE EP—HNTC	Harper & Row		0-06-064020-0	1973	7.95
9.214	Marshall, I. H.	EPS JOHN—NICNT	Eerdmans		0-8028-2189-2	1978	12.95
9.215	Stott	EPS JOHN—TNTC	Eerdmans	p	0-8028-1418-2	1964	3.95
9.216	Gaebelein	EXP BIB COM, 12	Zondervan		0-310-36540-6	1981	19.95
9.217	Danker	INVITATION TO EP, 4	Doubleday	p	0-385-14799-6	1980	3.95
9.218	Perkins	JOHANNINE EP—NTM	Glazier		0-89453-144-1	1980	8.95
9.218p	(same)	(same)	(same)	p	0-686-65717-9	1980	4.95
9.219	Thüsing & Stöger	EPS JUDE & JN—NTSR	Crossroad		0-8245-0357-0	1971/1981	10.00
9.219p	(same)	(same)	(same)	p	0-8245-0132-2	1981	4.95
9.220	Selwyn	1 PETER	Baker	p	0-8010-8199-8	1947/1981	10.95
9.221	Bigg	1 & 2 PT & JD—ICC	Seabury		0-567-05036-X	1902[2]/1978	15.95
9.222	Mayor	EPS JUDE & 2 PET	Baker	p	0-8010-6082-6	1907/1979	8.95
9.223	(same)	(same)	Klock & Klock		0-86524-945-8	1907/1978	15.25
9.224	Reicke	JS JD 1 & 2 PET—AB	Doubleday		0-385-01374-4	1964/1978[2]	14.00

BB#	AUTHOR/EDITOR	SHORT TITLE	PUBLISHER	B	ISBN	DATE	PRICE
9.225	Kelly	1 & 2 PET, JUDE	Baker	p	0-8010-5430-3	1969/1981	8.95
9.226	Leaney	PET & JUDE—CBCNT	Cambridge		0-521-04216-X	1967	14.95
9.226p	(same)	(same)	(same)	p	0-521-09403-8	1967	6.50
9.227	Best	1 PETER—NCBC	Eerdmans	p	0-8028-1909-5	1982	5.95
9.228	Sidebottom	JS JD 2 PET—NCBC	Eerdmans	p	0-8028-1936-2	1982	5.95
9.229	Stibbs	1 PETER—TNTC	Eerdmans	p	0-8028-1416-6	1959	3.95
9.230	Green	2 PET & JUDE—TNTC	Eerdmans	p	0-8028-1417-4	1968	3.95
9.231	Gaebelein	EXP BIB COM, 12	Zondervan		0-310-36540-6	1981	19.95
9.232	Schwank & Stöger	1 & 2 PETER—NTSR	Crossroad		0-8245-0356-2	1971/1981	10.00
9.232p	(same)	(same)	(same)	p	0-8245-0131-4	1981	4.95
9.233	Senior	1 & 2 PETER—NTM	Glazier	p	0-89453-143-3	n.d.	8.95
9.233p	(same)	(same)	(same)	p	0-89453-208-1	n.d.	4.95
9.234	Martin & Elliott	JS 1 & 2 PT JD—ACNT	Augsburg	p	0-8066-1937-6	1982	7.50
9.235	Ropes	JAMES—ICC	Seabury		0-567-05035-1	1916/1978	13.95
9.236	Bigg	1 & 2 PT JD—ICC	Seabury		0-567-05036-X	1902²/1978	15.95
9.237	Mayor	JAMES	Baker	p	0-8010-6073-7	1913/1979	6.95
9.238	(same)	(same)	Klock & Klock		0-86524-971-7	1913/1977	19.25
9.239	Dibelius/Greeven	JAMES—HERMENEIA	Fortress		0-8006-6006-4	1976	24.95
9.240	Davids	JAMES—NIGTC	Eerdmans		0-8028-2388-2	1982	14.95
9.241	Reicke	JS JD 1 & 2 PET—AB	Doubleday		0-385-01374-4	1964/1978²	14.00
9.242	Laws	JAMES—HNTC	Harper & Row		0-06-064918-6	1980	14.95
9.243	Kelly	1 & 2 PET, JUDE	Baker	p	0-8010-5430-3	1969/1981	8.95
9.244	Tasker	JAMES—TNTC	Eerdmans	p	0-8028-1415-8	1957	2.95
9.245	Green	2 PET, JUDE—TNTC	Eerdmans	p	0-8028-1417-4	1968	3.95
9.246	Sidebottom	JS JD 2 PET—NCBC	Eerdmans	p	0-8028-1936-2	1982	5.95
9.247	Adamson	JAMES—NICNT	Eerdmans		0-8028-2377-7	1976	10.95
9.248	Williams	LTRS JN & JS—CBCNT	Cambridge		0-521-04206-2	1965	14.95
9.248p	(same)	(same)	(same)	p	0-521-09250-7	1965	6.50
9.249	Leaney	PET & JUDE—CBCNT	Cambridge		0-521-04216-X	1967	14.95

BB#	AUTHOR/EDITOR	SHORT TITLE	PUBLISHER	B	ISBN	DATE	PRICE
9.249p	(same)	(same)	(same)	p	0-521-09403-8	1967	6.50
9.250	Gaebelein	EXP BIB COM, 12	Zondervan		0-310-36540-6	1981	19.95
9.251	Kugelman	JAMES & JUDE—NTM	Glazier		0-89453-143-3	n.d.	8.95
9.251p	(same)	(same)	(same)	p	0-686-69905-5	n.d.	4.95
9.252	Schierse & Knock	HEBR & JAMES—NTSR	Crossroad		0-8245-0355-4	1969/1981	10.00
9.252p	(same)	(same)	(same)	p	0-8245-0130-6	1981	4.95
9.253	Thüsing & Stöger	JUDE & JOHN—NTSR	Crossroad		0-8245-0357-0	1981	10.00
9.253p	(same)	(same)	(same)	p	0-8245-0132-2	1981	4.95
9.254	Martin & Elliott	JS 1 & 2 PT JD—ACNT	Augsburg	p	0-8066-1937-6	1982	7.50
9.255	Charles	REVELATION, 1—ICC	Seabury		0-567-05038-6	1920	17.00
9.256	Charles	REVELATION, 2—ICC	Seabury		0-567-05039-4	1920	17.00
9.257	Swete	REVELATION	Kregel		0-8254-3716-4	1911/1978	14.95
9.258	Beckwith	APOCALYPSE JOHN	Baker		0-8010-0761-5	1919/1979	12.95
9.259	Sweet	REVELATION—NWPC	Westminster		0-664-21375-8	1979	14.95
9.259p	(same)	(same)	(same)	p	0-664-24264-6	1979	8.95
9.260	Caird	REVELATION—HNTC	Harper & Row		0-06-061296-7	1966	14.50
9.261	Ford	REVELATION—AB	Doubleday		0-385-00895-3	1975	18.00
9.262	Glasson	REVELATION—CBCNT	Cambridge		0-521-04208-9	1965	14.95
9.262p	(same)	(same)	(same)	p	0-521-09256-6	1965	6.50
9.263	Mounce	REVELATION—NICNT	Eerdmans		0-8028-2348-3	1977	12.95
9.264	Beasley-Murray	REVELATION—NCBC	Eerdmans	p	0-8028-1885-4	1981ʳ	7.95
9.265	Morris	REVELATION—TNTC	Eerdmans	p	0-8028-1419-0	1957	4.95
9.266	Gaebelein	EXP BIB COM, 12	Zondervan		0-310-36540-6	1981	19.95
9.267	Schick	REVELATION 1,—NTSR	Crossroad		0-8245-0358-9	1971/1981	10.00
9.267p	(same)	(same)	(same)	p	0-8245-0133-0	1981	4.95
9.268	Schick	REVELATION 2,—NTSR	Crossroad		0-8245-0359-7	1981	10.00
9.268p	(same)	(same)	(same)	p	0-8245-0134-9	1981	4.95
9.269	Collins	APOCALYPSE—NTM	Glazier		0-89453-145-X	1979	8.95
9.269p	(same)	(same)	(same)	p	0-89453-210-3	1979	4.95
9.270	Fiorenza	INVITATION TO REV	Doubleday	p	0-385-14800-3	1981	3.95

INDEX

LIBRARY USE ONLY